FALSE TONGUES
AND
SUNDAY BREAD
▼▼▼▼▼▼▼▼▼▼▼▼▼▼▼▼▼▼▼▼▼▼▼▼▼▼▼▼▼▼▼▼

FALSE TONGUES
AND
SUNDAY BREAD

A GUATEMALAN
AND MAYAN
COOKBOOK

COPELAND MARKS

M. EVANS

Lanham • New York • Boulder • Toronto • Plymouth, UK

The illustrations in this book include pre-Hispanic Mayan hiero-
glyphs and symbolic representations of Mayan dieties. They are taken
from the few codices that survived the Spanish conquest.

Library of Congress Cataloging-in-Publication Data

Marks, Copeland.
  False tongues and Sunday bread.

  Bibliography: p. 397
  Includes index.
  1. Cookery, Guatemalan.   2. Cookery, Maya.   I. Title.
TX716.G8M37   1985   641.597281   85–16102

ISBN 978-1-59077-276-8

Distributed by
NATIONAL BOOK NETWORK

M Evans
An imprint of Rowman & Littlefield
4501 Forbes Boulevard. Suite 200
Lanham, Maryland 20706
www.rowman.com

Design by Ronald F. Shey/Donnelley/ROCAPPI, Inc.

Manufactured in the United States of America

CONTENTS

FOREWORD

Copeland Marks has made a meticulous study of a little-known culinary region of the Americas, the once-great Mayan empire that stretched from the mother city of Tikal in Guatemala, north into Mexico's Yucatán peninsula through the modern state of Campeche to Palenque in Chiapas, and south to Copán in Honduras in Central America. The great stone cities are now in ruins. Mayan glory had already begun to fade by the time of the Spanish Conquest in the sixteenth century. Surprisingly, much has survived the centuries, including the magnificent weavings and the food.

Having worked in the region myself, I know that his task cannot have been an easy one, as he has not just recorded echoes from the past but has given us the modern kitchen with all its traditional qualities. The cuisines of the region are, of course, dominated by the indigenous foods. Most of them, like tomatoes, corn, the common bean, chiles and sweet peppers, were first cultivated in Mexico, where it is believed agriculture in the Americas was born millennia ago. These still form the basis of the kitchen, though nowadays with the foods introduced by the Conquest and by the spread of modern trade, all the foods of the world are available. The Guatemalan kitchen of today reflects this, and it has also been modified by modern cooking methods and kitchen tools such as the blender and food processor. This has made the dishes more accessible to the modern cook, and Copeland Marks gives us clearly written and easy-to-follow recipes for dishes that are delectable, with the added merit of being healthful.

There are many recipes for dried beans and rice, poultry, vegetable dishes and salads, as well as vegetarian dishes and unusual desserts. There are entertaining headnotes, useful menu suggestions and a discussion of ingredients and cooking methods. But beyond this, Copeland Marks has made an important contribution to the literature of the kitchen. He deserves the title of food historian.

ELISABETH LAMBERT ORTIZ

ACKNOWLEDGMENTS

The Guatemalan and Central American men and women who assisted me were wonderful. Whether a simple Indian in her tribal village or an elegant upper-class woman in Guatemala City, they cooperated with me with amusement and with pride in their own culture. My profound thanks to all.

Luzvina de Argueta
Olivia Asij
Mercedes Barreiro
Jaime Bischof
Nicolasa Mejia de Boj
Maruca de Bolanos of El Salvador
Carmen Brenes of Costa Rica
Clemente Cano
Melita de Castillo
Odette G. de Cobos
Carmen Cho
Maria Angelina Aldana de Diaz
Helen Margoth Dugan
Alvaro Diaz Fahardo of Nicaragua
Leslie Fairhurst

Maria Isaura Arevalo Fonsea
Aurora Sierra Franco
Julia Alicia Galvez
Dora Alicia Cristales Galvez
Maria Laiva de Gamboa
Esperanza Garcia
Zoila de Gonzalez
Maria Lucia Pocon de Granados
Joan Hempstead
Patricia Cobos de Lamport
Elvira de Leal
Michele de Leal
Maria de Leon
Stella Chinchilla de Leon
Virginia Cobos de Llarena

9

Anacleta Lopez
Peter and Sandy Garcia Martinez
Victoria Marroquin
Mirtala Merida
Alfonso Miron
Olga de Miron
Marie Elena de Morales
Josefa Morales
Candido Mathias Organis
Oscar Armando Palencia
Maria Luz Munoz de Pereira
Cristy de la Roca
Hesse de Roman of Honduras

Angelica Garcia Rosales
Felipa Cosme Mucum de Cruz Rosales
Francisca de Rosales
Yolanda de Rosales
Francisco Luna Ruiz
Maria Chel Santiago
Ana Smith
Isa Deldago de Smith
Everilda Pichola de Sol
Josefina de Solorzano
Martita de Taque
Carlota de Valdez
Olimpia Hidalgo Vidaurre

INTRODUCTION

S everal years ago I approached a number of people in Guatemala City and told them I wanted to write a book on the cuisine of Guatemala. The comment was received with utter disbelief that there was a cuisine at all; people claimed that the highland Indians ate only beans, tortillas and tamales, and that if there was any semblance of a cooking style it occurred only in the large cities.

I had been collecting the textiles of the Maya for twenty years, moving from one village to another where the great tribal textile tradition was still extant, and I had been impressed by the variety of foods in the daily markets as well as the selection of spices and seasonings available. On the basis of my intuition, I knew that there must be a cuisine, notwithstanding the fact that none of the restaurants serving tourists was presenting the authentic typical foods and that there was no real bibliography of cookbooks in English one could study.

So I returned to the village weavers known to me, all of them women, and proceeded to talk about food and record the daily and ceremonial recipes based upon my observation and actual cooking activities with them.

It wasn't all that easy. At one point I was bitten by a mad dog in the village of San Juan Sacatepéquez and thereafter took sixteen anti-rabies injections in the stomach. On another occasion in the highlands our station wagon transmission fell off with a tremendous crash on the edge of a precipice. Then there was the time our Indian bus was surrounded by leftist guerillas and there was a shoot-out as I tried to clarify a miniature tamale recipe given me by an Indian woman cowering, with me, on the floor of the bus. In a moment of panic it occurred to me that there must be an easier way to record a cuisine that the city folk informed me did not exist. If a mad dog resulted in only two recipes and a broken axle about four major recipes, what would my expectations be for an earthquake, an army revolt or a street mugging?

However, after the guerilla incident, the veil lifted and I was able to collect considerable evidence that the cuisine of the Guatemala Maya was in reality two separate cuisines—one of the highland Indian with its pre-Hispanic style and the other of the Spanish Colonial era, which had been developed by the new race, the Ladinos, who were a mixture of the old and the new.

Later on I recognized a third division, a minor satellite, that had developed independently of the other two in the town of Livingston on Guatemala's Caribbean coast. It was here that indentured labor from India and Africa was brought in by the British to work in the sugarcane and forests of British Honduras (now known as Belize). These people developed a vivid style of cooking that was tropical, based on seafood, bananas and coconut milk. Examples of this style are included in the recipes.

After Guatemala, the four small countries of Central America have their own special culinary magic that is astonishingly unique to each country. Although El Salvador, Honduras, Nicaragua and Costa Rica emerged historically from a common origin, both pre-Hispanic and after the Spanish Conquest in the fifteenth-sixteenth centuries, they took different directions in their kitchens. Geography has a vital control over diet, and people in the tropical lowlands throughout Central America eat differently from those in the mountainous highlands.

A common theme that permeates the cooking of Central America reflects their pre-Hispanic Indian origins. Corn, tortillas, beans, squash, hot chiles and tomatoes are basic. After the Spanish arrived, the foods of Europe and Asia, such as rice, were introduced and integrated into the cuisines. As the centuries moved on, each region, before the political demarcations took place in 1823, began to find itself in a culinary way in direct proportion to the Indian population.

Guatemala, with the largest number of Indians, the home of the Maya, has logically developed its cooking in direct proportion to their number, leaning heavily on the turkey and the fruits and vegetables that originated botanically in Central America. Next came El Salvador and Honduras, with some Indian tribes or villages but with less Indian influence on the cookery, which depends more on Spanish ideas. Nicaragua, with its Miskito Indians, a Caribbean coastal group, has a mixture of foods that can be considered eclectic. Costa Rica is an almost exclusively non-Indian nation and the cooking is based on the fertile tropical countryside and indigenous adaptations of the foods, both old and new, of the region.

To sum up, although Mayan tribes and their offshoots roamed freely up and down the Central American region in pre-Hispanic times, their culinary influence diminished the farther away they moved from Guatemala toward South America. Thus Costa Rica has the least attachment to the foods of the ancient Indians. Architectural vestiges of lost civilizations are found in all of Central America, but the cooking that is available to us in modern times is based upon historical influences plus contemporary modes and preferences.

There is, of course, a substantial amount of overlapping in the sheer numbers of recipes that have been devised. Along the hot and steaming Caribbean coasts of all these countries, for example, coconut milk is used in preparing bread, chicken and fish dishes.

The differences found in the cooking of each country have put a special stamp on it that is identifiable. For instance, the Pupusas (Stuffed Tortillas) of El Salvador (see Index) are not duplicated in Costa Rica. People of those countries know their own cooking but are unfamiliar with the foods of their neighbors a few miles away as the crow flies. I have cooked with men and women of Central America and each one was determined to demonstrate national identity through their food and to make their differences known.

El Salvador faces the Pacific Ocean, yet it is not particularly interested in seafood. The cuisine is varied and has the usual tortilla, rice and bean dishes. Yet it rises above this to a substantial degree with an assortment of highly sophisticated poultry and beef dishes, of which an outstanding example is Gallo en Chicha (Capon in Fruit Wine, see Index). The national dessert, La Semita, which is a pineapple torte (see Index), cannot be faulted. The early Spanish influence predominates and, since there is very little Indian life, the reliance on pre-Hispanic foods is not as observable as in Guatemala.

Honduras has two ocean outlets, on the Pacific and Caribbean, is sparsely populated for its size, and can boast of the famous archaeological site at Copán. Two of the most extraordinary soups in all of Central America (in my opinion) are prepared in Honduras, although one might not consider soup appropriate or popular in a semitropical country. Sopa de Hombre (A Man's Seafood Soup) and the Mondongo (Tripe Soup, see Index for pages) are justly famous in their hearty, country village way. Both use the foods of the tropics—chayote, plantain, banana, yuca, achiote and coconut milk.

Nicaraguan food does not fit into any easy category. Rather, it is based on tropical foods artfully prepared and essentially simple. A preponderance of yuca, green plantain and red bean dishes are balanced with Nacatamal (see Index), one of the best tamales in Central America. Festive poultry dishes for special occasions and the well-known Carne a la Parilla (see Index), charcoal-grilled steak bathed in an assertive marinade, are popular preparations. The Miskito Indians of mixed blood also contribute their ideas of Caribbean-style dishes.

INGREDIENTS AND COOKING METHODS

ACHIOTE: Also called *annatto* in most bottled products found in the United States. It is distributed locally by the Goya Company in two forms. There are bottles of small red granules that can be dissolved in hot corn oil (1 teaspoon granules to 2 teaspoons hot oil), and you may also find it already dissolved in lard and sold in cans. The Guatemalans prefer to use lard in their cooking, but I believe the use of corn oil is healthier.

Achiote is a red/orange vegetable coloring made from the seeds of a small tree, annatto (*Bixa orellana*), which I have seen growing wild in different regions of Guatemala. In regional marketplaces, village women will sell a smoothly ground red paste prepared from the seeds, which they have pulled away from what appears to be a 3-inch pod. I have seen and photographed a woman sitting in her

15

doorstep in Livingston stripping the achiote seeds, her hands a bright red as though she had dipped them into a bucket of blood.

Achiote is all-pervasive in regional foods and can be purchased anywhere in Guatemala. I have bought it in pressed circles, the size of a dime and carefully wrapped in minute plastic bags; in a paste, 15 cents worth; or as a firm nugget wrapped and tied in tiny dried cornhusks and strung like a necklace.

Its main purpose in these recipes is to add color. I have been told that too much achiote will alter the flavor of the food in a negative manner but have yet to discover in what way this occurs.

BREADFRUIT *(Artocarpus communis):* Not a fruit at all in the dessert sense, but a starchy breadlike ball with a warty skin, growing on a beautiful tropical tree. The breadfruit is eaten in Livingston and tropical coastal Guatemala, fried in slices, plain boiled, or cut into cubes and then boiled and mashed. The breadfruit is native to Southeast Asia.

CACAO *(Theobroma cacao):* Made from cacao beans grown in the tropical and semitropical regions of Guatemala and found in almost all of the Indian marketplaces there, the chocolate can be purchased in small cakes or in larger industrial tablets. The homemade cakes are used principally to prepare hot chocolate. The beans are not readily available here, but sometimes you will find the Mixco chocolate (see Index for section on this chocolate).

CASSAVA *(Manihot utilissima):* Also called yuca and tapioca; this is grown all over the tropics. This plant should not be confused with the ornamental plant, yucca, found in the Western United States. Cassava is prepared in the same way as potatoes, that is, boiled, mashed or fried. It is also prepared as a dessert in Nicaragua and in soups in Honduras. This root is not so well known in the United States but always seems to be available in Latin-American groceries.

CHAYOTE, *Huisquil,* also *Guisquil (Sechium edule):* This marvelous vegetable, whose botanical origin is Central America, is found all over Guatemala from the chilly highlands down to the tropical coast. Everyone eats them—boiled, mashed, fried, baked, in salads, as a vegetable or a dessert such as Chancletas (Stuffed Chayotes, see Index). They come in various sizes, shapes and colors but are essentially pear-shaped with a firm, sometimes hairy skin, which can be a dense charcoal green to a pale green. The *perulero*, a first cousin to the *huisquil*, is pale beige or eggshell and is a small, rounder version with a less intense flavor. Chayote is available in Latin-American markets, always in New York's Chinatown, and in many supermarkets.

CHICHA: The dictionary definition of *chicha* is "a popular alcoholic beverage," and this may have been what it was intended to be. However, it would be more accurate to describe *chicha* as a country or regional liquor that is also and perhaps principally used in cooking. The *chicha* from Salcajá is made from quince, apple, cherry, apricot, peach and nance (wild, yellow cherry), mixed with a white rum and allowed to ferment for a month or more. Some say it is not really ready for six months. In other regions, it is prepared differently, sometimes with and sometimes without fruit. Our use of it here is mainly in the preparation of poultry and meat, as in Gallo en Chicha (see Index). Several recipes from different areas are included as well as a suggested substitute.

CHICHARRONES: Crispy fried pork rinds used in so many ways in Central America. The Guatemalans include them in their famous salad, Chojin (see Index), while the Hondurans and Nicaraguans add it to their Vigoron salads with cassava (see Index). Since most of the fat is fried out of the rind, these make a good crisp appetizer to serve with drinks. They are usually purchased by the ounce bag in meat markets and Latin-American groceries.

CHILE (*Capsicum frutescens*): This is a long story, a history that started botanically in Mexico and Guatemala and moved via Columbus throughout the rest of the world. Characterized by variable pungency, different sizes and shapes and a high vitamin C content, the chile has become an important and essential ingredient for daily consumption in all walks of life.

The two chiles most often used in this book are the *chile guaque* and the *chile pasa*.

The *chile pasa*, also known as *pasilla*, looks like a large, dark dried prune. It is found dried in the marketplaces of Guatemala and used in *pepián* dishes (see Squash Seeds in this section) as well as mole. It is more often known in the United States by its Mexican name of *chile pasilla*.

The *chile guaque* is a long, reddish brown, smooth dried chile; it is known most frequently in the United States by its Mexican name of *chile guajillo.*

The *chile de Cobán,* or Cobán chile, is perhaps the best-known and most popular chile in Guatemala. Sold dried everywhere, the small round balls, about ½ inch in diameter, have the dark smoky flavor of the wood fire drying process that gives the food a marvelous extra taste. Unfortunately, this chile is not available to my knowledge outside of Guatemala. I use them as a standard chile in my own kitchen simply because they are always available to me.

The *diente de perro* (dog's tooth) is shaped like a dog's canine about 1 inch long; it is bright red and has a heat that must be dealt with cautiously. I noticed this chile was available in Livingston on the Caribbean, a town known to prefer black pepper to the chile.

The *chile chiltepe,* which is the size of a green pea, is dynamic and intense. It is generally used fresh in a *salsa picante* (hot sauce) with a vinaigrette base.

The long (3 to 4 inches) slender, red *chile chocolate* is also found in marketplaces of Guatemala. Large quantities are grown in eastern Guatemala and are sold around the countryside by traders who come to the village fairs. A medium hot chile.

The *chile zambo* is about 2 inches long, broad, red and medium hot; it is sold dried. The flavor is reminiscent of the Cobán chile.

And so it goes. There are those who recognize and utilize all the chiles for their regional dishes and claim to be able to detect the nuances of flavors. What the chiles all have in common is a pungency that is habit-forming and without which food is insipid and without character.

It should be pointed out that the heat intensity of any of the chiles is variable. One should be prepared for a lack of standardization when using both fresh and dried chiles. It is the capsaicin in the chile that is responsible for the heat. Using chiles, cutting them and then touching sensitive lips, tongue and especially the eyes, can be extremely unpleasant. Caution should be used. Wash hands with soap after working with chiles.

CHIRMOL: Essentially a tomato sauce seasoned with onion and garlic. It can be prepared fresh or fried, smooth or coarse, and is used to flavor appetizers and fritters. Every household has its own variation on the same theme—a little chile, a few tomatillos, oil or not, etc.

The *chirmol* is as Guatemalan as black beans. You will find several recipes (with slight variations) in this book.

CILANTRO *(Coriandrum sativum):* Also known as culantro and Chinese parsley; fresh coriander is a leafy, aromatic herb that is probably the most popular if not ubiquitous in Guatemala. It is also used throughout the Middle East and in Asia as a condiment, garnish and seasoning.

COCONUT AND COCONUT MILK *(Cocos nucifera):* Guatemala is fortunately situated on the Pacific ocean and the Caribbean sea, and no sight is more characteristic of the tropics than the coconut palms that proliferate along the coast. The Caribbean particularly attracts our attention with the unique cuisine of Livingston and its use of coconut milk and freshly grated coconut.

Here is a standard method of extracting rich coconut milk, which I have also used in preparing recipes from Indonesia, where the coconut is king.

RICH COCONUT MILK

1 ripe coconut, with a brown, hard shell
4 to 5 cups very hot water

1. Bake the coconut in a 400° F. oven for 15 to 20 minutes; a little more will not harm. Remove coconut from the oven and give it several hard whacks with a hammer to break it open and into 4 or 5 pieces. The coconut *water* will drain away and is not used unless specifically called for, as in Cocada (Coconut Conserve, see Index).

2. Pry away the coconut meat from the shell; use a dull knife to eliminate the possibility of running the knife through one's fingers. Cut the meat into 1-inch-wide strips and then into horizontal thin slices.

3. Put about 3 cups of the slices into a blender container and pour in 4 cups of water (the less water, the richer the coconut milk). Process for about 1 minute, which will be enough time to cut up the coconut and release the milk. Pour the mixture through a metal sieve and squeeze out the coconut fragments. The liquid that remains is coconut milk. It can be stored in the refrigerator for 3 days, or it can be frozen in plastic containers for future use.

When preparing grated coconut to be used in the Trifle (Coconut Milk Cake, see Index), trim the brown skin from the coconut meat after slicing it into strips. This will keep the coconut white when using it in desserts. Grate all you need on a hand grater or in a food processor.

EPAZOTE *(Chenopodium ambrosioides)*: It seems as if this herb grows wild all over the Guatemala highlands; it is used to flavor regional dishes as well as for medicinal purposes. It does have a mild antiseptic flavor that is ingratiating. In the recipe Caldo de Huevo Para la Goma (Egg Soup for a Hangover, see Index), the epazote produces a fine egg soup and cures a hangover at the same time, or so I have been told. Fresh epazote is generally available throughout the year in Oriental markets.

GUISADO: A preparation of meats that uses many seasonings. Usually the meats are first browned in oil and the spices, liquids and other ingredients are added later.

HUICOY: A hard-shelled pumpkin/squash similar in texture to the Hubbard squash in the United States. The West Indian calabaza, which is sold whole or in pieces in Latin-American stores, is also similar in texture to the Guatemala *huicoy*. I have noticed that Korean vegetable shops in New York also sell the calabaza, which has a smooth skin. The *huicoy* is shaped like one of the pre-Columbian Colima pots in my collection, with vertical ridges and indentations around the exterior.

HUISQUIL: *see* Chayote.

MASA: The use of this word in the recipes always refers to ground cornmeal (tortilla flour), the same texture used for tortillas and tamales (*masa harina,* corn flour), which has been moistened with sufficient water to shape into a ball with the consistency of putty. The proportion is 2 cups of the corn flour to 1 cup of warm water. The Quaker brand of *masa harina* is available in supermarkets in the United States.

The *masa* does become, in fact, a dough that is also used to thicken sauces. Rather than put in the dry cornmeal, the Maya have devised this method to make it easier to handle and control the development of the thickening.

MASHAN or MAXAN: The leaf of the Palmyra palm tree that is the standard wrapper for tamales, steamed fish, farmer's cheeses or any other type of market food that is to be carried home. Glossy green with fine ridges, the leaf appears impervious as plastic and as useful. When used with tamales it does impart what could be described as a clean, natural flavor rather than one that is distinctive. Foil can be used in its place.

MIEL (honey): There are two kinds of honey in Guatemala and one must be specific. There is bees' honey, which has been the great sweetener since pre-Hispanic times. The Mayan codices that still exist have calligraphic references and drawings of the honey god. There is mention of honey and of the Mayans getting drunk on fermented honey in a Cakchiquel Indian annal.

I am a collector of Guatemala honey from each region where I happen to be traveling. It is usually purchased from an occasional roadside stand or village marketplace, packed in empty whiskey bottles and absolutely natural. Since there is no standardized flavor, the variety is unlimited.

The second type is "white honey," that prepared from sugar and water and used in regional desserts. After sugarcane was introduced into Central America by Columbus, sugar replaced bees' honey as it has all over the world. You will find several recipes for white honey (syrup) in these pages—some simple syrups, some flavored.

MIL TOMATE or TOMATILLO (the Mexican name) (*Physalis ixocarpa*): The small, green, acid tomatolike fruit that is used in many recipes. The fruit itself is about ¾ inch in diameter, although I have seen larger versions of this in Mexican food shops. The Guatemala type is small and quite acid. I am using with an easy conscience the canned *mil tomates* from a California company. These are convenient, available and do not torpedo the flavor.

MOLE: A Mexican word for a stew of meats with various spices. It does not necessarily include chocolate, as some people mistakenly believe. Among the Guatemalan versions, Mole de Conejo (Mountain Rabbit, see Index) is in fact colored with achiote to give it an orange/pink color. On the other hand, the Plátanos en Mole (Plantain in Chocolate Sauce), a dessert (see Index) does have chocolate, which combines very well indeed with the fried plantain.

NANCE or NANTZE *(Byrsonima cotinifolia, B. crassifolia)*: A yellow, cherrylike fruit that grows on a large and lovely tropical tree in the semitropical regions. The trees produce a profusion of the slightly acid fruits, which are used in preparing the *chicha* of Salcajá. Also cooked as a fruit compote.

NARANJA AGRIA: *see* Sour Orange Juice.

PACAYA *(Chamaedorea tepejolote):* One of the most interesting and ubiquitous sights in the tropical markets of Guatemala is the pacaya, the edible flower pod of the pacaya palm tree. The flower of the palm is 8 to 12 inches long, sometimes longer, and about 2 inches thick at the base, enclosed by a firm, green fibrous casing. The pointed buds are similar in appearance to bamboo shoots, which I used to see in India and Indonesia. The rather thick, green, tough casing is removed to reveal the delicate embryonic fronds of the palm in a pale cream color.

The flower must be cooked in several changes of hot water to remove some of the bitter taste. It is then used in salads and especially dipped into an egg batter and fried as a fritter called Recado de Pacaya (see Index).

Taking a bus into the highlands or tropical regions of Guatemala is a good way to encounter the pacaya fritters. At every bus stop along the highway, women of the nearby villages hawk their pacaya, hard-cooked eggs, tortillas, sauce in old mayonnaise jars, cooked chickens and soft drinks to the travelers. A pacaya fritter wrapped in a tortilla with a bit of *chirmol* and a dash of salt is difficult to refuse.

PEPIÁN: *see* Squash Seeds.

PEPITORIA: *see* Squash Seeds.

PIEDRA or METATE: No Indian household is without the grinding stone, a flat, gray lava stone platform with the rounded pestle that is used like a rolling pin to crush seeds and vegetables. The *piedra* comes in many different sizes; it is the original of the blender. The homes very often have more than one *piedra*, which means "stone." For example, the *piedra* that grinds the freshly roasted coffee is not used for sauces since it might contaminate the flavor.

The best *piedras* are cut in the town of Nahualá, and it is a common sight to see them sold on the roadside of the Pan American Highway. Occasionally, one encounters a pre-Columbian *piedra* with a smooth surface and decorations.

The Indian women insist that the taste of food is better when prepared with the *piedra* since the food is crushed in a rolling motion whereas in a blender or food processor the seeds or whatever are cut in a circular motion.

PINOL: Another Mayan method of preparing meat in which the *pinol*, toasted dry corn kernels, are ground to a powder and used as the major ingredient in a recipe along with poultry. It is probably of Cakchiquel Indian origin.

PLANTAIN or PLÁTANO *(Musa sapientum L.):* All plantains are bananas but not all bananas are plantains. A truism that hardly describes the versatility and popularity of this fruit/vegetable (it can be utilized in both guises). Eaten principally in the semitropical lowlands and in the larger cities, it is an essential food prepared in a number of ways that reflect its adaptability. It is not, however, eaten by the Maya in the chilly highland villages where the plantain does not grow and where their diet is based on local produce.

Plantain is always cooked; there are several recipes in these pages.

PULIQUÉ: I have been unsuccessful in tracing the source of this word, which refers to a system of preparing meats. Unlike a *guisado*, in which the meat is first browned, a *puliqué* omits oil of any kind. The meats and the seasonings are cooked together at the same time. It is a Mayan method of preparation and the word has become a part of the language without any known etymology.

RAPADURA: Also called *panela*. The unrefined dark brown sugar that is sold in square cakes weighing about 2 pounds each. Also packed two to a woven basket of sugar cakes with rounded tops. This is the sugar of the countryside, a peasant sugar with an intense caramel flavor that can be eaten out of hand as a village sweet or in various dessert dishes. Syrups *(miel)* made with *rapadura* are infinitely more delicious than those made of our own packaged brown sugars which, however, are a logical substitute.

RECADO: No exposure to Guatemalan cooking can be taken without the mention of *recado*. This is the sauce in which meats, poultry, tamales or any other typical foods are prepared, bathed or mixed. The *recado* is the sauce that is the flavor of the preparation. It usually consists of standard items like onion, garlic, tomatoes, spices and the thickening medium.

Sauces can be thickened with moistened cornmeal, toasted

bread crumbs, French-style bread softened in water or broth, toasted cornstarch (rarely, but effective), toasted or fresh tortillas, flour and toasted raw rice. Each method has its partisans and makes its special contribution to the taste. All of them are used in this book, but I find that bread crumbs, toasted rice and tortillas have a kind of magic that I am partial to.

SOUR ORANGE JUICE: *Naranja agria*, bitter orange, or sour or Seville orange (*Citrus aurantium*), is not our supermarket variety of sweet juice orange. This one has a sour bite. It is used in cooking in Guatemala and El Salvador where an acid flavor is necessary to combine with meat in Salpicón (Chopped Beef Appetizer, see Index) and salads as in the Salsa of El Salvador (see Index). Elisabeth Lambert Ortiz, in her *The Book of Latin American Cooking*, suggests one third lemon or lime juice to two thirds sweet orange as a substitute. I have also used 1 teaspoon cider vinegar to 3 tablespoons sweet orange juice.

SQUASH SEEDS: These are the pepitas that are toasted to a crisp brown, then ground to a powder to become *pepitoria*, an essential ingredient of Mayan foods. Usually available in health-food stores here, squash seeds should be integrated into our cooking since they provide a nutlike flavor and assist in thickening sauces. Pumpkin seeds may be used in place of the squash seeds.

Pepián indicates a particular, and classic, method of preparing meats, whereby the meat is cooked in water before the sauce and flavoring ingredients are added. *Pepitoria* is usually one of the ingredients and probably that is what gives it the name.

TOASTING TECHNIQUE: This is nothing more than putting sesame or squash seeds, dry or fresh chiles, onion, garlic, tomatoes, or anything else required in a recipe, in a dry skillet without oil or liquid. These items are lightly toasted or browned over moderately low heat, which may take 10 to 15 minutes.

Alternately, whole tomatoes, onions, garlic or even tortillas may be toasted or lightly charred in an oven broiler or over charcoal. The toasting enhances the flavor of the seasonings and also darkens the color of the sauces, both of which are important to a recipe.

TORTILLA FLOUR: *see* Masa.

YUCA: *see* Cassava.

RICE
AND
BEANS

Rice and beans, beans and rice—the staples of Central American cooking.

The beans used may be red, white or black, but we are principally concerned with the black beans of Guatemala, without which the cuisine for the majority of the people would be unthinkable. Not like the baked pea beans of Boston, these are rich black beans, prepared whole, as a soup, as a paste or purée, in any sort of textural combination that appeals to one. Personal preference is the guide.

Some Guatemalans claim that the beans grown in the Parramos district are the very best, and ask for them in the markets as though they were individually marked with the place of origin. And a farmer in the Jutiapa district told me emphatically that the beans of *his* town were better and showed me sacks being filled for sale throughout the country.

Black beans are eaten at any time during the day. They are fine at breakfast with white cheese and tortillas. They can be served as an

25

appetizer, at luncheons and dinner buffets. In the Caribbean areas they are combined with rice, and they sustain the peasant all day long when not much else is available. They are delicious cooked any way you want them.

As for the rice, it was introduced by the Spanish back in the days of the conquistadores; it flowed from Asia via Spain to the highlands of Guatemala and was accepted as part of the foreign cooking the new arrivals brought with them from the Old World. But the Mayans also retained their traditional foods, just adding the rice to them, so that rice is now considered a staple in the mestizo kitchen.

FRIJOLES NEGROS PARADOS

WHOLE BLACK BEANS

GUATEMALA

This dish is the everyday fare par excellence of the Guatemala people, regardless of their economic or social status. It is eaten with tortillas or bread for breakfast or at any other time of day. The basis of several other bean recipes, it is used in bean purées and also provides the bean liquid called for in Arroz Negro (Black Rice, see Index).

1 pound dried black beans
6 cups water
½ teaspoon salt, or to taste
¼ cup chopped onion
1 garlic clove, chopped

1. Soak the beans overnight in the water.
2. The next day cook the beans in the same water with the salt, onion and garlic for about 1 hour, or until they are soft but still retain their shape. The finished dish will have a substantial amount of liquid. Serve warm.

SERVES 6 TO 8

FRIJOLES NEGROS COLADOS

BLACK BEAN PURÉE

ANTIGUA, GUATEMALA

1 pound dried black beans
6 cups water
¼ cup chopped onion
1 garlic clove, chopped
1 teaspoon salt, or to taste
¼ cup onion crisps (see Note)

1. Soak the beans overnight in the water.
2. The next day cook the beans, onion, garlic and salt for about 1½ hours, or until beans are soft.
3. Purée the mixture in a food processor until smooth. Press the purée through a metal sieve to make it completely smooth.
4. Add the onion crisps and simmer again slowly to reduce the consistency to a thick but silky paste. Serve warm with *tostados*.

SERVES 6 TO 8

Note: Prepare the onion crisps in this manner: Fry ½ cup of fine-chopped onions in 3 tablespoons corn oil over low heat for 3 to 4 minutes, until they are light brown. Remove crisps from the oil and drain on paper towels. Then incorporate them in the purée.

FRIJOLES NEGROS VOLTEADOS

FRIED BLACK BEAN PASTE

GUATEMALA

This takes the Black Bean Purée one step farther. More liquid is cooked out of it until it will hold its shape in a roll and can be sliced. The *Volteados* is a classic treatment of black beans. At breakfast, brunch or any other time this dish is universally popular. Any quantity can be made, reheated the next day, used as an appetizer with tortilla crisps (*tostados*) or included as a vegetable for any meal.

2 cups Frijoles Negros Colados (Black Bean Purée, preceding recipe)
1 tablespoon corn oil

1. Heat the oil in a skillet over moderate to low heat. Add the bean purée and mix well with a wooden spoon. Continue to stir as the liquid evaporates and the purée thickens.

2. Continue this process until the purée comes away easily from the skillet and begins to take form. Shaking the pan back and forth briskly will help in developing the *maleta* or sausage shape characteristic of this dish. Complete forming the "sausage" by rolling it with your hands.

3. Serve warm with tortillas, farmer cheese, thick cream or French bread, or with all together.

SERVES 6 TO 8

HABAS EN ZAPATADAS

FAVA BEANS IN THEIR SHOES
GUATEMALA CITY

Fava beans are of Spanish origin rather than being indigenous to Central America. When eating them, each diner traditionally squeezes the beans out of the rather tough skins and deposits the skins on a plate. These are the "shoes" of the beans.

½ pound dried fava beans
4 cups water
1 teaspoon salt, or to taste
4 cups beef or chicken broth
1 tablespoon corn oil
1 stalk of epazote, 5 inches

1. Soak the beans in water and salt overnight.

2. The next day cook them over moderate heat until soft, about 1½ hours.

3. Pour off the liquid and replace it with the broth. Add the oil and epazote and simmer the soup over moderate heat for 10 minutes. Serve hot.

SERVES 4 TO 6

Variation: Replace the dried favas with canned beans. Pour off the liquid and add the broth, oil and epazote. Simmer.

HABAS VOLTEADOS

FAVA BEAN PASTE

GUATEMALA CITY

½ pound dried fava beans
4 cups water
1 teaspoon salt, or to taste
½ cup fine-chopped onion
3 tablespoons corn oil

1. Soak the beans overnight in the water and salt.

2. The next day cook them over moderate heat until soft, about 1½ hours. Remove the tough skins (also known as the "nail"), pour off the liquid, and process the beans to a smooth paste.

3. Fry the onion in the oil over moderate heat in a skillet until light brown and crisp. Add the fava paste and fry over low heat, stirring from time to time to evaporate the moisture. Then shake the pan back and forth to form a *maleta,* or a round sausagelike roll of the dried, smoothly fried paste.

4. Serve warm as a breakfast food, side vegetable or as an appetizer with tortillas, either fresh or toasted.

SERVES 4 TO 6

Variation: Canned fava beans, not always available, can be used as the easy way out, eliminating the soaking and cooking procedures. Process and fry as directed.

FRIJOLES COLORADOS

RED BEANS

EL SALVADOR

1 pound dried red beans
4 cups water

¼ cup chopped onion
2 garlic cloves, chopped
½ teaspoon salt

1. Soak the beans in the water overnight.
2. The next day combine beans and soaking liquid with the remaining ingredients and cook over moderate heat for about 1 hour, until beans are soft.
3. Use the cooked beans in the recipes that follow.

SERVES 6

FRIJOLES GUISADOS

RED BEANS, VEGETARIAN STYLE

EL SALVADOR

2 tablespoons corn oil
½ cup sliced sweet green pepper
¼ cup thin-sliced onion
1 teaspoon salt
2 cups cooked red beans and liquid
¼ teaspoon orégano
2 tablespoons grated Parmesan-style cheese
Sour cream

1. Heat the oil in a skillet over moderate heat. Add the green pepper, onion and salt. Stir-fry for 2 minutes. Add the beans and stir well. Mash 2 tablespoons of the beans in a corner of the skillet and mix with the rest to provide thickening.
2. Continue frying until the beans are quite dry. At the last moment add the orégano and mix well.
3. Serve warm as an appetizer or principal dish sprinkled with cheese and sour cream to taste. Accompany with toast, tortillas or *tostados.*

SERVES 3 OR 4

FRIJOLES COLORADOS CON MARRANO

RED BEAN AND PORK PURÉE

EL SALVADOR

1 tablespoon corn oil
½ pound boneless pork, cut into ½-inch cubes
½ cup sliced onion
1 garlic clove, sliced
½ cup chopped tomato
½ cup sliced sweet red pepper
½ cup sliced sweet green pepper
3 bay leaves
⅛ teaspoon freshly ground black pepper
½ teaspoon sugar
¼ teaspoon orégano
1 pound red beans, cooked, including liquid
2 tablespoons grated cheese
¾ cup sour cream
6 strips of sweet red pepper

1. Heat the oil in a pan over moderate heat and fry the pork until it changes color. Add the onion, garlic, tomato and red and green pepper, and stir-fry for 10 minutes. Add the bay leaves, black pepper, sugar and orégano, and continue to fry for a few minutes longer.

2. Add the cooked beans and liquid and mix well. Simmer over moderate/low heat for 1 hour, or until the pork is soft.

3. Process the bean mixture to a smooth purée.

4. Serve the purée in the center of a round dish. Sprinkle purée with grated cheese and spoon sour cream around the perimeter. Spread the petals of a red flower (strips of sweet red pepper) out from the center of the dish. Serve warm.

SERVES 6 TO 8

Note: Cubes of beef chuck may be substituted for the pork.

TORTAS DE ARROZ

RICE PANCAKES

COSTA RICA

2 cups cooked rice, ground but not puréed (see Note)
3 tablespoons sugar
2 tablespoons butter, melted
2 eggs, beaten
¼ cup corn oil
Additional sugar for sprinkling

1. Mix all ingredients except the oil and additional sugar and shape into pancakes about 3 inches in diameter and ½ inch thick.

2. Heat the oil in a skillet over moderate heat and brown the pancakes on both sides. Drain briefly on paper towels.

3. Serve warm. Traditionally pancakes are served with a sprinkling of sugar and a bowl of sour cream.

SERVES 4

Note: *To cook the rice for grinding:*

1 cup rice
2 teaspoons corn oil
1½ cups water
½ teaspoon salt

Brown the rice lightly in the oil over moderate heat for 2 minutes. Add the water and salt and bring to a boil. Reduce heat to low, cover the pot, and cook for 10 to 12 minutes. Let the rice cool before grinding. This can be prepared early in the day for later use.

FRITANGA

FRIED RICE

ANTIGUA, GUATEMALA

This *fritanga* is frequently served as a breakfast food in Antigua, but it can be eaten at any meal. It is reminiscent of Chinese fried rice without the soy sauce.

¼ cup chopped onion
2 garlic cloves, chopped
2 tablespoons oil
4 cups cold cooked white rice
½ cup ½-inch cubes of cooked beef
½ cup ½-inch cubes of cooked chayote (huisquil)
¼ cup ½-inch cubes of tomato
½ teaspoon salt, or to taste

1. Fry the onion and garlic in the oil in a skillet over moderate heat for 3 minutes. Add the rice and stir-fry for 2 minutes more.

2. Add all the other ingredients and stir-fry well for 3 minutes more. Serve warm.

SERVES 6

ARROZ BLANCO CON COCO

WHITE RICE IN COCONUT MILK

LIVINGSTON, GUATEMALA

1 tablespoon chopped onion
2 teaspoons corn oil
1 cup raw rice, rinsed in cold water and drained well
1½ cups Rich Coconut Milk (see Index)
¼ teaspoon salt (optional)

1. Fry the onion in oil over moderate heat for 1 minute. Add the rice and fry for 2 minutes, stirring continuously.
2. Add the coconut milk, and salt if used. Bring to a boil, then reduce heat to low. Simmer in a covered pan for 20 minutes. Stir once after 10 minutes. Serve warm.

SERVES 4 TO 6

ARROZ NEGRO

BLACK RICE

GUATEMALA CITY

2 tablespoons fine-chopped onion
1 tablespoon corn oil
1 cup raw rice, rinsed in cold water and drained well
1¾ cups black bean liquid (see Note)
1 tablespoon chopped sweet red pepper
¼ teaspoon salt, or to taste

1. Fry the onion in the oil over moderate heat for 1 minute. Add the rice and fry for 2 minutes more, stirring continuously.

2. Add the black bean liquid, sweet pepper and salt. Stir well. Bring to a boil, then reduce heat to low and simmer for 15 to 20 minutes. The rice should be dry, gray/black in color, with a nutty flavor. Serve warm.

SERVES 4

Note: The black bean liquid is that taken from the Frijoles Negros Parados (Whole Black Beans, see Index). Remove ¼ cup cooked beans and 1½ cups of the liquid. Process to a smooth purée in a food processor.

SOPA DE ARROZ CHAPÍN

GUATEMALAN RICE

GUATEMALA

1 cup raw rice, rinsed in cold water and drained well
1 tablespoon corn oil
1 tablespoon fine-chopped onion
1 garlic clove, chopped
2 tablespoons grated carrot
1 tablespoon fine-chopped sweet red pepper
1 tablespoon chopped ripe tomato
½ teaspoon salt, or to taste
1¼ cups water or chicken broth

1. Fry the rice in the oil in a skillet over moderate heat for 2 minutes, or until the rice turns a light tan color. Add the onion, garlic, carrot and sweet pepper, and fry for 2 minutes more.

2. Add the tomato, salt and water or broth. Cover the pan, bring to a boil, turn heat to low, and cook for 12 to 15 minutes more. Stir once.

3. Allow the rice to remain covered for 10 minutes or more before serving. Serve warm.

SERVES 4

Note: Rice always tastes better when it has been allowed to rest for a short time before serving. The various seasonings have an opportunity to be absorbed by the kernels as the rice steams in its own heat in a covered pan.

ARROZ Y FRIJOLES COLORADOS

RICE AND BEANS

GUATEMALA

This is one of the classic dishes of the Guatemala people who live in towns along the Caribbean coast. It is so common that it is known by its English name even in a Spanish-speaking country. Usually served as a side dish, it also makes a tasty appetizer when served with a few drops of Salsa Picante (see Index) on a *tostado*.

½ cup dried small red beans
2½ cups water
½ teaspoon salt
1½ cups Rich Coconut Milk (see Index)
1 tablespoon chopped onion
1 whole garlic clove
1 tablespoon chopped sweet red pepper
2 teaspoons corn oil
1 cup raw rice
¼ teaspoon thyme

1. Soak the beans in the water overnight.

2. Simmer beans in the same water with the salt over moderate heat until soft, about 45 minutes. Drain beans and reserve the liquid.

3. Prepare the coconut milk, using warm bean liquid instead of water.

4. Fry the onion, garlic and sweet pepper in the oil for 1 minute. Add the rice and fry for 2 minutes, stirring constantly. Add the coconut milk, beans and thyme. Bring to a boil, then immediately reduce heat to low, cover the pan, and simmer for 20 minutes. Stir once or twice during this process.

SERVES 4 TO 6

FRIJOLES CON ARROZ

RICE AND BEANS

PUERTO BARRIOS, GUATEMALA

This slightly different recipe for Rice and Beans includes tomatoes, green pepper and bay leaves for flavoring.

1 pound dried red kidney beans
4 cups water
1 cup sliced tomatoes
½ cup sliced green sweet pepper
2 tablespoons chopped onion
2 bay leaves
1 teaspoon thyme
1 teaspoon salt, or to taste
3 cups raw rice
½ cup Rich Coconut Milk (see Index)

1. Soak the beans overnight in the water.

2. The next day add the tomatoes, sweet pepper, onion, bay leaves, thyme and salt. Bring to a boil and cook in a covered large saucepan for 45 minutes, or until the beans have softened.

3. Add the rice and coconut milk and stir well. Bring this mixture to a boil and reduce heat to low. Cook for about 20 minutes, until the rice has absorbed all the liquid. Stir once or twice during the cooking process to blend all the seasonings. Serve warm or at room temperature.

SERVES 8

TAMALES, TORTILLAS AND BREAD

Several cultures in Asia, principally the Indonesians, wrap seasoned foods in green leaves, such as banana leaves, and steam them over hot water until cooked. In Central America, they use the same technique with tamales whether the dough in the steaming packages is made from cornmeal, potatoes or green bananas. It is a simple and essentially healthful method of cooking food without the calories added by frying in oil.

On certain days, but not daily, the market women bring their tamales in for sale. They may be the Tamales Negros (Black Tamales), colored with chocolate and usually eaten on festival holidays, or the simple Paches which can be found almost anytime. Other regional tamales, such as the Guineo (Green Banana Tamale, see Index) are prepared by the townswomen who specialize in cooking such things and are for special orders only. So one can always find these wonderful pre-Hispanic creations in Guatemala or the other Central American countries. I usually arrange somehow, when there, to have them for breakfast or a light evening supper.

Tortillas are another matter. It is not an uncommon sight to see the market women dispensing them daily to eager buyers by the dozens, like votive offerings at a shrine. Mornings are the time to buy them. Warm and tender, they retain their intrinsic texture for the day when wrapped in a towel and a plastic bag. In the cities tortillas are rarely prepared at home when they can be purchased so easily and cheaply. In the Mayan villages, the homemaker lives off the land and makes her tortillas from scratch—mixing the *masa* on a grinding stone, then baking them, without oil, on a dry, clay platter known as a *comal*.

Bread competes with tortillas as the great filler. The name for French bread (*pan Français*), which came to Guatemala via Mexico and France, has become part of the local vocabulary. It refers to the small rolls that are baked and sold twelve to the rectangular pan all over Guatemala. Small village bakers prepare the bread in this style rather than in the long loaves we associate with French bread.

The homemade breads include cornbread and Sunday bread, but the best bread in Guatemala is the coconut bread, a specialty of Livingston on the Caribbean coast.

TAMALITOS PACHES

LITTLE CORNMEAL TAMALES

COBÁN, GUATEMALA

2 pounds (8 cups) tortilla flour (masa harina)
1 cup cold water
1 teaspoon salt, or to taste
½ cup corn oil
3 cups water
Corn leaves or aluminum foil

1. Mix the first 4 ingredients together into a paste.

2. Shape the *tamalitos,* using about 1 heaping tablespoon of the paste for each. Wrap them in corn leaves or aluminum foil. If using foil, seal the ends by a twist of the wrist.

3. Cook them in a large saucepan containing 3 cups water. The *tamalitos* should be covered at all times.

MAKES 18 TO 20 TAMALITOS

Note: The *paches* are served traditionally with a spiced turkey soup, although they can be served with anything at any time. *Paches* can be rewarmed the following day by boiling them, while they are still in their wrappers, in an inch of water for 10 minutes.

CHUCHITOS

CORNMEAL DUMPLINGS STUFFED WITH MEAT

SAN JUAN OBISPO, ANTIGUA, GUATEMALA

1 pound boneless chicken, pork or turkey
1 tablespoon oil
2 cups sliced ripe tomatoes
1 chile guaque (guajillo), seeds and stem removed
2 tablespoons water
1 pound (4 cups) tortilla flour (masa harina)
8 tablespoons lard or margarine, at room temperature
1½ cups cold water
1 teaspoon salt
Fresh green or dried cornhusks, wet

1. Cut the chicken, pork or turkey into 1-inch cubes. Fry them in the oil in a skillet over moderate heat for 3 minutes. Set aside.

2. Process the tomatoes, chile pepper and 2 tablespoons water into a smooth sauce. Set aside.

3. Mix the flour, lard, 1½ cups cold water and the salt together into a thick mush. Put ½ cup mush in each wet cornhusk, push an indentation into the mush, and add 1 tablespoon sauce and a chunk of meat. Cover the stuffing with the mush and wrap the dumpling into a sausage shape with the corn leaves.

4. Steam the *chuchitos* over hot water over moderate heat for 1½ hours.

5. Unwrap and eat them warm or at room temperature.

MAKES 10 DUMPLINGS

TAMALES COLORADOS

RED TAMALES—A RECIPE FOR 100 TAMALES

GUATEMALA CITY

Tamales take time and effort, and a Guatemalan considers it worthwhile to undertake this project only when preparing for a crowd. Hence this recipe for 100 tamales—enough to sell to the neighbors. The same recipe, reduced, follows and will be of more practical use in the American kitchen.

Dough (Masa)

8 pounds tortilla flour (masa harina)
25 quarts water
¼ cup salt, or to taste
3 to 5 pounds lard, butter or margarine

Sauce (Recado)

25 pounds ripe red tomatoes
2 chiles guaque (guajillo)
2 tablespoons chile zambo or chile of Cobán, or any red hot chile
    flakes
2 tablespoons chile chocolate (optional, if you prefer a more
    pungent sauce)
3 cups sliced sweet red peppers
1 teaspoon achiote
¼ cup corn oil

Meat

10 pounds boneless pork, or boned chicken or turkey

1. Combine all the dough ingredients and cook together over moderate to low heat for 1½ hours, stirring the mixture continuously so it does not stick. The *masa* is usually cooked in a large clay pot over a wood fire using a wooden pole to stir the heavy, thick mixture. The more fat you use, the richer the dough. When ready, the dough should be a smooth purée.

2. Combine all the sauce ingredients except the oil and simmer together over moderate heat for 20 minutes.

3. Process the mixture into a smooth sauce. Heat the oil in a large skillet or pan and fry the sauce for 5 minutes, then simmer over low heat for 15 minutes more. Set aside.

4. Use pork, chicken or turkey as a center for the tamale. Use one or two kinds of raw meat, cut into 1-inch cubes. Beef is not used.

Assembling and Cooking the Tamale

Mashan leaves, large and small, or foil (12 inches square)
1 cup cooked masa
¼ cup sauce
1 or 2 cubes of meat

1. Put the *masa* in the center of a small mashan leaf, about 4 inches square, which rests on a larger leaf, about 12 × 5 inches. Make a well in the center of the *masa*. Put in the sauce and meat. Swirl the sauce around a bit.

2. Fold both ends of the leaves to the center and fold them over each other to seal. Then turn over one end of the leaf and stand the tamale on its end to pack in the contents. Then turn over the other leaf end to make a bundle 6 inches long by 4 inches wide. Tie the bundle with a grass stalk or string. This is the prepared tamale.

3. Place mashan leaves on the bottom of the cooking pot and put the tamales flat one on top of the other and around the sides of the pot. Fill the cooking pot one third up the side with water. Cover the tamales with more leaves before covering the pot. Cook over moderate heat for 1 hour.

(recipe continues)

4. Serve tamales hot or at least warm. Unwrap the leaves and trim them square with scissors. Use leaves as a plate but put them on another plate for convenience.

MAKES 100 TAMALES

Note: Tamales will keep in the refrigerator for 3 or 4 days. They can be reheated, one or two at a time or a larger number. Simply pour 1 inch of water into a pot, bring it to a boil with the tamales, then reduce the heat, cover, and simmer for 10 minutes.

TAMALES COLORADOS

RED TAMALES

GUATEMALA CITY

Dough (Masa)

4 cups tortilla flour
8 cups water
1 teaspoon salt
4 tablespoons lard or vegetable shortening

Sauce (Recado)

2 pounds ripe tomatoes, fresh or canned
¼ chile guaque (guajillo), broken up
1 teaspoon dried hot red chile flakes
¼ cup sliced sweet red pepper
¼ teaspoon achiote, melted in 1 teaspoon hot oil
2 teaspoons corn oil

Meat

2 pounds boneless chicken, turkey or pork

1. Combine all the dough ingredients in a 4-quart pot and cook together over moderately low heat for about 30 minutes, stirring the mixture continuously so that it does not stick.

2. Combine all the sauce ingredients except the oil and cook together over moderate heat for 20 minutes.

3. Process the mixture into a smooth sauce. Heat the oil in a large skillet or pan and fry the sauce for 5 minutes, then simmer over low heat for 15 minutes more. Set aside.

4. Chicken, turkey or pork can be used as a center for the tamale. Use one or two kinds of uncooked meat cut into 1-inch cubes.

Assembling the Tamale

Mashan leaves, large and small
1 cup cooked masa
¼ cup sauce
1 or 2 cubes of meat

1. Assemble the tamales in the same manner as for the larger recipe. All other aspects of cooking and serving are the same.

MAKES 10 TAMALES

GUINEO OR BIMENA

GREEN BANANA TAMALE

LIVINGSTON, GUATEMALA

Bimena is the name of the tamale in the Caribe language. *Guineo* is actually the green banana itself.

1½ pounds boneless pork, cut into 2-inch pieces
4 cups water
1 tablespoon lemon juice
1 teaspoon salt, or to taste
4 tablespoons corn oil
¼ teaspoon achiote
3 tablespoons flour
¼ cup cold water
½ teaspoon freshly ground black pepper
1 teaspoon Worcestershire sauce
2 pounds green bananas
1 cup Rich Coconut Milk (see Index)
Mashan leaves or aluminum foil
¼ cup diced cooked carrots
¼ cup cooked diced chayote (huisquil)

1. Soak the pork, 2 cups water and the lemon juice together for 1 hour. Drain well.

2. Add 2 more cups water and 1 teaspoon salt to the pork. Simmer in a covered pan over moderate heat for 1 hour. Drain and set aside.

3. Make the sauce: Put 2 tablespoons of oil in a skillet and add the achiote to dissolve it. Blend the flour into the cold water with the pepper and Worcestershire sauce. Add the flour mixture to the oil and cook over moderate heat for a moment to thicken. Set aside.

4. Grate the bananas by hand or in a processor to a smooth paste. Add the coconut milk and remaining 2 tablespoons oil and mix well.

5. Assemble the tamale: Take a mashan leaf or 10-inch square of foil, and put ½ cup banana paste on the center. Press into the paste 2 cubes of pork, 2 teaspoons of the cooked vegetables and 1 tablespoon of the sauce. Top this with 1 tablespoon more of banana paste.

6. Fold the sides of the leaf or foil toward the center. Then fold both ends toward the middle to shape a tamale 5 inches long and 2 inches wide. Tie up the tamale with a string in the center if using the leaf, but this is not necessary if using foil.

7. Put several mashan leaves on the bottom of a saucepan. Add the tamales, cover them with a few more leaves, and cover everything with boiling water. Cover the pan and cook over moderate heat for 30 minutes.

8. Unwrap the tamales and serve them hot or at room temperature.

MAKES 10 TAMALES

Note: The tamales may be refrigerated for several days and reheated in boiling water for 10 minutes. When using foil, the tamales can also be steamed in a Chinese-style steamer over hot water for 30 minutes, rather than cooking them in water.

PACHES DE PAPA QUEZALTECOS

POTATO TAMALES, QUEZALTENANGO STYLE

GUATEMALA

2 pounds potatoes, about 8
3 cups water
1 pound ripe tomatoes, sliced
2 scallions, sliced
4 garlic cloves, sliced
½ cup sliced sweet red pepper
1 chile pasa, seeds and stem removed
6 tablespoons margarine, melted
2 cups tortilla flour (masa harina)
2 teaspoons salt
1½ teaspoons ground allspice
1½ teaspoons pepper
¼ teaspoon achiote, dissolved in 2 teaspoons hot water
Mashan leaves or aluminum foil cut into 12-inch squares

1. Cook the potatoes in their jackets in 2 cups water over moderate heat until they are soft but not overdone, about 20 minutes. Cool and peel. Process to a smooth dry purée.

2. Cook together 1 cup water, the tomatoes, scallions, garlic, sweet pepper and chile pasa over low heat for 20 minutes. Process to a smooth sauce and strain through a metal sieve to remove any lumps. There should be about 2½ cups sauce.

3. Mix together into a smooth, moist paste the mashed potatoes, sauce, margarine, tortilla flour, salt, allspice, pepper and dissolved achiote. Mix well.

4. Put ¾ cup of this mixture onto a leaf or foil and fold it into a rectangle to make a tamale 5 inches long and 2 inches wide. Pack it firmly when folding.

5. Steam the tamale over moderate to high heat for 30 minutes. Serve warm, with a liberal squeeze of lemon.

MAKES 15

Variation: *Paches* very often have a 2-inch cube of cooked pork pushed into the center of the potato mash, before it is folded over and steamed. A 1-inch cube of cooked ham may be used in place of the fresh pork.

NACATAMAL

CLASSIC TAMALE
NICARAGUA

In my opinion, this is one of the finest of all the tamales in Central America. It is beloved by the Nicaraguans and is the national tamale. Traditionally the wrapper is made from banana leaves; several sheets of them are needed to seal off the dough from the water. It is tightly tied up with bamboo or some type of thick string.

The *nacatamal* is cooked in, not steamed over, hot water and must therefore be tightly bound up. Aluminum foil works well and is always available to us.

The word *nacatamal* is a play on words; *nacata* is a word of the indigenous Indian population which means "food." *Mal* is the Spanish word meaning "bad." It is "bad food" only in that it is so good that one is apt to eat too much and then must face the usual consequences of overeating.

Filling

1 pound boneless pork, chicken or turkey
¼ cup sour orange juice
1 teaspoon salt
2 teaspoons achiote
1 garlic clove, crushed

(recipe continues)

Dough (Masa)

1 pound (4 cups) tortilla flour (masa harina)
1 cup milk
2 tablespoons lard or vegetable shortening
1 tablespoon sour orange juice
½ teaspoon salt
½ cup mashed potatoes
Aluminum foil, cut into 15-inch squares

Garnishes

For 7 or 8 tamales, plan on 2 slices of each vegetable and 1 teaspoon
of rice for each tamale.

Potatoes, sliced ⅛ inch thick and 2 inches square
Tomatoes, sliced thin
Onion, sliced thin
Sweet red pepper, sliced thin
Fresh mint leaves and stems
Raw rice, well rinsed
Raisins (optional)
Stuffed olives (optional)
Dried prunes (optional)
Fresh hot chile, sliced thin (optional)

1. Combine the pork, chicken or turkey with remaining filling ingredients as a marinade, and let the meat marinate overnight.

2. Combine the dough ingredients in a large saucepan, mix well,
and cook over moderate to low heat for about 30 minutes, until it
becomes a moist but firm dough that holds together. This can be
done the day before and the dough refrigerated.

3. Put ¾ cup of the corn dough in the center of a foil wrapper. Push
2 slices of potatoes into the mound of dough near the bottom, then
1 piece of meat into the center. Cover the mound with 2 slices of
tomato, 2 of onion, 2 of sweet red pepper. Top this with 3 mint
leaves and put 1 teaspoon rice on top. If you also use the optional
items (recommended since they give the tamale more richness), then

push them into the dough around the perimeter. Add 1 teaspoon of the liquid from the meat marinade.

4. Bring both ends of the foil together to the center and fold them over ½ inch to seal tightly. Fold over one end tightly, stand the package on its end to shake everything down, and tighten the wrapping. Fold over the other end and seal. The tamale should be about 5 inches long and 4 inches wide.

5. Put the tamales in a pan large enough to hold all of them in one layer and fill it up with water to cover. Cover the pan. Bring to a boil over high heat, then reduce heat and cook over moderate to low heat for about 4 hours. Replenish the water as it evaporates. Some cooks claim that 5 or even 6 hours is required, but this applies only to wood fires.

6. Unwrap the tamales when ready and serve hot.

MAKES 7 OR 8 TAMALES

Variation: Individual *nacatamals* can be prepared as appetizers. Follow the same steps and use the same ingredients but shape them much reduced in size. The miniature *nacatamal* is 3 inches long and 1 inch wide when all wrapped up. Cook for 2 to 3 hours only.

TAMALES NEGROS

BLACK TAMALES
QUEZALTENANGO, GUATEMALA

The *tamale negro* is sweet and rich with the unconventional flavors of chocolate, chile and cinnamon, but sharpened with olives, raisins and prunes. It is an expensive tamale to prepare in Guatemala and one that is offered only on the special occasions worthy of its appearance. The *tamale negro* reflects the vibrancy of the modern Quezaltenango cooking, although it is drawn from earliest Mayan times.

Sauce (Recado)

2 tablespoons squash seeds, toasted
2 tablespoons sesame seeds, toasted
1 chile pasa, toasted
1 chile guaque, toasted
1 teaspoon ground cinnamon
¼ cup toasted bread crumbs, preferably French bread
2 pounds ripe tomatoes, sliced
2 ounces bitter chocolate, melted
½ cup water
1 pound boneless chicken

Dough

2 pounds tortilla flour (masa harina)
6 cups water
¼ cup sugar
½ pound butter or margarine, melted

1. Prepare a smooth sauce in the food processor with all the sauce ingredients except the chicken. Cook the sauce and the chicken together in a covered pan over moderate to low heat for 20 minutes.

2. Remove the chicken and cut it into 2-inch cubes. Set aside the chicken and the sauce.

3. Mix the dough ingredients together and simmer in a pan over low heat for 30 minutes, stirring frequently, until the mash is thick and smooth. Set aside.

Assembling the Tamale

Aluminum foil cut into 12-inch squares
1 small dried pitted prune for each tamale
2 raisins for each tamale
2 pitted green olives for each tamale

1. Put ½ cup of the dough in the center of the foil sheet. Smooth it out to a rectangle 4 by 5 inches and 1 inch thick. Top this with 2 tablespoons of the sauce and 1 cube of chicken. Around the side gently press in the prune, raisins and olives.

2. Fold the foil toward the center, seal it, then give the ends a twist around to seal the ends. Cook in a steamer over moderate heat for 1½ hours.

3. To serve, unfold the foil and cut around the edges with scissors, leaving the center part of the foil intact. It is your plate. Serve hot.

SERVES 7 OR 8

ENCHILADAS

CRISP TORTILLAS—AN OPEN SANDWICH

GUATEMALA CITY

12 thin tortillas, about 4 inches in diameter
½ cup corn oil

Sauce

1 tablespoon chopped onion
2 teaspoons corn oil
¼ teaspoon thyme
3 bay leaves
½ teaspoon salt, or to taste
1 cup canned peeled tomatoes, processed to a smooth purée

Pickled Vegetables

4 cups shredded cabbage
1 cup shredded carrots
1 cup shredded cooked beets, canned or fresh
¼ cup white or cider vinegar
2 tablespoons lemon juice
1 teaspoon thyme
¼ teaspoon orégano

Garnishes

½ cup grated Parmesan-type cheese
½ cup fine-chopped parsley
½ cup thin-sliced onion rounds
2 hard-cooked eggs, sliced

1. Fry the tortillas in moderately hot oil until brown and crisp. Drain on paper towels.

2. Make the sauce: Fry the onion in oil in a skillet over moderate heat. Add the thyme, bay leaves and salt, and fry for 2 minutes more. Add the tomato purée and simmer over low heat for 5 minutes to thicken the sauce. Set aside.

3. Prepare the vegetables: Blanch the cabbage in boiling water for 5 minutes. Drain well. Blanch the shredded carrots in boiling water for 5 minutes. Drain well. Mix together the cabbage, carrots, beets, vinegar, lemon juice, thyme and orégano. Set aside.

4. Assemble the enchilada as follows: Spread 2 teaspoons sauce on the fried tortilla. On that sprinkle 1 teaspoon cheese, 2 slices of onion and ½ teaspoon parsley. Over that arrange 2 or 3 tablespoons of the pickled vegetables. On that mound add 2 teaspoons sauce, 2 slices of onions and ½ teaspoon parsley. Over that place 1 slice of egg and ½ teaspoon cheese.

The enchilada is now piled with about 3 inches of ingredients in, more or less, the shape of a pyramid.

MAKES 12 ENCHILADAS

Note: In order for the enchilada to remain crisp, it should be assembled at the time of serving rather than in advance. The sauces and vegetables make the tortilla soggy if combined in advance.

Variation: A meat sauce can be used in place of the completely vegetarian tomato sauce.

2 teaspoons corn oil
1 tablespoon chopped onion
1 garlic clove, chopped
½ pound ground beef or pork
½ teaspoon salt
¼ teaspoon freshly ground black pepper
⅛ teaspoon grated nutmeg
½ cup canned peeled tomato, processed to a smooth purée

Heat the oil in a skillet over moderate heat and fry the onion, garlic and beef or pork for 2 minutes. Add the salt, pepper and nutmeg, and fry for 1 minute more. Mix well. Add the tomato purée and simmer over low heat for 5 minutes. If you use pork, fry slowly for 10 minutes. Cool and set aside for use with the enchiladas.

ENCHILADAS SALVADOREÑAS

OPEN TORTILLA SANDWICHES

EL SALVADOR

½ cup corn oil
8 fresh tortillas
½ pound ground beef or pork
½ teaspoon salt
¼ teaspoon freshly ground black pepper
1 tablespoon capers, chopped
½ cup julienne of carrots
¼ cup lightly cooked green snap beans, sliced thin
¼ cup thin-sliced onion
1 tablespoon cider vinegar
½ teaspoon sugar
½ cup tomato sauce (see Note)
3 tablespoons grated cheese
2 hard-cooked eggs, sliced

1. Heat the oil in a skillet and over moderate heat fry the tortillas until crisp but not overdone. Drain on paper towels. Set aside.

2. Remove all the oil except 1 tablespoon from the skillet. Fry the beef or pork, salt, pepper and capers together for 3 minutes, or until the meat is cooked. Set aside.

3. Prepare a simple salad by mixing the carrots, green beans, onion, vinegar and sugar together. Set aside.

4. Assemble the enchiladas as follows: Spread 1 tablespoon beef on the bottom of the crisp tortilla. Top with 1 tablespoon of the salad. Top that with 1 tablespoon tomato sauce. Sprinkle with 1 teaspoon cheese and top with a slice of egg. Serve immediately.

MAKES 8 ENCHILADAS

Note: For the tomato sauce, you may use any of the *chirmol* sauces from Guatemala (Simple Tomato Sauce, see Index). Tomato sauces are made all over Central America and are interchangeable in use, although the individual ingredients may vary.

ENCHILADAS

OPEN TORTILLA SANDWICHES

HONDURAS

Enchiladas are crisp-fried flat tortillas. They are prepared the same way as Tacos (see Index), with the same stuffings, sauce and garnishes. The principal difference is that tacos are rolled up, whereas enchiladas are served like an open sandwich.

The layers of the enchilada start with the meat stuffing on the bottom of the pile and then one layer after another is added. The list that follows shows the order of ingredients, from the sauce on top to the meat.

Sauce
Cheese
Avocado, sliced egg
Potato, tomato
Shredded cabbage
Chicken or beef stuffing
Tortillas

Serve the warm sauce separately for each person to pour as much as wanted over the piled-high sandwich.

PICADO DE ZANAHORIA

TORTILLA CRISPS WITH CARROT— AN APPETIZER

COBÁN, GUATEMALA

½ cup corn oil
12 tortillas
½ cup chopped onion
1 garlic clove, chopped
1 cup chopped sweet red pepper
1 pound ground beef
½ teaspoon thyme
½ teaspoon freshly ground black pepper
2 teaspoons vinegar
½ teaspoon salt
2 cups grated carrots

Sauce

2 cups chopped ripe tomatoes
¼ cup chopped onion
½ teaspoon orégano
¼ teaspoon salt

1. Heat the oil in a skillet over moderate heat. Fry the tortillas on both sides until they are crisp and brown, about 3 minutes. Drain on paper towels.

2. Remove all the oil in the skillet except 1 tablespoon. Fry the onion, garlic and sweet pepper over moderate heat for 2 minutes. Add the beef and stir-fry for 5 minutes, then add the thyme, black pepper, vinegar and salt. Continue to fry for 2 minutes more to distribute all the seasonings.

3. In another skillet, stir-fry the carrots in 2 teaspoons of oil for 3 minutes. Set aside.

4. Make the sauce: Simmer everything together in a dry skillet over low heat for 5 minutes. Process the mixture into a smooth sauce.

Strain through a metal sieve to remove any particles.

5. To serve, put 2 teaspoons sauce over the toasted tortilla. Top this with 2 tablespoons of the beef mixture. Cover this with 1 tablespoon of the carrots. Serve warm or at room temperature.

SERVES 12

DOBLADAS

DOUBLED-OVER TORTILLAS— AN APPETIZER

GUATEMALA

1 cup farmer cheese
2 tablespoons chopped sweet red pepper
2 tablespoons chopped onion
½ teaspoon freshly ground black pepper
½ teaspoon salt
10 tortillas
¼ cup or more corn oil

1. Mix the cheese, sweet pepper, onion, black pepper and salt together into a fairly smooth paste.

2. Put 1 heaping tablespoon of the cheese mixture on the lower half of the tortilla and fold the top over carefully to make a half-moon shape. Press lightly.

3. Heat the oil in a skillet over moderate heat. Fry the *dobladas* until crisp on both sides. Drain them briefly on paper towels. Serve warm.

SERVES 10

Variation: Use 2 cups of the meat and vegetable stuffing from the Chiles Rellenos (Stuffed Peppers, see Index) in place of the cheese.

PUPUSAS

STUFFED TORTILLAS

EL SALVADOR

Pupusas are El Salvador's most popular snack and can be eaten any-time as an appetizer, at lunch or when hunger tempts. When not made at home, they are often sold in *pupuserias*, a sort of pizza parlor that prepares and serves the *pupusas*, along with cold drinks, to the public, *à la carte*, fresh and hot. They sell for 20 cents each for those made with *chicharrones* and 25 cents each for the ones made with cheese and beans.

2 pounds prepared ground tortilla flour (masa harina)
Chicharrone, Cheese or Black Bean Stuffing (recipes follow)

1. Mix the prepared ground tortilla flour (*masa harina*) with water according to the directions on the package. The moist mixture is known as *masa*. Prepare tortillas by using 2 full tablespoons of the *masa* for each. Shape it into a tortilla 2½ inches in diameter and ¼ inch thick.

2. Scoop 1 tablespoon of chicharrone, cheese or black bean stuffing and put it into the center of a tortilla. Top this with another tortilla and press the edges together carefully to make a *pupusa*. Seal the edges with the tines of a fork so that the stuffing will not leak out.

3. Bake the *pupusas* on a hot, dry griddle or skillet over moderate heat for 6 to 8 minutes, or until brown on both sides.

4. Serve hot with any type of cabbage salad or pickled vegetables.

Chicharrone Stuffing

½ pound chicharrones (pork rinds)
¼ cup chopped sweet red pepper
2 cups sliced ripe tomatoes
¾ cup sliced onion
½ teaspoon salt, or to taste

1. Process everything together into a relatively smooth paste. Refrigerate for 1 day before using.

Cheese Stuffing

¾ cup farmer cheese
¼ cup feta cheese

1. Mash the cheeses and mix together. Refrigerate for several hours or 1 day before using.

Black Bean Stuffing

1 cup of prepared Frijoles Volteados (Black Bean Paste, see Index)

SERVES 10

Variations: *Pupusas* are also prepared using 2 or 3 different stuffings together. For example, put cheese and beans side by side on each tortilla, then cover with a second tortilla.

REPOCHETAS

STUFFED TORTILLA SANDWICHES

NICARAGUA

12 fresh tortillas
8 ounces cream cheese, at room temperature
½ cup corn oil
2 cups cabbage salad

1. Prepare a sandwich by smearing 1 tablespoon or more of cream cheese over the surface of a tortilla. Press another tortilla on top and seal the two together.

2. Heat the oil and over moderate heat brown the sandwich on both sides until crisp, about 3 minutes. Drain on paper towels.

3. Cut the sandwich into halves and garnish each piece with cabbage salad.

SERVES 12

CHILAQUILAS

FRESH TORTILLA TURNOVERS

COSTA RICA

Served at all occasions for lunch and dinner, but does very well as an important appetizer with drinks.

3 eggs, separated
1 teaspoon flour
¼ cup corn oil
1 recipe of Picadillo (Chopped Beef and Vegetables, see Index)
8 fresh tortillas

1. Beat the whites of the eggs until stiff. Fold in the lightly beaten yolks, sprinkle the flour over all, and fold it in.

2. Heat the oil in a skillet over moderate heat. Put 1 heaping tablespoon of the *picadillo* in the center of each tortilla and fold it in half. Dip it into the beaten eggs to coat both sides, and brown the turnover in the oil.

3. Drain briefly on paper towels and serve warm.

SERVES 8

CHILAQUILAS

STUFFED TORTILLAS
COBÁN, GUATEMALA

This is a simple, family-style preparation that can be put together easily and served as an appetizer for dedicated vegetarians.

1 pound farmer cheese, cut into ¼-inch-thick slices
12 tortillas
3 eggs, separated
2 teaspoons flour
½ teaspoon salt
¼ cup corn oil

1. Put 1 slice of the cheese on the bottom half of each tortilla and fold it over to form a half-moon.

2. Beat the egg whites until they are stiff but still moist. Add the flour, salt and the slightly beaten yolks. Mix.

3. Heat the oil in a skillet over moderate heat. Dip the stuffed tortilla into the egg batter and cook in the oil on both sides for about 5 minutes, or until brown.

4. Serve warm with a Chirmol (Simple Tomato Sauce, see Index).

SERVES 6

CHILAQUILAS DE TORTILLAS

STUFFED BAKED TORTILLAS

GUATEMALA CITY

This is a more glorified version of the Stuffed Tortillas—a party dish that may be prepared hours ahead and baked just before serving.

4 eggs, separated
½ teaspoon salt, or to taste
1 teaspoon flour
1½ cups farmer cheese
¼ cup chopped onion
½ cup chopped sweet red pepper
½ teaspoon freshly ground black pepper
12 tortillas
4 tablespoons corn oil
2 cups Chirmol (Simple Tomato Sauce, see Index)

1. Beat the egg whites with ¼ teaspoon salt until stiff. Fold in the beaten yolks and the flour.

2. Mix the cheese, onion, sweet pepper, black pepper and a pinch of salt. Put 2 tablespoons of the cheese filling on each tortilla and fold the tortilla over in half. Should it crack in folding, it will not matter since the egg batter will hold everything together.

3. Heat the oil in a skillet over moderate heat. Dip the stuffed tortillas into the egg batter and fry in the oil until light brown on each side, about 3 minutes.

4. Place the tortillas in a single layer in a heatproof glass baking dish and cover them with the tomato sauce. Add a second layer of tortillas if necessary. Bake in a 375° F. oven for 20 minutes. Serve warm.

SERVES 12

Variation: In place of the tortillas, you may make sandwiches of chayote with the same filling and sauce. For 8 chayotes, use 1 cup of farmer cheese plus all the other ingredients in the stuffed tortillas and proceed as follows:

1. Peel the chayote and cut it into ¼-inch-thick slices the long way. Blanch the slices in boiling water for 5 minutes. Drain and dry the slices well.

2. Make a sandwich with 2 slices of chayote with the cheese mixture in between. Dip sandwich into the egg batter and brown in the oil.

3. Place the stuffed chayotes in a single layer in a heatproof glass baking dish, cover with the tomato sauce, and bake in a 375° F. oven for 20 minutes. Serve warm.

PASTELITOS DE CHUCHOS

LITTLE PASTRY DOGS

EL SALVADOR

These appetizers are easily made. They make a popular addition to any cocktail party or coffee-time snack.

2 cups masa prepared with ½ teaspoon dissolved achiote and ¼
    teaspoon salt
1 cup prepared Picadillo (see Index)
½ cup corn oil

1. Form the *masa* into tortillas 3 inches in diameter and ¼ inch thick. Put 1 tablespoon of the *picadillo* in the center of the tortilla and fold it over into a half-moon. Press the edges down with the tines of a fork.

2. Heat the oil. Fry the *pastelitos* over medium heat until brown on both sides. Drain on paper towels. Serve warm.

MAKES 10

TACOS

FRIED STUFFED TORTILLA ROLLS

HONDURAS

Sauce

1 cup sliced tomato
½ cup sliced sweet red pepper
1 cup sliced celery
1 tablespoon chopped leek
½ cup sliced onion
½ teaspoon salt
¼ teaspoon freshly ground black pepper
1 tablespoon corn oil
4 ounces canned tomato paste
1½ cups water
Meat Stuffing or Chicken Stuffing (recipes follow)
20 fresh tortillas, preferably thin ones
1 cup corn oil
1 cup shredded cabbage, mixed with 1 tablespoon lemon juice
4 hard-cooked eggs, sliced
1 cup sliced boiled potatoes
1 ripe avocado, sliced
1 small ripe tomato, sliced
¼ cup grated mild cheese

1. Prepare the sauce: Fry vegetables and salt and pepper together in the oil over moderate to low heat for 10 minutes. Process this into a smooth paste.

2. Return mixture to the pan, add the tomato paste and water, bring to a boil, and simmer for 10 minutes to reduce the liquid somewhat. The sauce will still be very thin. Set aside.

3. Make whichever stuffing you plan to use.

4. Put 1 heaping tablespoon of the beef or chicken stuffing on one end of the tortilla. Roll it up firmly. Tie it together with a few turns of sewing thread. Prepare all the tacos this way.

5. Heat the oil in a skillet and over moderate heat brown the tortillas on all sides. Drain briefly on paper towels.

6. Place the tacos on a large serving platter. Cover them with the cabbage. Then garnish with the sliced eggs, potatoes, avocado and tomato and sprinkle the cheese over all.

7. Serve the sauce separately.

Meat Stuffing

1 tablespoon corn oil
½ pound ground beef
¼ teaspoon orégano
¼ teaspoon thyme
1 bay leaf
¼ teaspoon salt
¼ teaspoon pepper
¼ cup chopped sweet red pepper
¼ cup chopped onion
½ cup chopped tomato

1. Heat the oil in a skillet and fry the beef over moderate heat until the color changes.

2. Add all the other ingredients and fry over moderate heat for about 10 minutes, until all the liquid evaporates. Set aside.

Chicken Stuffing

2 cups cooked chicken, shredded
Other ingredients as above

1. Combine the chicken with the same herbs, seasoning and vegetables as those used for beef. Fry over moderate heat in oil for about 10 minutes, until all the liquid evaporates. Set aside.

MAKES 20 TACOS

SOPA DE TORTILLA

DRY TORTILLA FRY

GUATEMALA CITY

This tortilla fry is a staple in homes in Guatemala City since it replaces rice or bread and is both easy to prepare and economical. For vegetarians anywhere, it could easily become an indispensable addition to their repertoire.

10 tortillas, 5 inches in diameter
3 tablespoons butter or margarine
2 tablespoons chopped onion
2 tablespoons chopped tomato
¼ cup chopped fresh mint
1 teaspoon salt, or to taste
¾ cup water or beef broth

1. Cut the tortillas into 1-inch-wide strips. Cut the strips into 1-inch-long diamond-shaped pieces. There will be about 3 cups.
2. Melt the butter or margarine in a large skillet over moderate heat. Add the tortillas and brown them lightly for 10 minutes. Add the onion, tomato, mint and salt, stir well, and fry for 2 minutes.
3. Add the water or broth, cover the skillet, and simmer over low heat for 10 minutes. Remove the cover and fry for 5 minutes more to dry out the moisture. *Do not stir* after the water has been added since the tortillas will disintegrate into a mush.
4. Serve warm with any meat or soup dish in place of rice.

SERVES 6

TORTILLAS DE ELOTE

CORN KERNEL PANCAKES

GUATEMALA CITY

2 ears of fresh corn
½ cup milk
1 cinnamon stick, 2 inches
2 tablespoons butter or margarine
¼ cup sugar
2 tablespoons flour
Corn oil

1. Cut away the kernels from the corn cobs to make 1 cup kernels, and process them into a smooth paste. Set aside.

2. Simmer the milk and cinnamon stick over low heat for 3 minutes. Add the butter and sugar and mix well. Add the flour and the corn paste. Mix well. Remove the cinnamon stick.

3. Heat 1 tablespoon oil in a skillet over low heat. Add 2 tablespoons of the batter for each small pancake and brown lightly on both sides.

4. Serve warm with honey or thick cream. My own preference is to cover them with cream and dribble a teaspoon of honey over all.

MAKES 8 TO 10 PANCAKES

Note: These are dessert tortillas and can be made as sweet as you wish by adding or subtracting the sugar in the batter. Also, canned corn kernels may be substituted. Use a 12-ounce can, drained.

CHIBOLITAS DE MASA

CORN FLOUR CROUTONS

GUATEMALA

These croutons are traditionally served with black beans. They are also fine as croutons in any kind of soup or as nibbles with drinks.

2 cups masa (tortilla flour, moistened)
½ cup grated Parmesan-style cheese
1 teaspoon dried hot red chile flakes
½ teaspoon salt
½ cup corn oil

1. Mix the *masa*, cheese, chile flakes and salt together. Prepare a small dough ball with 1 heaping teaspoon of dough, rolling it into a firm ball. Prepare all the dough in this manner.

2. Heat the oil in a skillet or wok over moderate heat. Fry the balls (*chibolitas*), a few at a time, until lightly golden brown. Drain them on paper towels.

MAKES 14 TO 16 CROUTONS

TORTILLAS DE HARINA CON COCO

COCONUT MILK TORTILLAS

LIVINGSTON, GUATEMALA

I believe that tortillas had their origin in India as chappatis and were brought over by the early Hindu laborers and adapted to local conditions over a period of years. I learned this recipe from a woman of Indian origin.

4 cups all-purpose flour
1½ cups Rich Coconut Milk (see Index)
½ teaspoon salt
1 teaspoon baking soda
2 tablespoons corn oil

1. Mix everything together. Knead the dough until smooth, about 5 minutes. Set it aside, covered with a cloth, for 20 minutes.

2. Divide the dough into 6 parts. Roll, or pat out by hand, tortillas 5 inches in diameter and about ⅜ inch thick.

3. Cook the tortillas in a dry skillet over moderate to low heat for about 10 minutes, or until browned on both sides.

4. Serve with any meat or fish dish. Excellent with preserves or jams for breakfast or teas.

SERVES 6

Note: The dough can be refrigerated in a plastic bag for up to 1 week and used as needed.

Variation: The tortillas can also be fried in corn oil in this manner: Roll out the tortillas as described. Cut the tortilla into halves and cut a 2-inch slash all the way through in each half. This is to allow the hot oil to bubble through and cook the center. Fry the half-moons in ¼ cup oil over moderate heat until they are brown on both sides. Drain on paper towels.

Or, fry the whole tortilla in oil, slashed twice in the center but not cut into halves.

PAN BUN

BUN BREAD, A SWEET ROLL

LIVINGSTON, GUATEMALA

Many of the food names in Livingston owe their origin to English, Spanish or Caribe languages. This sweet roll is a combination of Spanish (*pan*) and the English (bun), reflecting the racial mixture of the people as well as the mixed origins of their cooking.

1 package (¼ ounce) dry yeast
¼ cup plus 1 teaspoon sugar
½ cup warm water (110° to 115°F)
3 to 3¼ cups flour
¼ teaspoon salt
1 egg
½ teaspoon vanilla extract
½ teaspoon grated nutmeg or ground aniseed (preferably aniseed)
½ cup Rich Coconut Milk (see Index)
3 tablespoons corn oil

1. Dissolve the yeast and 1 teaspoon sugar in the warm water and proof for 10 minutes.

2. Mix the flour, salt, ¼ cup sugar, the egg, vanilla, nutmeg or aniseed, coconut milk and oil together by hand or in a processor. Add the yeast mixture and mix well.

3. Knead the dough on a floured board for 5 minutes. Dust the board with flour for easy manipulation to produce a smooth, manageable dough. Let the dough rise in a warm spot covered with a towel for 30 minutes, or until doubled in bulk.

4. Punch down the dough and cut it into 4 equal long strips. Roll each one out between the palms of your hands to make long "cigars" about ½ inch thick.

5. Cut each "cigar" into halves. Roll the strands 3 times around from the center in the shape of a shell. Let the buns rise in a greased pan, covered, for 1 hour.

6. Bake in a 375°F. oven for 30 minutes.

MAKES 8 BUNS

PAN DE BANANA MADURA

RIPE BANANA BREAD

LIVINGSTON, GUATEMALA

This bread does not rise very much. It is moist, with texture, and the ingredients reflect the regional flavors of the Caribe. This bread makes a nice change from our usual banana bread.

1½ pounds ripe bananas, about 6, peeled
1½ cups Rich Coconut Milk (see Index)
12 tablespoons (1½ sticks) margarine, at room temperature
2 cups flour
½ teaspoon salt
2 teaspoons baking soda
1 teaspoon grated nutmeg
½ teaspoon vanilla extract
2 tablespoons raisins (optional)

1. Process the bananas and coconut milk into a smooth paste. Add the margarine and combine smoothly.

2. Add the flour, salt, baking soda, nutmeg, vanilla and raisins. Mix well.

3. Pour into a buttered pan, 12 × 16 inches, and bake in a preheated 350°F. oven for 30 minutes.

MAKES 1 LOAF

PAN DE COCO

COCONUT BREAD

LIVINGSTON, GUATEMALA

This is the traditional coconut bread of Livingston, which is sold on the streets by the bakers' children. The women also circulate around this Victorian town carrying straw baskets covered by a clean cotton towel, selling the buns at two for 25 cents. They go fast.

1 package (¼ ounce) dry yeast
2 teaspoons sugar
⅓ cup warm water (110° to 115°F.)
3½ cups all-purpose flour
¼ teaspoon salt
3 tablespoons corn oil
1 cup Rich Coconut Milk (see Index)

1. Dissolve the yeast and sugar in the warm water. Let the yeast proof until the mixture becomes foamy, about 10 minutes. In the hot, tropical climate of Livingston, the yeast proofs easily and quickly.

2. Mix the flour and salt together. Add the oil, coconut milk and the yeast mixture. Mix and knead for at least 5 minutes, or until well blended, when the dough will be smooth and will not stick. Add additional flour if necessary.

3. Form the dough into a long loaf, cover with a towel, and let it rise for about 30 minutes. It should have doubled in bulk.

4. Cut the loaf into 3 long strips. Divide each strip into halves to make 2 buns. Knead these for a minute and set aside.

5. Flatten the round buns so they are about 3 inches in diameter. Put them on an ungreased cookie sheet and let them rise until doubled in size, about 40 minutes.

6. Bake the buns in a preheated 375°F. oven for about 25 minutes.

MAKES 6 BUNS

Note: This dough may also be prepared as a single loaf of bread. It will keep well in the refrigerator for a week without deteriorating and is excellent sliced and toasted.

PAN DE MAÍZ

TORTILLA FLOUR CORNBREAD
EL SALVADOR

This is the rough common bread of the countryside—the staff of life in El Salvador. For princes and peasants alike, cornbread may be considered the supreme "comfort food."

½ pound (1 cup) vegetable shortening or margarine
1 pound brown sugar
1½ pounds (6 cups) masa (tortilla flour, moistened)
1½ pounds cottage cheese
3 cups light cream
2 whole eggs
4 egg yolks
1 teaspoon salt
2 teaspoons ground anised
4 egg whites, beaten stiff

1. Cream the shortening and brown sugar together. Add the *masa,* cottage cheese, cream, whole eggs, egg yolks, salt and aniseed. Mix well. Fold in the stiffly beaten egg whites.

2. Pour the mixture into a shallow 8-inch-square pan. Bake in a preheated 350°F. oven for 30 minutes, or until done. Test the bread with a toothpick.

3. Serve warm or at room temperature. This cornbread does not rise high and is customarily 1 to 1½ inches high when baked.

MAKES 1 LOAF

QUESADILLA

SUNDAY BREAD

EL SALVADOR

This cheese-flavored, rather solid mixture is known as Sunday Bread since it is served as a national ritual on Sundays in Salvadoran homes.

A special-size metal baking pan is used for this bread. It is 1 inch deep and 7 × 10 inches in size. The bread mixture is poured to fill half the depth of the pan and the baked bread is, therefore, only about 1 inch high. The *quesadilla* can be baked in any conventional-size cake pan, but traditionally it has this shape.

9 eggs, separated
1 cup sugar
1 cup rice flour
1¼ cups all-purpose flour
1½ teaspoons baking powder
1 pound (4 sticks) margarine, melted and cooled
¾ cup grated mild cheese
2 cups sour cream
1 teaspoon sesame seeds

1. Beat the egg whites until stiff. Add the yolks one by one, beating continuously. Add the sugar and continue beating.

2. Mix the two flours together with the baking powder. Fold the mixture into the eggs. Stir in the margarine. Add the cheese, then the sour cream, folding them into the mixture.

3. Cut a sheet of wax paper the size of the greased baking pan and place it in the bottom of the pan. Pour the bread mixture into the pan and sprinkle with the sesame seeds.

4. Bake in a preheated 350°F. oven for 20 to 25 minutes, or until lightly browned. Serve warm or at room temperature.

MAKES 1 LOAF

SOUPS

C*aldo* (soup) is one word that is mentioned constantly in the numerous *comedores* (village restaurants) around the Guatemala highlands. These are not to be confused with the drive-ins of the cities, but go way back to the Colonial period when one could find in such a place fried eggs and a few tortillas, sometimes nothing more.

In recent years, when I was traveling around the country searching for the Mayan textiles in the weaving villages, the *comedor* was still a welcome sign painted on an adobe wall. It meant that here would be something simple and traditional to eat, the sweetened strong coffee, the ubiquitous fried eggs and the soups.

It was the soups, either chicken or beef, steaming on the *poyo*, or wood-burning stove, that one could count on. The beef soup with vegetables fulfilled all the requirements of an itinerant textile collector or the drivers of the beer trucks who traveled everywhere along the narrow, rocky and forbidding roads. In the Ixil Indian village of Nebaj, the kitchen was also the warmest room during a distinctly chilly and damp rainy season.

The soups of the highlands, such as the Caldo de Res (Boiled Beef and Vegetable Soup) of Cobán (see Index) made an entire

79

meal—filling, nourishing and tasty. Not many things were omitted and the spices and seasonings grown in the region were utilized. At altitudes of five to nine thousand feet, what better way to sustain body and soul?

The tropical coastal soups of Livingston and Puerto San José rely on an unlimited supply of fish and seafood, with or without the creamy richness of coconut milk. It is an entirely different cuisine from that of the highland Maya, but nevertheless Guatemalan and unforgettable.

CALDO DE CARNERO

LAMB SOUP
CONCEPCIÓN CHIQUIRICHAPA, GUATEMALA

Concepción Chiquirichapa is a poor, dusty, small Mam Indian village a few miles from Quezaltenango where the people speak Quiché. The recipes given here are the simple fare the people eat at fiestas, marriages or other ceremonial days. They grow potatoes on the dusty, gray, volcanic lava hills and so potatoes are a cheap and popular item in their diet. In this village, for some reason, very little pork is eaten, in a country where pork is ordinarily favored. All meat is costly and they prefer chicken, beef and lamb or mutton when they go to the expense of buying meat for a special occasion. In spite of the simplicity of their life-style, the women weave beautiful and intricate traditional costumes.

2 pounds lamb, with or without some bone, cut into 2-inch cubes
½ cup sliced onion
½ teaspoon salt, or to taste
4 cups water

1. Over moderate heat cook everything together in a saucepan until lamb is tender, about 1½ hours.
2. Serve hot. Eat with small tamales.

SERVES 6

POLLO EN CALDO

CHICKEN SOUP

CONCEPCIÓN CHIQUIRICHAPA, GUATEMALA

1 chicken, 3 pounds, cut into serving pieces, loose skin and fat
   discarded
4 cups water
½ teaspoon salt, or to taste
½ cup epazote leaves
6 small whole potatoes, unpeeled

1. Cook the chicken in the water with salt and epazote leaves until
it becomes tender, about 20 minutes.

2. Add the potatoes and simmer over moderate heat until the potatoes are soft.

3. Serve hot. Chicken, broth and potato are served to each person
and each one peels his own potato. Serve with small tamales.

SERVES 6

CALDO DE POLLO

CHICKEN SOUP
EL RANCHO, PROGRESSO, GUATEMALA

This recipe comes from El Rancho, a small whistle stop in the semidesert region of Progresso. Although nothing more than a group of wooden shacks and a few houses, it is a popular stop for fruit, cold drinks and fresh coconuts. This *caldo* is a good example of the variety of foods found in a country where even a crossroads bus stop can furnish a completely different country soup.

1 chicken, 3 pounds, cut into serving pieces, loose skin and fat
    discarded
4 cups water
1 teaspoon salt, or to taste
1 large potato, quartered
2 carrots, halved
1 chayote (huisquil), quartered
1 medium-size onion, halved
¼ cup fresh mint leaves
1/4 cup chopped cilantro, leaves and stems

1. Cook the chicken in the water with the salt over moderate heat until it becomes tender, about 25 minutes.

2. Add the potato, carrots, chayote and onion. Simmer over low heat for 20 minutes.

3. Add the mint and cilantro and simmer for 3 minutes more. The vegetables should be soft but not overcooked. Serve hot.

Cucumber Salad

This salad is a traditional accompaniment to the chicken soup.

1 cup thin-sliced cucumbers
¼ cup sliced tomatoes

¼ cup thin-sliced scallion rings, from white part of scallions
½ teaspoon salt, or to taste
3 tablespoons lemon or lime juice, or more

1. Mix everything together. Chill. Serve with the *caldo*.

SERVES 6

CALDO DE HUEVO PARA LA GOMA

EGG SOUP FOR A HANGOVER

SAN PEDRO AYAMPUC, GUATEMALA

In San Pedro Ayampuc this soup is reputed to cure a hangover. For those who have not been celebrating, the soup is a delicious luncheon dish, enhanced by the unusual flavor of the epazote leaves.

2 cups water
½ teaspoon or more chopped fresh hot chile
¼ cup chopped tomato
2 scallions, green part only, chopped
½ cup chopped fresh epazote leaves
½ teaspoon salt, or to taste
2 eggs

1. Bring the water to a boil in a saucepan over moderate heat. Add the chile, tomato, scallions, epazote leaves and salt. Simmer for 15 minutes.

2. Drop the eggs carefully into the simmering soup and poach them until they are firm, about 10 minutes. Make certain that the yolks are not broken. Serve hot.

SERVES 2

SOPA DE ROSQUILLAS

CORN RINGS IN BROTH
NICARAGUA

This soup is traditionally prepared for the seven Fridays prior to Easter Sunday. These days are known as the *Cuaresma* or Lent.

Corn Rings

4 cups tortilla flour (masa harina)
½ cup grated Parmesan-style cheese
3 tablespoons margarine, at room temperature
½ cup water, or more if necessary
Corn oil for frying

Soup

8 cups chicken or beef broth
¼ cup chopped onion
¼ cup chopped tomato
½ cup chopped sweet red pepper
2 eggs, beaten
Salt

1. Mix together the flour, cheese, margarine and enough water to prepare a firm dough. Prepare the corn rings (*rosquillas*) by rolling dough out into 4-inch-long tubes about ½ inch thick. Shape a circle and press the joining edges firmly to seal.

2. Heat the oil in a skillet and brown the rings over moderate heat for about 2 minutes. Remove and drain on paper towels.

3. Bring the broth to a boil over moderate heat and add the onion, tomato and sweet pepper. Cook for 2 minutes. Add the eggs, dribbled in a slow stream into the soup pot. Add salt to taste.

4. Add 2 corn rings per serving and simmer for 3 minutes more.

5. Serve hot. This is traditionally served with boiled slices of green plantain.

SERVES 6

SOPA CALDOSA DE FRIJOL BLANCO

WHITE BEAN SOUP

JALAPA, GUATEMALA

½ pound dried white beans
6 cups water
1 teaspoon salt, or to taste
½ cup sliced tomato
¼ cup sliced onion
1 garlic clove, sliced
¼ teaspoon black pepper
1 tablespoon chopped mint or cilantro

1. Soak the beans overnight in 3 cups water.

2. The next day, discard the water, add an additional 3 cups and the teaspoon of salt, and cook over moderate heat for about 1½ hours, or until the beans are soft. Process them into a smooth paste.

3. Process the tomato, onion, garlic and black pepper into a smooth paste. Add this to the beans and simmer over low heat for 1 hour. Since this is a soup, add ½ cup water if it appears too thick.

4. Just before serving, add the mint or cilantro; each provides its own intrinsic flavor. Simmer for 10 minutes more.

5. Serve hot with toasted croutons or tortillas, if you wish.

SERVES 4

SOPA DE FRIJOLES

RED BEAN SOUP

NICARAGUA

This is the most typical soup of Nicaragua; it is eaten throughout the country. Unlike the Guatemalans, who dine almost exclusively on black beans, the Nicaraguans prefer red beans. This soup may be made in quantity and refrigerated for several days. When ready to serve, heat to boiling and add eggs.

½ cup dried red beans
4 cups water
3 garlic cloves, sliced
½ teaspoon salt, or to taste
⅓ cup chopped onion
1 tablespoon corn oil
¼ cup coarse-chopped chicharrones
¼ teaspoon freshly ground black pepper
¼ cup chopped sweet red pepper
4 medium-size eggs, at room temperature

1. Soak the beans overnight in the water.

2. The next day cook the beans, garlic and salt in the soaking water until soft, about 1 hour. Process the mixture into a smooth purée.

3. Fry the onion in the oil over moderate heat until lightly crisp. Add the *chicharrones*, black pepper and sweet red pepper. Add this mixture to the beans. Simmer the soup over moderate to low heat for 10 minutes.

4. Pour the hot soup into a bowl. Break 1 egg carefully into each bowl. The heat of the soup will partially cook the egg, the more completely the longer one waits.

SERVES 4

SOPA DE FRIJOLES NEGROS

BLACK BEAN SOUP

ANTIGUA, GUATEMALA

1 pound black beans
10 cups water
½ pound bacon, chopped
6 garlic cloves, chopped
½ cup chopped onion
Spanish sherry
Thick cream

1. Cover the beans with water and soak them overnight.

2. The next day cook them over moderate to low heat for 1½ hours, or until they are soft. Purée the beans in a food processor until smooth.

3. Fry the bacon in a dry skillet long enough to render all the fat. Remove the crisp bacon and drain on paper towels.

4. Pour off all but 2 teaspoons fat and fry the garlic and onion until soft and golden. Purée these with ½ cup of the bean purée and the bacon crisps and return the mixture to the bean pot.

5. Simmer the soup slowly over low heat for 30 minutes. There should be about 8 cups of soup remaining.

6. Serve each bowl of warm soup with 1 teaspoon of sherry and 1 tablespoon or more of thick cream.

SERVES 8

SOPA DE RES

BEEF SOUP

NICARAGUA

2 pounds beef chuck, plus a few bones
8 cups water
2 teaspoons salt, or to taste
4 garlic cloves, sliced
1 pound cassava, peeled and cut into 2-inch pieces
1 chayote (huisquil), peeled and cut into 6 pieces
1 ear of corn, cut into 2-inch pieces
½ pound cabbage, cut into 4 chunks
½ cup chopped tomato
½ cup chopped onion
1 tablespoon chopped fresh cilantro
½ cup chopped sweet red pepper
2 tablespoons sour orange juice

1. Cook the beef and bones in the water with the salt and garlic over moderate heat for about 2 hours, until the meat is nearly tender.

2. Add the cassava, chayote, corn, cabbage, tomato, onion, cilantro, sweet pepper and orange juice. Simmer over moderate to low heat for another 30 minutes, or until the vegetables are soft. Serve meat and vegetables hot. You may remove the bones if you wish.

SERVES 6

Note: This is also a popular method of preparing oxtail. Substitute the oxtail for the chuck but increase the cooking time to 3 hours before adding the vegetables.

CALDO DE RES

BOILED BEEF AND VEGETABLE SOUP

COBÁN, GUATEMALA

2 pounds beef chuck, cut into 3-inch pieces
1 pound beef bones
6 cups water
1 teaspoon salt, or to taste
1 garlic clove, chopped
2 whole garlic cloves
1 large onion, sliced
2 carrots, halved
2 chayotes (huisquils), peeled and quartered
1 ripe plantain, peeled and cut into 2-inch pieces
¼ cup chopped cilantro, leaves and stems
¼ teaspoon achiote
1 pound cabbage, quartered
1 cup green snap beans, whole
1 cup 2-inch pieces of squash, green or yellow

1. In a large heavy saucepan, cook the beef, bones and water with the salt, garlic and onion over moderate heat for 1 hour or more, until the beef is nearly tender.

2. Add the carrots, chayotes, plantain, cilantro and achiote and simmer over moderate heat for 15 minutes.

3. Add the cabbage, green beans and squash and continue cooking until the vegetables are soft but still retain their shape.

4. Remove and discard the bones. Serve the *caldo* hot in soup bowls with the meat and vegetables, or serve the broth first and the meat and vegetables as a separate course. The soup will be colored a light yellow by the achiote.

SERVES 6 TO 8

ARROZ CON CARNE ENSOPADA

BEEF AND RICE IN BROTH

NICARAGUA

This is a family-style soup that has real substance. It is a popular dish in Nicaragua, with such typical seasonings as the ubiquitous sweet red pepper, sour orange juice and the favored, but less often used, mint.

1 pound beef chuck
8 cups water
½ cup tomato cubes
¼ cup thin-sliced onions
3 garlic cloves, sliced thin
1 cup cubed sweet red pepper
1 cup raw rice, well rinsed and drained
2 tablespoons chopped mint
1 teaspoon salt, or to taste
¼ cup sour orange juice

1. Cook the beef in the water for 1½ to 2 hours, or until tender.

2. Remove the beef from the broth and cut into 1-inch cubes. Measure the broth and add enough water to make 8 cups. The additional water should replace the liquid lost in cooking.

3. Put the beef back in the broth and add all the other ingredients. Bring to a boil over moderate to low heat and simmer for 20 minutes, until the rice has softened but is not mushy. Adjust salt, if necessary. Serve hot.

SERVES 6

CALDO DE RES

BEEF SOUP WITH VEGETABLES

HUEHUETENANGO, GUATEMALA

Beef soup is ubiquitous in the cool highlands. This one is a family-style, clear, strong soup served for lunch or dinner. A complete meal for soup lovers on cool days.

2 pounds beef chuck, cut into 2-inch cubes
1 pound beef bones
1 teaspoon salt, or to taste
8 cups water
½ cup chopped cilantro
1 garlic clove, whole
5 small potatoes, peeled and halved
1½ cups 3-inch pieces of carrot
2 chayotes (huisquils), peeled and quartered
3 whole small onions, cut one quarter through, crisscrossed
3 whole small ripe tomatoes, cut one quarter through
1 cup green snap beans, cut into 2-inch pieces (optional)

1. Prepare a strong broth by cooking the beef, bones and salt in the water over moderate heat until beef is tender, about 1½ hours. Remove and discard the bones.

2. Add the cilantro, garlic and vegetables, but as each vegetable takes a different time to cook, add the potatoes first, the carrot and chayotes 10 minutes later and 10 minutes after that add the onions, tomatoes and green beans.

3. Simmer the soup slowly until all the vegetables are soft but not overcooked. Adjust the salt to taste.

4. Serve the broth hot in a bowl with both meat and an assortment of vegetables.

SERVES 6

SOPA DE ALBÓNDIGAS

MEATBALL AND VEGETABLE SOUP
CHIQUIMULILLA, GUATEMALA

When is a *sopa* not a soup and when *is* it a soup and served as such? There are *sopas* with ample broth that are unquestionably soups, then there are *sopas* thickened with tortillas or rice, which are dry and have a category of their own. This *sopa de albóndigas* is the second kind where the vegetables and the meatballs make it a family-style soup that is a complete meal.

Meatballs

1 pound ground beef
12 mint leaves, chopped
6 leaves and stems of cilantro, chopped
2 tablespoons chopped onion
2 tablespoons chopped tomato
½ teaspoon salt, or to taste
¼ teaspoon pepper

Vegetables, Broth and Pasta

4 cups strong beef broth
1 chayote (huisquil), cut into julienne
1 cup julienne pieces of carrot
¼ cup sliced leek, white part only
½ cup shredded cabbage
½ cup pasta such as shells or macaroni

1. Make the meatballs: Mix everything together and shape into miniature meatballs ¾ inch in diameter.

2: Bring the broth to a low simmer and add the vegetables. Add the meatballs and top them with the pasta. Cover, and simmer over low heat for 30 minutes.

3. Serve hot in bowls, with tortillas or French bread.

SERVES 6

SOPA DE ALBÓNDIGAS

MEATBALL SOUP

GUATEMALA CITY

2 garlic cloves, chopped fine
2 tablespoons fine-chopped onion
¼ cup fine-chopped peeled ripe tomato
1 tablespoon corn oil
½ teaspoon salt, or to taste
¼ teaspoon freshly ground black pepper
1 pound ground beef
2 eggs, beaten
¼ cup toasted bread crumbs
6 cups strong chicken or beef broth
3 sprigs of fresh mint, about ¼ cup chopped
Flour

1. Fry the garlic, onion and tomato in the oil in a skillet over moderate heat for 3 minutes. Add the salt and pepper. Cool the sauce and process to a smooth paste. Add this to the beef with the eggs and bread crumbs and process until well mixed.

2. Bring the broth to a moderate simmer with the mint.

3. Prepare the meatballs with 1 heaping tablespoon of the beef mixture for each. Roll them lightly in flour and drop into the simmering broth. Cook for 15 minutes. The meatballs when well cooked will float to the top of the broth. Serve hot.

SERVES 6

CALDO COLORADO

CEREMONIAL LAMB SOUP

CUNÉN, GUATEMALA

Cunén, in the Department of Quiché, nestles in the hills and over-looks the Río Negro River far below. In the old days a visitor coming into Cunén on market days would see this *caldo*, an old traditional food of the village, steaming away in large clay pots. For a few centavos one could be served bowls of this hot, spicy nourishing soup.

Nowadays the *caldo* is infrequently cooked by the younger generation since style and taste in traditional foods change just as the colors and designs of the traditional costumes have changed or disappeared altogether.

2 pounds boneless lamb, cut into 2-inch cubes
8 cups water
½ teaspoon achiote
1 teaspoon dried hot red chile flakes
4 scallions, green part only, chopped
¼ teaspoon ground cloves
1 teaspoon thyme
¼ cup chopped fresh cilantro
1 teaspoon salt, or to taste
½ teaspoon whole allspice berries
1 pound potatoes, cut into ½-inch cubes to make about 3 cups

1. Cook the lamb cubes in the water over moderate heat for 1 hour, until the meat is nearly done.

2. Add all the other ingredients to the lamb and simmer uncovered, slowly for 1 more hour, so that about one quarter of the liquid evaporates and the flavors intensify. This soup has substantial liquid when finished. Serve hot.

SERVES 6

CALDO DE CARNERO

LAMB SOUP

TODOS LOS SANTOS
CUCHUMATÁN, GUATEMALA

The *caldo* is a popular preparation in a truly fabulous mountain village high in the Cuchumatanes mountains. Isolated for centuries in a cool climate that often becomes cold because of its elevation of eight to ten thousand feet, both men and women still wear striking tribal costumes that are predominantly red and white, with intricate designs woven on a back strap loom. The costume is unmistakable whether one should see it in Huehuetenango, Quezaltenango or Guatemala City.

Lamb is the principal meat for these agricultural people, which is logical since the mountainous terrain lends itself to sheep raising.

2 pounds boneless lamb, or shank or shoulder with bone, cut into
    3-inch pieces
4 cups water
½ teaspoon achiote
1 teaspoon salt, or to taste
10 fresh mint leaves
2 stalks of cilantro, about 5 inches long
¼ cup chopped onion
½ teaspoon chopped fresh hot chile, or dried hot red chile flakes
3 cups thick slices of peeled potatoes

1. Bring the lamb and water to a boil in a saucepan over moderate heat. Add the achiote, salt, mint, cilantro, onion and chile. Simmer over moderate heat in a covered pan for 1 hour, or until the lamb is tender.

2. Add the potato slices. Simmer for 15 minutes more, until the potatoes are creamy soft. Serve hot.

SERVES 6

MONDONGO HONDUREÑO

HONDURAN TRIPE SOUP

HONDURAS

This is the most popular, classic soup of Honduras. It is rich in flavor and texture and with enough substantial ingredients to sink a battleship. One of my all-time favorite soups.

Tripe

3 pounds cleaned beef tripe
½ cup lemon juice or sour orange juice
10 garlic cloves, peeled
1 teaspoon salt
6 cups water

Pig's Feet

3 pig's feet, quartered
8 cups water
1 teaspoon salt

Sauce (Sofrito)

2 tablespoons corn oil
1 cup chopped ripe tomato
¼ cup chopped onion
4 garlic cloves, chopped
2 tablespoons chopped fresh coriander
½ cup chopped sweet red pepper
½ teaspoon salt
½ teaspoon black pepper

Vegetables

3 cups coarse cubes of cabbage
1½ cups cubed potatoes
1½ cups sliced carrots
1 cup 1-inch pieces of green snap beans
½ cup ½-inch cubes of chayote (huisquil)
1 ripe plantain, peeled, cut into ½-inch cubes
2 green bananas, peeled, cut into ½-inch-thick slices
2 cups 2-inch pieces of cooked cassava

1 to 2 teaspoons achiote
Oil
½ cup toasted bread crumbs, for thickening
Lime slices

1. Put all the tripe ingredients in a pot and cook until tripe is tender, about 2 hours. In a pressure cooker, cook for 1 hour. Drain the tripe and cut into ½-inch cubes.

2. Put the pig's feet, water and salt in a pan and cook over moderate heat until soft, about 2 hours. A pressure cooker will reduce the time by half.

3. Cool the feet and remove the small bones. Cut the gelatinous meat into ½-inch cubes. Reserve the broth, about 6 cups.

4. Make the sauce: Heat the oil in a skillet over moderate heat and fry everything together for 3 minutes.

5. Add all the vegetables listed and fry for 10 minutes more. Mix well.

6. Dissolve enough achiote in hot oil to produce a light rose color in the soup. Try 1 teaspoon dissolved; if this is not enough, add another teaspoon of this vegetable coloring.

7. Pour the broth reserved from pig's feet into a large soup pan. Add the sauce (*sofrito*) and the vegetables, which have been fried together. Add the tripe and the pig's feet. Add the dissolved achiote and bring the soup to a boil over moderate heat. Simmer the soup over low heat for 20 minutes. During this time adjust the achiote coloring and

(recipe continues)

the salt. Should the soup appear too thick, add ½ to 1 cup of water and continue to simmer to integrate the flavors.

8. Lastly, add the bread crumbs. Try ¼ cup and simmer for 10 minutes. Should the soup still be too thin for one's taste, add the other ¼ cup crumbs.

9. Serve the soup hot in generous quantities, with slices of lime.

SERVES 12 TO 14

SOPA DE HOMBRE

A MAN'S SEAFOOD SOUP

HONDURAS

This recipe is from the Caribbean coast of Honduras where the seafood is fresh, plentiful and cheap. But, cheap though it is, not a scrap of meat goes to waste when a soup of this caliber is served. The fish head and the crab shells are not discarded before they have been carefully inspected for any edible shreds that can be salvaged. The scene is usually of a very informal nature, with the men in shirt sleeves and the tablecloth nonexistent. Named "A Man's Soup," so they say, because it will resolve all the languors of a hangover after a heavy weekend of carousing. The implication is that women would never overindulge and need this kind of revival.

3½ cups Honduran Coconut Milk (see Note)
¼ cup chopped onion
½ cup chopped sweet red pepper
3 cups chopped ripe tomatoes
3 tablespoons chopped parsley
2 teaspoons salt
1 teaspoon pepper
½ teaspoon dried hot red chile flakes
4 cups water
1 fish head, halved (scrod, sea bass, red snapper)
20 small clams, well rinsed
4 small blue crabs, shells removed but not discarded
4 large stone crabs or similar type
1 pound large shrimps, peeled and deveined
1 large green plantain, peeled and cut into ½-inch cubes
½ cup tomato paste
½ cup toasted bread crumbs
Lime slices

1. Bring the coconut milk to a boil in a large pan over moderate heat. Add the onion, sweet pepper, tomatoes, parsley, salt, black pepper and hot chile flakes. Add 2 cups water and bring everything to a boil.

2. Add the fish head and simmer for 10 minutes to extract the flavor. Add the clams, crabs including shells, shrimps, green plantain, tomato paste and the balance of the water, 2 cups. Bring to a boil and simmer, covered, over moderate to low heat for 30 minutes.

3. Add the bread crumbs for thickening and simmer for 10 minutes more. Serve hot with slices of lime.

SERVES 12 TO 14

Note: How to prepare Honduran Coconut Milk: Crack open a young coconut carefully to catch all the coconut water. Slice the coconut meat into small pieces. Bring the coconut water plus 2 more cups water to a boil and pour it over the meat in a blender. Blend for 1 minute. Pour the mixture into a cheesecloth-lined sieve and squeeze out all the coconut milk. Discard coconut.

SOPA DE CAMARONCILLOS

DRIED SHRIMP SOUP

GUATEMALA

This recipe was named after the grandmother of the Aparicio family who originated it in Guatemala City. It is a personal recipe, but it is also one of the soups of the country.

In Guatemala dried shrimps are found in both city and small village markets. They are harvested and dried on both the Pacific and Caribbean coasts. The flavor of the dried shrimps is intense. They are also lightly salted. They are available here in Oriental markets.

2 cups water
¼ cup sliced onion
5 ounces dried shrimps, peeled
2 cups chicken or beef broth
¾ cup ¼-inch potato cubes
A few threads of saffron
4 tablespoons butter
3 tablespoons flour
¼ cup thin-sliced celery
¼ teaspoon freshly ground black pepper
½ cup cream or milk
1 tablespoon chopped parsley or fresh cilantro
¼ cup sliced scallions, green part only

1. Bring 1 cup water to a boil with the onion and add the dried shrimps. Cook over moderate heat for 5 minutes, then process the mixture to a smooth purée. Pour the purée into a large pan with the chicken or beef broth.

2. Cook the potato cubes, saffron and the second cup of water together until potatoes are soft but still firm.

3. Melt the butter in a skillet and stir the flour in smoothly. Add this to the shrimp and broth pot, bring to a boil, and simmer over

low heat. Add the potatoes, celery, black pepper and cream or milk. Stir continuously.

4. Add the parsley and scallions and simmer for 5 minutes more to blend the flavors. Serve warm.

SERVES 6

SOPA DE PEPINO

CUCUMBER SOUP

SAN BERNARDINO
SUCHITEPÉQUEZ,
GUATEMALA

A smooth, tasty but mildly flavored soup assembled in the Guatemalan manner. An interesting change from the cold cucumber soup we are used to.

1 pound small cucumbers (Kirby type), sliced, not peeled
½ cup chopped celery
1 tablespoon chopped parsley
1 sweet green or red pepper, chopped
1 tablespoon corn oil
3 cups chicken or beef broth
½ teaspoon salt, or to taste

1. Fry the cucumbers, celery, parsley and sweet pepper in the oil in a skillet over moderate to low heat for 5 minutes. Cool. Process to a smooth paste.

2. Add the paste to the broth with salt and simmer over low heat for 15 minutes. Serve hot.

SERVES 6

SOPA DE GARBANZO

CHICK-PEA PURÉE IN BROTH
GUATEMALA CITY

Chick-peas are eaten in many parts of Guatemala including distant highland villages. Swiss chard (*acelga*) is a popular green and more conspicuous in the markets than spinach. Chick-peas and chard complement each other.

1 pound chick-peas, cooked
8 cups beef broth
1 teaspoon salt, or to taste
½ pound Swiss chard, cut into thin slices

1. Process the chick-peas to a smooth paste with 2 cups of broth. Add the purée to the rest of the broth. Add the salt and bring to a boil over moderate heat.

2. Add the chard and simmer in a covered pan over low heat for 10 minutes. Stir well. Serve hot.

SERVES 6 TO 8

SOPA DE ALBÓNDIGAS DE PAPA

POTATO BALLS IN BROTH
GUATEMALA CITY

¼ cup chopped tomato
¼ cup chopped sweet red or green pepper
1 tablespoon chopped onion
1 teaspoon corn oil
1 pound potatoes, cooked until soft but still firm
1 tablespoon flour

3 tablespoons grated Parmesan-style cheese
3 cups chicken or beef broth
½ teaspoon salt, or to taste

1. Fry the tomato, sweet pepper and onion in the oil over moderate heat for 2 minutes. Stir the resulting sauce well.

2. Process the cooked potatoes, flour, the fried sauce and the cheese into a fairly smooth mixture.

3. Bring the broth to a boil over moderate heat and drop heaping teaspoons of the potato mixture, made into balls, into the broth. Cook for 2 minutes but do not stir since the potato balls might disintegrate. Serve broth and potato balls hot.

SERVES 4 TO 6

CALDO DE PAPA

POTATO SOUP

JOYABAJ, GUATEMALA

1 pound pototoes, about 4, peeled and sliced
¼ cup sliced onion
2 tablespoons cilantro
1 teaspoon salt, or to taste
4 cups water
½ cup tomato, processed to a smooth paste
½ teaspoon achiote
¼ cup masa (cornmeal moistened with water)

1. Over moderate heat cook the potatoes, onion, cilantro and salt in the water until vegetables are soft.

2. Add the tomato paste, achiote, and *masa* to thicken the soup; stir well. Simmer over low heat for 10 minutes. Serve hot.

SERVES 4 TO 6

CHICKEN, TURKEY AND DUCK

Poultry running around the roads, gardens, farms and on the loose must be one of the commonest sights in the Guatemala countryside. The stately turkey has the right of way since it is most often eaten (or sacrificed) as a ceremonial object, and its preparation coincides with a fiesta or national holiday. Turkeys have a special mystique derived from pre-Hispanic times when the Mayans raised them in corrals or caught the turkey in the wild. It was a North American bird, unknown in Europe and Asia until after the Spanish Conquest.

The turkey had an odyssey of its own. Taken to Spain after the Conquest, it was not long before it turned up in Portugal. The Portuguese, in turn, carried it to their possession, Goa, on the south

Indian coast. And so when the Emperor Jahangir sent one of his courtiers from Delhi to search through India and bring back various animal curiosities for his private zoo, a zebra and a turkey were included. Monsur, the famous court painter, painted several miniatures of the turkey about 1612. These paintings, now in museums, provide us with the evidence of how and when the turkey arrived in India.

Only the turkey, half wild as it is in the domesticated state, has the wild look, on the alert from attack. At night it flies off the ground to a perch or tree limb to escape predators. The vagaries of the weather in the highlands result in a high mortality for the chicks and so turkeys are expensive and eaten on special occasions. In El Salvador, the reverse is true. The weather is agreeable and the turkey is common and of reasonable price.

Hens and roosters are eaten any time. One can buy the supermarket variety, fed on commercial feeds and relying on the spices and seasonings to revive flavors lost in the feedlot. Or one can find the native chicken with its firm flesh and rather long legs developed by running in the village lanes. The Indian women in the villages exclaim with scorn at the taste of the commercial chicken—and with some justice.

Ducks and pigeons have their own admirers. In fact, almost anything with wings can be prepared in the Guatemalan fashion

GALLINA RELLENA NAVIDEÑA

STUFFED CHICKEN FOR CHRISTMAS
NICARAGUA

This is a special preparation for Christmas using a combination of local ingredients, such as papaya, chayote and sweet peppers, and those with a European origin, such as capers, olives and raisins.

3 tablespoons butter
1 tablespoon prepared mustard
1 whole chicken, 3½ pounds, loose fat removed
1 tablespoon corn oil
3 cups water
1 pound potatoes, peeled and cubed
1 cup peeled chayote (huisquil) cubes
1 cup peeled green papaya cubes
1 tablespoon raisins
1 teaspoon capers
20 small pitted green olives
½ cup chopped onion
½ cup coarse-chopped sweet red or green pepper
¼ cup chopped tomato
½ teaspoon salt
¼ teaspoon pepper
¼ teaspoon achiote, dissolved
1 tablespoon cider vinegar
1 cup red wine

1. Mix the butter and mustard together. Rub the chicken inside and out with the mixture.

2. Heat the oil in a flameproof casserole over moderate heat and brown the chicken on all sides for 5 minutes. Set aside.

3. Bring the 3 cups water to a boil and add the potatoes, chayote and papaya cubes along with the raisins, capers, olives, onion, sweet pepper, tomato, salt, pepper, achiote and cider vinegar. Cook together over moderate heat for 5 minutes. Drain the vegetables and reserve 1 cup of the cooking liquid.

4. Stuff the chicken firmly with the vegetable mixture. It is not necessary to sew up the opening, merely fold over the skin flaps.

5. Return the chicken to the melted butter/mustard mixture in the casserole. Surround the chicken with the balance of the vegetable mixture. Add the wine and the reserved cup of liquid.

6. Roast uncovered in a 350°F. oven for 1½ hours. Serve warm.

SERVES 6

POLLO ENCEBOLLADO

CHICKEN WITH ONIONS

EL SALVADOR

2 teaspoons prepared mustard
1 teaspoon Worcestershire sauce
½ teaspoon salt
¼ teaspoon freshly ground black pepper
1 teaspoon thyme
1 chicken, 3 pounds, cut into serving pieces, loose skin and fat
    discarded
2 tablespoons corn oil
3 cups small onions, peeled and cut into quarters
½ cup water

1. Combine the mustard, Worcestershire sauce, salt, black pepper and thyme. Rub the mixture over the chicken pieces and let them marinate for 1 hour.

2. Heat the oil in a skillet and lightly brown the chicken over moderate heat for 5 minutes. Remove the pieces and set aside.

3. Fry the onions in the same oil in the skillet until translucent, about 5 minutes.

4. Return the chicken to the skillet, add the water, and cover the pan. Simmer over moderate to low heat for 30 minutes, or until the chicken is done. Serve warm.

SERVES 4

POLLO DESHUESADO RELLENO

STUFFED BONELESS CHICKEN

GUATEMALA

Dona Maria Isaura taught me how to bone and stuff a chicken in the small, agricultural town of Taxisco in the Department of Santa Rosa. Her working class *comedor* did not serve this, since it was too elegant for everyday fare. Also, since she had no oven and everything in this hot town was usually cooked over outdoor wood fires, on brick and cement stoves, the chicken was roasted at the bakery down the street.

1 teaspoon salt
1 teaspoon white or cider vinegar
3 teaspoons prepared mustard
1 chicken, 3½ pounds, boned whole (see Note)
¼ cup fine-chopped onion
2 garlic cloves, chopped fine
¼ teaspoon achiote
2 tablespoons chopped ripe tomato
½ teaspoon freshly ground black pepper
2 bay leaves
2 tablespoons capers
½ teaspoon thyme
1 tablespoon corn oil
½ pound ground beef
½ cup carrot cubes, cooked for 2 minutes
½ cup green peas, cooked for 2 minutes
½ cup sliced green snap beans, cooked for 2 minutes
1 large potato, cooked whole and cut into ¼-inch cubes
1 scallion, green leaves only

1. Mix 1 teaspoon salt, the vinegar and mustard together and rub this into the interior skin and meat of the chicken. Refrigerate for 1 hour.

2. Make the stuffing: Fry the onion, garlic, achiote, tomato, black pepper, 1 bay leaf, capers and ¼ teaspoon thyme in the oil for 2 minutes. Add the ground beef, carrot cubes, peas, green beans and potato; stir-fry for 3 minutes. Cool the mixture. Remove the bay leaf.

3. Fill the skin, legs and wings with the mixture and sew up the bird. Repair any torn skin at this time. Sprinkle the outer skin with ¼ teaspoon thyme and 1 bay leaf, and lay the scallion leaves over the top of the chicken.

4. Coat a roasting pan with oil and roast the chicken in a 400°F. oven for 1 hour, or until brown and crisp.

SERVES 4

Note *(To Bone a Raw Chicken)*: Start with the back and cut the skin from the tail to the neck, removing all the meat and skin from the bone in a cutting, pushing motion.

Cut the thigh bone from the body and push the meat down to the leg. Cut off the thigh bone. Cut the leg skin ½ inch from the bottom. Push all the thigh meat down and off, pull out the leg bone, and remove it.

Next take the wings, cut through the bone at the shoulder and push down the meat and skin of the first part of the wing. Remove the bone. Continue with the second part of the wing, push down to the end, and remove the 2 thin bones. The wing tip should be cut off and discarded.

Now attack the breast by cutting it from the body on both sides, removing all the meat with the skin. Cut through the tail, which should remain attached to the complete skin to give the stuffed chicken shape. The chicken is now boned.

GALLO EN CHICHA

CAPON IN FRUIT WINE

EL SALVADOR

The *gallo en chicha* could also be known as "Monday Rooster." Cockfights are held in El Salvador on Sundays and the losers of this bizarre pastime are sold to Monday's hungry diners. Since we do not have losers here as a source, a supermarket capon is a reasonable substitute.

2 tablespoons coarse salt
¼ cup lemon juice
1 capon or oven-roaster, 5 pounds, loose skin and fat discarded,
    cut into serving pieces, with solid meat cut into 3-inch cubes
6 cups chicha (see following recipe)
1 cup sliced onion
5 garlic cloves, put through a garlic press
¼ pound (1 stick) butter
1 tablespoon prepared mustard
1 teaspoon salt
½ teaspoon pepper
1 tablespoon Worcestershire sauce
3 tablespoons corn oil
1 cup water
1½ cups white table wine
1 pound boneless pork, cut into thin strips
¼ cup capers
20 small pickling onions, peeled

An Additional Sauce

½ cup French bread crumbs, moistened with water
2 tablespoons sesame seeds, toasted in a skillet
2 cups tomato slices, toasted in a dry skillet
2 garlic cloves, toasted in a dry skillet
1 cup sweet red pepper pieces, toasted
½ chile pasa, seeds and stem removed
½ chile guaque, seeds and stem removed

Side Dishes

6 hard-cooked eggs, chopped
2 ripe plantains with black skins, peeled, cut into long diagonal
    slices, and browned in corn oil
4 cups cooked rice, any style, either plain or seasoned
½ cup canned red chile pimiento strips
½ cup stuffed green olives
2 cups fresh cooked green peas

1. Mix the coarse salt and lemon juice together and rub the capon pieces with the mixture. Let the capon stand for 2 hours.

2. Rinse the pieces with cold water and dry them well. Add them to the *chicha* with 1 cup onion and the puréed garlic and let stand in a covered dish in the refrigerator overnight.

3. The next day, mix the butter, mustard, salt, pepper and Worcestershire together. Dry the capon and cover the pieces generously with the butter mixture. Heat the oil in a large skillet or pan and fry the pieces over moderate heat for 3 minutes, or just enough to change the color.

4. Add the *chicha* marinade mixture, 1 cup water and the white wine. Bring the mixture to a boil and add the pork strips and capers. Cook over moderate heat for 30 minutes, then add the small onions.

5. Prepare the additional sauce: Grind all the sauce ingredients into a smooth sauce with 1 cup of broth from the simmering capon. Add this sauce to the capon pot.

6. Continue to cook everything for about 2 hours, until the capon is tender. The sauce will have thickened but should it appear to have too much liquid, remove the cover from the pot.

7. Prepare the side dishes.

8. Serve the capon warm in soup plates with amounts of sauce according to preference. Each diner then adds some or all of the side dish items to the capon—a sprinkling of egg, slices of plantain or anything else.

This is a rich, somewhat exaggerated family-style dinner. There should be enough of the side dishes to accommodate the diners' appetites generously.

SERVES 12

LA CHICHA

FRUIT WINE

EL SALVADOR

There are many recipes for *chicha* but this is the one traditionally used in Gallo en Chicha.

6 quarts water
2 ripe medium-size pineapples, sliced with the skin
2 pounds white or brown sugar
½ cup tamarind paste, dissolved in 1 cup water
6 cloves, crushed
1 cinnamon stick, 4 inches
12 whole allspice berries

1. Mix everything together in a glass or stone crock. Let the mixture ferment in a warm spot for 3 days.
2. Strain and bottle the wine. Refrigerate it until ready for use.

Note: Pineapple vinegar is prepared in the same way with the same ingredients. Omit the tamarind and let the mixture ferment for 5 days. The result is a light fruit vinegar.

GALLO EN CHICHA

ROOSTER COOKED IN FRUIT WINE

GUATEMALA CITY

½ cup tomato chunks
2 garlic cloves, sliced
½ teaspon black pepper
1 teaspoon salt, or to taste
2 cups Chicha (Fruit Wine) (see Note)

1 capon or oven-roaster, 4 pounds, cut into serving pieces, loose
    skin and fat discarded
2 tablespoons corn oil
6 whole cloves
2 bay leaves
1 cinnamon stick, 1 inch

1. Prepare a smooth sauce in a processor with the tomato, garlic, black pepper, salt and 1 cup *chicha*. Set aside.

2. Fry the capon pieces in the oil in a large skillet over moderate heat for 5 minutes. Add the sauce, the balance of the *chicha* (1 cup), the cloves, bay leaves and cinnamon stick.

3. Stir well and simmer over moderate heat for about 45 minutes, or until the capon is tender and the sause is reduced and thickened.

4. Serve warm with rice, tortillas and typical salads.

SERVES 8

Note: The *chicha* in Guatemala is a somewhat contraband fruit liquor made in the town of Salcajá. I bought my bottle from an under-the-table grocery store with very little difficulty. The *chicha* is reputed to have been made with peaches, pineapple, quince and nance, a sort of wild yellow cherry. The mixture is allowed to ferment for 6 months, then strained and bottled. It is a semisweet, fruity wine, light red in color, and can pack a punch.

A home substitute can be quickly made with a fruit vinegar (cider or pineapple) mixed with *panela,* the village dark brown sugar. Should you try it this way, dissolve ½ cup dark brown sugar in 1 cup vinegar. This will produce that light sweet-and-sour flavor that is characteristic of the Gallo en Chicha.

ARROZ CON POLLO CHAPINA

CHICKEN AND RICE, GUATEMALA STYLE

GUATEMALA CITY

This dish is a first cousin to the Spanish Paella Valenciana and reveals its origin with the olives, capers and saffron, which do not grow in Guatemala, and the general technique of assembly. Like all of the preparations of Spanish origin, the Arroz con Pollo Chapina has become a classic of the country and has been absorbed into the mainstream of the cuisine without reference to its European origin.

1 chicken, 3 pounds, cut up for frying, loose skin and fat discarded
1 tablespoon corn oil
1 teaspoon salt, or to taste
¼ teaspoon black pepper
½ cup chopped onion
1 garlic clove, chopped fine
½ cup chopped peeled ripe tomato
1½ cups raw rice
1 cup sliced carrots
⅓ cup stuffed green olives
1 tablespoon capers (optional, but desirable)
2½ cups chicken broth, homemade
5 saffron threads, dissolved in broth (optional)
1 cup green peas, fresh or frozen
½ cup sweet red chile pimiento, cut into strips (canned)
1 hard-cooked egg, sliced
2 tablespoons grated Parmesan-style cheese

1. In a 4-quart serving skillet or flameproof casserole brown the chicken in the oil over moderate heat for 20 minutes. Sprinkle with ½ teaspoon salt and the black pepper. Remove the chicken and set aside.

2. In the same skillet in the accumulated chicken fat, fry the onion, garlic and tomato for 2 minutes. Add the rice and fry for 2 minutes more. Add the carrots, olives and capers and mix everything together.

3. Pour in the broth and add saffron and chicken pieces. Bring to a boil, reduce heat to low, cover the skillet, and simmer until the broth has been absorbed, about 10 minutes. Add the green peas.

4. Cover the skillet with aluminum foil and punch 8 holes in the top to allow steam to escape. Bake in a 300°F. oven for 30 minutes. Fluff up the mixture once or twice during the baking time.

5. Serve warm. Decorate the surface with the chile pimiento strips and egg slices and sprinkle with the cheese. The rice should be dry, loose and not sticky. This dish is usually served with fried ripe plantain slices, a Salsa Picante, and Encurtidos (Pickled Vegetables, see Index).

SERVES 6

POLLO GUISADO

CHICKEN SAUTÉ

CHIQUIMULA, GUATEMALA

1 chicken, 3½ pounds, cut into serving pieces, loose skin and fat discarded
2 tablespoons corn oil
1 cup water or chicken broth
⅛ teaspoon achiote
½ cup sliced ripe tomato
½ cup sliced sweet green pepper
½ cup sliced onion
1 garlic clove, chopped
2 bay leaves
1 teaspoon thyme
½ teaspoon salt, or to taste

1. Fry the chicken pieces in the oil in a large skillet for 5 minutes. Add the water or broth, achiote, tomato, green pepper, onion, garlic, bay leaves, thyme and salt. Stir several times.

2. Cover the pan and simmer over moderate heat for about 40 minutes to cook the chicken and combine the seasonings. The *guisado* will have ample sauce.

3. Serve warm with Arroz y Frijoles Colorados (Rice and Beans, see Index).

SERVES 4

POLLO ENCEBOLLADO AL VAPOR

CHICKEN AND ONIONS

CHIQUIMULILLA, GUATEMALA

1 teaspoon salt
1 teaspoon orégano
2 tablespoons white or cider vinegar
1 chicken, 3 pounds, cut into serving pieces, loose skin and fat
    discarded
2 tablespoons butter
1 cup water or homemade chicken broth
1 tablespoon cornstarch
2 cups sliced onions

1. Mix the salt, orégano and vinegar together. Pour over the chicken and marinate for 1 hour.

2. Remove chicken from the vinegar mixture and reserve the vinegar. Brown the chicken in the butter over moderate heat for 15 minutes. Add the water or broth and cover the skillet. Simmer over low heat for 15 minutes.

3. Toast the cornstarch in a dry skillet over low heat until it browns lightly. Dissolve this in ½ cup of chicken broth from the pot.

4. Add the onion slices and the dissolved cornstarch to the chicken and mix around slightly. Cover the skillet and simmer over low heat for 10 minutes. Stir once or twice. The sauce will have reduced and thickened.

5. Serve warm with rice or purée of potato.

SERVES 4

Note: *Al Vapor* means to cook the chicken over low heat in a tightly covered pan with little liquid. It is in effect a steaming process so that all the flavors are locked into the chicken and the sauce.

POLLO EN CREMA

CHICKEN IN CREAM SAUCE
JALAPA, GUATEMALA

Jalapa is a center for dairy products in the eastern region of Guatemala. Milk, rich thick cream and several types of cheese both fresh and dry are produced for sale around the country. The cheeses are produced as a cottage industry in private homes where there are a few cows. The Pollo en Crema is the most popular dish in the town, and all the ingredients are produced in the vicinity. *Lorocos* are a member of the periwinkle flower family and are perhaps the most beloved of the edible flowers in Guatemala. During August and September in the Jalapa region, and elsewhere, small heaps of the green buds and opened small white flowers are for sale to be used in the Pollo en Crema, a rare and celebrated delicacy. We have nothing here to use as a substitute.

1 chicken, 3 pounds, cut into serving pieces; include giblets
½ cup water
1 cup sliced onion
1 cup sliced sweet red or green pepper
1 garlic clove, chopped fine
¼ teaspoon black pepper
1 teaspoon salt, or to taste
1 cup light cream

1. Put the chicken, water, onion, sweet pepper, garlic, black pepper and salt in a saucepan and bring to a boil over moderate heat.

2. Add the cream and simmer the mixture over moderate to low heat for about 40 minutes, or until the chicken is tender.

3. Serve warm with tortillas or French bread.

SERVES 4

Variation: Cook the chicken in water and salt for 10 minutes. Add the onion, garlic, pepper and cream and simmer over moderate to low heat for 20 minutes. Add the sweet red pepper and simmer for 15 minutes more. The sauce is reduced and thickened and the sweet pepper retains a more crunchy texture.

POLLO EN CREMA

CHICKEN IN CREAM
GUATEMALA CITY

In this recipe from Guatemala City the chicken is browned before cooking the sauce and is made piquant with the mint. The rich creamy red sauce is quite different from the sauce in the other recipes.

1 chicken, 3 pounds, cut into serving pieces; include giblets
2 tablespoons butter
½ teaspoon salt, or to taste
1 cup chopped ripe tomato
¼ cup chopped onion
1 garlic clove, chopped
¼ teaspoon black pepper
1 cup light or heavy cream
1 cup sliced sweet green pepper
1 sprig of mint

1. Fry the chicken pieces in 1 tablespoon butter with the salt in a skillet over moderate heat for 10 minutes.
2. In another skillet, fry the tomato, onion, garlic and black pepper in 1 tablespoon butter over moderate heat for 5 minutes.
3. Add the tomato mixture to the chicken with the cream and sweet pepper slices. Cover the skillet and simmer over low heat for 30 minutes.
4. Add the mint and simmer uncovered for 5 minutes more. Serve warm.

SERVES 4

POLLO CON LECHE DE COCO

CHICKEN IN COCONUT MILK

LIVINGSTON, GUATEMALA

½ cup chopped onion
3 tablespoons corn oil
3 cups coconut milk
1 chicken, 3 pounds, cut into serving pieces, loose skin and fat
discarded
½ cup chopped sweet green pepper
½ cup chopped sweet red pepper
¼ cup chopped cilantro
1 teaspoon salt, or to taste
⅛ teaspoon achiote

1. Fry the onion in 1 tablespoon oil in a large saucepan over moderate heat for 2 minutes. Add the coconut milk and bring it to a rolling boil. Stir frequently so the milk does not separate.

2. Meanwhile, brown the chicken in 2 tablespoons oil in a skillet over moderate heat for 5 minutes or so. Add the pieces to the coconut milk.

3. Add the sweet peppers, cilantro, salt and achiote. Continue to simmer over moderate heat, stirring and basting, for 30 minutes, or until the chicken is tender and the sauce is reduced and thickened.

4. Serve warm with Arroz y Frijoles Colorados (Rice and Beans, see Index) and its ample sauce.

SERVES 4

Note: Coconut milk is temperamental and requires correct handling. It is possible for the milk to separate and give a watery appearance to the sauce rather than the creamy consistency that we anticipate in this chicken preparation. Therefore, constant stirring will "homogenize" the milk as it is boiling.

Basting is an effective technique to assist in producing the lightly pink (from the achiote) creamy, thick (but not gummy) sauce.

POLLO GUISADO LIVINGSTON

CHICKEN IN VEGETABLE SAUCE

LIVINGSTON, GUATEMALA

1 chicken, 3 pounds, cut into serving pieces, loose skin and fat
  discarded
1 teaspoon salt
1 tablespoon flour
¼ cup corn oil
¼ cup thin-sliced celery
¼ cup sliced onion
½ cup thin-sliced leek, both white and tender green parts
¼ cup sliced sweet red pepper
2 garlic cloves, put through a press
1 cup Chirmol (Simple Tomato Sauce, see Index)
1 tablespoon white or cider vinegar
½ teaspoon black pepper

1. Dust the chicken pieces with salt and flour. Heat 3 tablespoons of
the oil in a skillet and brown the chicken over moderate heat for 5
minutes. Set aside.

2. In a large saucepan, heat 1 tablespoon oil and fry the celery,
onion, leek, sweet pepper and garlic over moderate heat for 5 minutes. Add the tomato sauce, vinegar and black pepper and stir-fry
for 5 minutes.

3. Add the browned chicken pieces to the sauce, mix well, cover the
pot, and cook over moderate heat for 15 minutes or more, or until
done.

4. Serve warm with Frijoles con Arroz (Beans and Rice) or Arroz
Blanco con Coco (White Rice in Coconut Milk) (see Index for
recipes).

SERVES 4

PINOL DE POLLO

CHICKEN IN TOASTED CORNMEAL GRUEL

SAN PEDRO SACATEPÉQUEZ, GUATEMALA

The *pinol* is a favorite food of both San Juan and San Pedro Sacate-péquez and is served by both for ceremonial religious days, special fiestas, wedding and birthday celebrations. As such, it is of great historical interest, but the whole recipe may be too large for most occasions. It may be halved with no loss of flavor. This recipe comes from an area renowned for the flowers grown for the Guatemala city market. The two towns, only 10 minutes apart over winding roads, are equally famous for their brilliant and yet completely different traditional Indian costumes.

My friend, Maria Lucia Pocon Archila de Granados of San Pedro, prepared this *pinol* with her sister Nicolasa on a cold but sunny day in November. San Pedro, at an altitude of about 7,000 feet, can be a very cold town where *pinol* and other soups are appropriate, nourishing, filling and infinitely delicious. The *pinol* was made in a large clay pot over a wood fire; the two sisters convinced me that both clay and wood were indispensable to reproduce the Mayan flavors of their village.

A vital step was toasting the dry corn kernels, which were grown on the family land. The kernels were toasted over a wood fire in a flat clay dish, about 24 inches in diameter, called the *comal*, until the aroma was released and the kernels turned light brown. They were then ground to a fine meal on the grinding stone (*piedra*), made of gray lava rock in the village of Nahualá. In San Pedro the base of the grinding stone is on 4 legs tilted slightly forward. The rounded oblong mallet is 2 or 3 inches wider than the base, making it much easier to reduce many kinds of foods to a smooth paste or powder in a back-breaking, back and forth, rubbing motion.

2 chickens, each 3½ pounds, cut into serving pieces; include giblets
12 cups water
2 tablespoons salt
1 pound beef bones
2 whole scallions
2 large sweet red peppers, about ½ pound
2 medium-size tomatoes, sliced
3 pounds (12 cups) masa harina, toasted in a dry skillet

1. Put the chicken pieces in a large pan with 8 cups water, the salt, beef bones and scallions. Bring to a boil over moderate heat and add the whole sweet red peppers to soften in the liquid for 5 minutes.

2. Process the tomatoes and red peppers to a smooth sauce and add it to the simmering chickens. Continue to cook for 40 minutes, or until the chicken is tender.

3. Remove the chicken and set aside. Remove and discard the beef bones, which were added to give the stock more body.

4. Moisten the toasted cornmeal with 4 cups water to the consistency of a heavy mush. Add this to the broth, stirring constantly to give it a relatively smooth consistency. Simmer this mixture over *low* heat for 30 minutes.

5. Serve generous portions of the light pink corn gruel in soup bowls. Serve the chicken on separate plates, but eat it together with the gruel. I prefer to serve the chicken and gruel together, which makes it more convenient to eat and also warms the chicken pieces, which have remained at room temperature. Traditionally served with tortillas and sweetened strong coffee.

SERVES 10

POLLO AL VAPOR

STEAMED CHICKEN

PUERTO SAN JOSÉ,
GUATEMALA

The cooks of San José insist that this chicken is really steamed, not fried in the oil. The onion and tomato provide enough liquid so that the effect is that of steaming. In any event, this is a most popular dish in the Pacific Coast seaport town. Worcestershire sauce was introduced in the port towns by visiting seamen longing for their own European seasonings. It is used as a standby condiment in the port towns on both the Pacific and Caribbean and is as remote from Mayan life as pizza.

1 chicken, 3 pounds, whole
2 teaspoons Worcestershire sauce
½ teaspoon salt, or to taste
¼ teaspoon black pepper
¼ cup lemon or lime juice
1 cup sliced onion
1 cup sliced tomato
2 tablespoons corn oil

1. Prick the chicken all over with a fork. Mix the Worcestershire sauce, salt, pepper and lemon juice together and rub this into the chicken inside and out. Let it stand for 30 minutes.

2. Fill the cavity of the chicken with the onion and tomato. Close the opening with a skewer.

3. Heat the oil in a skillet or heavy saucepan and put the chicken, breast side up, in the oil. Cover the pan and fry/steam over low heat for about 45 minutes, or until the chicken is tender. Baste several times with the accumulated juices during this process. Serve warm.

SERVES 4

POLLO RECADITO

CHICKEN IN THICK SAUCE
AGUACATÁN, GUATEMALA

This tasty chicken was prepared for me by an Aguacateca Indian family in the Department of Huehuetenango. These simple, uncomplicated people live in a town on the banks of the Río Negro, famous for growing garlic and onions. Their fields are beautifully managed, and green with a constant supply of water. The produce is known and in demand in Guatemala City. The women of the town weave spectacular headbands and wide ornate sashes for the men, and the traditional costumes are in daily use.

¼ cup tortilla flour (masa harina), moistened with ½ cup cold
    water
1 chicken, 3 pounds, cut into serving pieces
2 cups water
1 teaspoon salt, or to taste
4 scallions; cut the green parts into 2-inch pieces, leave the bulbs
    whole
3 stalks of epazote, 3-inch size
1 cup chopped tomato
⅛ teaspoon achiote

1. Moisten the tortilla flour to make a corn ball, which will be used as a thickening agent.
2. Cook the chicken in the water with the salt over moderate heat for 30 minutes. Then add the scallion greens and bulbs, epazote, tomato and achiote. Simmer for 10 minutes.
3. Add the corn ball and simmer for 10 minutes more. Stir well to dissolve the ball and thicken the sauce. Serve warm.

SERVES 4

PEPIÁN DE POLLO

CHICKEN IN RED SAUCE

HUEHUETENANGO, GUATEMALA

A *pepián* is made in several different ways in Guatemala, but it always includes squash seeds (*pepitoria*). All the preparations are delicious, reflecting the preference of the region. This recipe is pure magic.

1 chicken, 3½ pounds, cut into serving pieces, loose skin and fat
    discarded
4 cups water
1 teaspoon salt, or to taste
1½ cups chopped ripe tomatoes
½ cup chopped tomatillos (mil tomates)
1 chile pasa (pasilla), seeds and stem removed
1 chile guaque (guajillo), seeds and stem removed
½ cup sesame seeds
1 tablespoon squash seeds
1 cinnamon stick, 1 inch, broken up
2 teaspoons dried hot red chile flakes, or to taste
½ cup French bread, cubed and moistened with broth
¼ teaspoon achiote
1 tablespoon flour

1. Cook the chicken in 3 cups water with the salt over moderate heat for 30 minutes. Reserve broth for sauce.

2. Cook the tomatoes, tomatillos, chile pasa and chile guaque in 1 cup water over moderate heat for 10 minutes to soften them.

3. Toast the sesame seeds, squash seeds, cinnamon stick and hot chile flakes in a dry skillet over low heat for about 10 minutes, or until they are a light tan color.

4. Process the toasted ingredients, then the cooked tomato mixture, into a smooth paste. Add the bread, achiote and 2 cups of chicken broth with the flour. Process everything together until smooth.

5. Add this sauce to the chicken. Simmer over low heat for 15 minutes, or until the sauce is reduced to a thick, rich red paste and the chicken is done. Total cooking time of chicken and sauce should be about 45 minutes. Serve warm with tortillas and rice.

SERVES 4

POLLO ENCEBOLLADO

CHICKEN SMOTHERED IN ONIONS

CHIQUIMULILLA, GUATEMALA

1 chicken, 3 to 3½ pounds, cut into serving pieces, loose skin and
    fat discarded
2 tablespoons corn oil
1 teaspoon salt, or to taste
½ teaspoon freshly ground black pepper
¼ teaspoon grated nutmeg
1 cup sliced onion
½ cup orange juice
½ cup chicken broth

1. Fry the chicken in oil in a skillet over moderate heat for 5 minutes, turning the pieces several times. Add the salt, black pepper, nutmeg and onion slices, and continue frying for 2 minutes.

2. Add the orange juice and broth and cover the skillet. Simmer over moderate to low heat until the chicken is tender and the sauce is somewhat reduced, about 30 minutes.

3. Serve warm. Traditionally served with rice, a mixed salad, or noodles in a simple tomato sauce. As always, a Salsa Picante (see Index) is a popular adjunct to stimulate the taste buds.

SERVES 4

POLLO EN VERDURAS

CHICKEN WITH VEGETABLES

COBÁN, GUATEMALA

The people of Cobán are good cooks and have a flair for preparing potted chickens, well seasoned with a variety of vegetables and seasonings, which always seem to be available in their kitchens or the nearby municipal outdoor markets. The Cobán district is rich in soil and water and the rain forests are green and luxurious. It is here that the Kekchi Indians, speaking their own language and wearing their national costumes, continue the tradition of good cooking.

One should not be intimidated by the large number of ingredients and seasonings. The number of vegetables can be reduced; for example, you can omit the chayote and green beans without damaging the recipe. However, the variety is part of the mystique of this family or party dish.

½ cup sliced onion
2 garlic cloves, sliced
1 cup sliced ripe tomato
2 teaspoons salt, or to taste
½ teaspoon black pepper
1 whole clove
⅛ teaspoon grated nutmeg
6 cups water
2 tablespoons corn oil
½ cup coarse-chopped celery
1 large leek, white part only, chopped coarse
1 cup sliced sweet green pepper
1 chicken, 3½ pounds, cut into serving pieces; include giblets; loose
　　skin and fat discarded
3 bay leaves
¼ teaspoon thyme
¼ teaspoon achiote

1 cup ½-inch potato cubes
1 cup 2-inch carrot sticks
1 cup diagonally sliced green snap beans
1 cup green peas, fresh or frozen
1 chayote (huisquil), peeled and cut into 1-inch sticks
1 tablespoon flour, dissolved in ¼ cup broth

1. Process the onion, garlic, tomato slices, 1 teaspoon salt, the black pepper, clove and nutmeg into a paste with 1 cup water.

2. Heat the oil in a large skillet and fry the celery, leek and sweet green pepper for 2 minutes. Add the tomato mixture and fry for 3 minutes more.

3. Cook the chicken in the remaining 5 cups water with 1 teaspoon salt in a large saucepan over moderate heat for 20 minutes.

4. Add the fried tomato mixture, the bay leaves, thyme and achiote, and stir well. Add the vegetables one by one, depending upon the firmness, potatoes first, then carrots, green beans, peas and chayote. Mix well.

5. Add the dissolved flour and stir it into the chicken broth. Simmer the entire preparation over low heat for 15 to 30 minutes to distribute the seasonings, cook the vegetables and chicken, and thicken the soup/sauce. Serve warm in soup bowls.

SERVES 6

JOCON

CHICKEN IN GREEN SAUCE
HUEHUETENANGO, GUATEMALA

Jocon is a famous dish from Huehuetenango. It is copied but seldom equaled in other parts of the country. This recipe is an authentic example which I cooked with an old-time cook in her *comedor*, a four-table restaurant in back of the Municipal Market. The people in this area like hot chile pepper, but it should not be hot enough to overpower the fresh green flavor of the scallions and cilantro.

1 chicken, 3 pounds, cut into serving pieces, loose skin and fat discarded
4 cups water
1 teaspoon salt, or to taste
2 tortillas, sliced
1 tablespoon squash seeds (pepitoria)
½ cup sesame seeds
1 cup cilantro, packed
1 cup sliced scallions, green part only
½ cup sliced tomatillos (mil tomates)
1 to 2 teaspoons hot green chile slices
1 tablespoon corn oil

1. Cook the chicken in the water with the salt in a covered kettle until soft, about 30 minutes. Remove the chicken and set aside. Reserve the broth and soak the tortillas in it.

2. Toast the squash seeds and sesame seeds in a dry skillet over moderate to low heat until they turn a light tan color, about 10 minutes.

3. Prepare a sauce in the processor. First grind the squash and sesame seeds. Add the cilantro, scallions, tomatillos, hot chile pepper and 1 cup of the reserved broth. Add the soaked tortillas and process to a smooth paste.

4. Brown the chicken pieces in oil over moderate heat for 5 minutes.

Add the green sauce and the balance of the broth, about 2 cups. Simmer this over low heat for 15 minutes, until the sauce is reduced to a thick, rich, green consistency. Serve warm.

SERVES 4

JOCON

CHICKEN IN GREEN SAUCE

QUEZALTENANGO, GUATEMALA

This is another variation of the *jocon* from a different region of Guatemala. Flavored with garlic and thickened with flour instead of tortillas, it is still cooked by the same general method.

1 chicken, 3 pounds, cut into serving pieces, loose skin and fat
    discarded
1 small onion, quartered
1 teaspoon salt, or to taste
1½ cups water
½ cup sliced scallions, green part only
½ cup sliced tomatillos (mil tomates), or 1 large green tomato,
    sliced
½ cup chopped cilantro
2 garlic cloves, sliced
2 teaspoons flour
1 teaspoon hot green chile slices, or to taste

1. Cook the chicken, onion, and salt in 1 cup water in a saucepan over moderate heat for 30 minutes.
2. Meanwhile, process the scallions, tomatillos, cilantro, garlic, flour and chile into a smooth paste with ½ cup water.
3. Add the green sauce to the chicken and continue to cook over moderate to low heat for 20 minutes. Serve warm.

SERVES 4

PULIQUÉ DE POLLO DE LA COFRADÍA

CEREMONIAL CHICKEN

PANAJACHEL, GUATEMALA

This *puliqué* is prepared by the wife of the *cofradía* (the village headman responsible for religious ceremonies) during special ceremonial occasions such as the day of the patron Saint of this village, San Francisco. Hens are killed and clay pots are filled with meat, sauces and potatoes, simmering over wood fires, so that the faithful may partake of some food during the celebration.

1 hen, 4 pounds, cut into serving pieces, loose skin and fat
    discarded
4 cups water
1 teaspoon salt, or to taste
2 cups ripe tomato slices
¼ teaspoon achiote
4 scallions, chopped
¼ cup chopped cilantro
¼ cup masa (tortilla flour moistened with ½ cup cold water)
2 cups sliced potatoes, cut as for French fries

1. Cook the chicken in the water with the salt until tender, about 30 minutes over moderate heat. Remove the chicken and set aside.
2. Process into a smooth sauce the tomatoes, achiote, scallions and cilantro.
3. Add the sauce, *masa* and potatoes to the broth and simmer over low heat for 10 minutes. Add the chicken pieces and simmer for 15 minutes more. Serve warm with tamalitos.

SERVES 6

PULIQUÉ DE CARNES

A STEW OF TWO MEATS

SANTA CATARINA PALOPÓ, GUATEMALA

This is the tribal dish of the Cakchiquel-speaking village on the slopes of Lake Atitlán. The headman (*cofradía*), from whom I learned this *puliqué*, prepares it on November 23, the day of their patron saint, Santa Catarina. The *puliqué* is prepared in large quantities and served to the villagers with tortillas, tamalitos and gallons of sweetened coffee.

3 pounds boneless beef chuck, cut into 2-inch cubes
8 cups water
2 teaspoons salt, or to taste
1 chicken, 3 pounds, cut into serving pieces, loose skin and fat
    discarded
1 cup ripe tomato chunks
1 to 2 teaspoons chopped hot chile, fresh or dried
¼ teaspoon achiote
2 cups masa (moistened tortilla flour)
8 small potatoes (2 pounds), peeled, whole
1 cup small pickling onions, cut into halves
1 pound cabbage, cut into quarters
¼ cup cilantro, stems cut short

1. Cook the beef in the water with the salt over moderate heat for 45 minutes. Add the chicken pieces and cook for 20 minutes more, or until the meats are nearly done.
2. Prepare a smooth sauce in a processor with the tomato chunks, hot chile and achiote. Add this to the meats with the *masa* and simmer over moderate heat for 10 minutes.
3. Add the potatoes, onions, cabbage and cilantro and continue to simmer for 20 minutes more, or until all the vegetables are cooked. Adjust the salt during this process and add more hot chile if you would prefer a bit of a sting.
4. Serve meat, chicken and vegetables warm in bowls.

SERVES 8

GALLINA EN MOLE

HEN IN CHOCOLATE SAUCE

GUATEMALA CITY

1 stewing hen, 5½ to 6 pounds, cut into serving pieces, loose skin
   and fat discarded
6 cups water
1 tablespoon salt, or to taste
1 small ripe tomato, halved
2 scallions, halved
2 garlic cloves, peeled, whole

Sauce

1 chile pasa (pasilla), seeds and stem removed
½ cup water
1 teaspoon salt
6 tablespoons squash seeds (pepitoria)
5 tablespoons sesame seeds
1 chile guaque (guajillo)
1 cinnamon stick, 3 inches, broken into pieces
1 pound whole ripe tomatoes
6 garlic cloves, peeled
1 medium-size onion, peeled, whole
1 teaspoon minced gingerroot
¼ teaspoon black pepper
4 ounces semisweet chocolate, Mixco or native style
¾ cup toasted bread crumbs

1. Cook the hen in 6 cups water with the salt, tomato, scallions and
garlic in a large saucepan over moderate heat for 1 hour, or until the
meat is nearly done. Remove the hen and set aside. Strain and
reserve the broth.

2. Make the sauce: Cook the chile pasa in the water with the salt for
15 minutes. Drain.

3. In a large dry skillet toast the squash seeds, sesame seeds, chile guaque and cinnamon stick until lightly charred. In another skillet or under a grill, toast the whole tomatoes, garlic and onion.

4. Purée the sauce ingredients in a processor—the chile pasa, all the toasted items, the gingerroot, black pepper and 2 cups of the reserved broth. Press the sauce through a metal strainer and discard the residue.

5. Add sauce to the balance of the broth (about 3 cups) with the chocolate and bread crumbs. Simmer over low heat for 10 minutes to dissolve the chocolate and thicken the sauce with the crumbs.

6. Add the hen and simmer over low heat for 20 minutes more.

7. Serve warm with rice, tortillas and a variety of typical salads.

SERVES 8

Note: This is a classic preparation in Guatemalan style and as delicious as any.

GALLINA GUISADO

HEN IN TOMATO SAUCE
MIXCO, GUATEMALA

The *guisado* is the favorite dish traditionally served at fiestas and other ceremonial occasions in this town on the edge of Guatemala City. Mixco is famous for making the native chocolate used in traditional foods, for its *chicharrones* (at the Saturday market) and jellies of quince, apple and guava. In Colonial times the women of Mixco were used as wet nurses for the babies of the wealthy citizens of Guatemala City. They were admired then and now for their cleanliness and neat appearance.

1 stewing hen, 3½ to 4 pounds
1 small head of garlic, about 8 cloves, unpeeled
1 teaspoon salt, or to taste
1 pound small potatoes, 5 to 6, whole, unpeeled
4 cups water
3 cups sliced ripe tomatoes
½ cup sliced tomatillos (mil tomates)
½ teaspoon thyme
¼ cup sliced onion
1 bay leaf
1 tablespoon corn oil

1. Cook the whole hen, garlic, salt and potatoes in the water over moderate heat until the hen is almost done, about 45 minutes.

2. Remove the hen and cut it into serving pieces. Peel the potatoes and cut into 1-inch cubes. Discard the head or cloves of garlic. Reserve 2 cups broth.

3. Process into a smooth sauce the tomato slices, tomatillos, thyme and onion, with the reserved 2 cups broth. In a large enough saucepan over moderate heat fry the sauce with the bay leaf in the oil for 3 minutes.

4. Add the chicken pieces and the potato cubes and simmer over low heat for 15 minutes to distribute the seasonings and complete the cooking of the chicken and potatoes.

5. Serve warm with rice and Ensalada de Remolacha (Beet Salad, see Index).

SERVES 4

MOLLEJAS (TITILES)

CHICKEN GIZZARDS IN WINE SAUCE

NICARAGUA

1 pound chicken gizzards, cut into lobes
2 cups water
6 garlic cloves, chopped
1 tablespoon corn oil
1 teaspoon achiote, dissolved in hot oil
¼ cup sliced onion
¼ cup sliced tomato
1 teaspoon salt, or to taste
½ teaspoon black pepper
¾ cup chopped sweet red pepper
1 tablespoon Worcestershire sauce
½ cup white table wine

1. Cook the gizzards in water with the garlic over moderate heat for about 45 minutes, or until done.

2. Add the oil, achiote, onion, tomato, salt, black pepper, sweet red pepper, Worcestershire sauce and wine. Simmer over moderate heat for 15 minutes, until the seasonings have been blended and the sauce is somewhat reduced.

3. Serve warm with rice and tortillas.

Note: The *titiles* may also be served as an appetizer with drinks. Serve with a small amount of sauce.

SERVES 6

PAN CON CHUMPÉ

TURKEY SANDWICH
EL SALVADOR

These famous sandwiches are a national addiction; they are sold by vendors all over the country, customarily sold and served at 5 P.M. and onward.

French bread
Butter
Escabeche (Cooked Pickled Salad, see Index)
Roast turkey or chicken, sliced
Sliced young cucumbers, peeled
Sliced radishes
Sliced tomato
Watercress

1. Butter the bread or toast.

2. Prepare the sandwiches in this manner using as much filling as you wish: For each sandwich use 1 heaping tablespoon *escabeche;* push into this 1 or 2 slices of turkey, 2 slices of cucumber, a slice or two of radish, 1 slice of tomato. Add 2 sprigs of watercress to the sandwich so that 2 inches of the green leaves stick out as an adornment.

CHUNTO

SPICED TURKEY STEW
COBÁN, GUATEMALA

Every family in Cobán claims to have the original or "real" *chunto* with its own variation. This version is spicier than others. The famous chile of Cobán may be added or not, depending upon family tradition and personal preference. A Salsa Picante (see Index) served separately caters to those with a penchant for chile.

Braising or stewing turkey may seem unappealing to those of us who are used to roasting the bird, but I promise you will find this method produces a dish tastier than and not as dry as roast turkey. Served in a soup bowl with plenty of French bread or tortillas to sop it up, it may become a family favorite.

4 large onions, whole (2 cups)
6 garlic cloves, peeled, whole
2 ripe tomatoes, whole (1 cup)
1 chile pasa (pasilla), seeds and stem removed
½ teaspoon achiote
6 peppercorns
2 small sweet red peppers, chopped, seeded, stems removed
    (1 cup)
10 cups water
1 turkey, 10 pounds, cut into serving pieces; include giblets
2 teaspoons salt, or to taste
½ cup chopped fresh mint
½ cup chopped cilantro
1 small whole head of garlic (8 cloves), unpeeled

1. Put the onion, peeled garlic cloves, tomatoes, chile pasa, achiote, peppercorns and sweet peppers in a skillet and toast over moderate heat for 5 to 10 minutes, until the various skins are lightly browned.

2. Process these with 1 cup of water into a smooth sauce.

3. Put the turkey, 9 cups water and the salt in a large heavy saucepan or roasting pan and bring to a boil over moderate heat. Add the sauce, mint, cilantro and the whole head of garlic. Simmer for about 1½ hours, until the turkey is tender and the seasonings well blended.

SERVES 12 GENEROUSLY

PEPIÁN DE CHUMPIPE

TURKEY IN DARK RED SAUCE
HUEHUETENANGO, GUATEMALA

This is a classic Mayan preparation beloved by all Guatemalans. The preparation of the turkey and its ancient religious connotation adds prestige to the cook and the diner. The *pepián* is expensive to prepare in the Mayan highlands since the village turkeys raised in the peasant compounds can cost about $2.00 per pound—a lot of money but in this recipe worth every centavo.

1 turkey, 10 pounds, cut into serving portions, including heart,
    liver and gizzard
10 cups water
1 tablespoon salt, or to taste
1½ cups sesame seeds
1 teaspoon peppercorns
1 cup squash seeds (pepitoria)
1 cinnamon stick, 3 inches, broken into pieces
2 cups ripe tomatoes
½ cup tomatillos (mil tomates)
1 tablespoon dried hot red chile flakes
3 small sweet red peppers, seeds and stems removed
½ teaspoon achiote
1 cup toasted bread crumbs

1. Pull off the loose skin and fat from the turkey and discard. Cut the breast and thighs into reasonable serving pieces, not too large. Cook the turkey in the water with the salt in a large saucepan or roasting pan over moderate heat for about 1 hour, until tender.

2. In a dry skillet over low heat, toast the sesame seeds, peppercorns, squash seeds and cinnamon stick until light tan in color. Set aside.

3. Meanwhile, char the red tomatoes and green tomatillos in a dry skillet over low heat for 5 minutes. Peel off the skins.

4. Prepare a smooth sauce (*recado*) in a processor with the toasted

sesame seeds, peppercorns, squash seeds, cinnamon, tomatoes and tomatillos, chile, sweet red peppers and achiote.

5. Add the sauce to the simmering turkey along with the toasted
bread crumbs and continue to simmer and stir over moderate to low
heat for about 30 minutes. The sauce will have thickened, and flavored the sufficiently cooked, tender turkey. There should be ample
sauce, but if the liquid has evaporated too quickly, add another ½
cup of water.

6. Serve warm. Traditionally served with rice and tortillas.

SERVES 12 GENEROUSLY

CHUMPIPE PRENSADO

PRESSED STUFFED BONELESS TURKEY

TAXISCO, GUATEMALA

The pressed turkey is an important buffet production, served cold or at room temperature. There, as here, it would not be everyday fare but reserved for celebrations, holidays and other important functions. The astonishing aspect is that I was taught this recipe by a simple woman in a small, provincial Guatemalan town that is entirely agricultural and where few if any big city culinary techniques appear. She assured me that this sophisticated and complicated recipe was known and used by many of the townspeople for special occasions. Boning a turkey is no everyday occurence. The essentially Spanish Colonial racial mixture of the population in this region reveals the source of the recipe.

2 teaspoons salt, or to taste
¼ cup white or cider vinegar
¼ cup prepared mustard
¼ pound margarine or butter
1 turkey, 10 pounds, boned (see Index for Stuffed Boneless
    Chicken)
½ cup fine-chopped tomato
½ cup fine-chopped onion
2 garlic cloves, chopped fine
1 tablespoon corn oil
4 bay leaves
1 teaspoon thyme
2 pounds ground beef
4 cups cooked diced carrots
4 cups cooked sliced green snap beans
4 cups diced cooked potatoes
4 cups green peas, fresh or frozen, lightly cooked
¼ cup capers

¼ cup stuffed olives
½ cup thin-sliced sweet red peppers
½ teaspoon freshly ground black pepper
8 hard-cooked eggs, shelled

Herb-Flavored Bath

4 cups water
2 scallions, sliced
½ teaspoon thyme
4 bay leaves
1 teaspoon salt

1. Mix 1 teaspoon salt, the vinegar, mustard and margarine together into a paste. Spread this all over the interior of the boneless turkey.

2. Fry the tomato, onion and garlic in the oil over moderate heat for 2 minutes. Add the bay leaves and thyme. Then add the ground beef, carrots, green beans, potatoes and green peas, and mix very well. Add the capers, olives, sweet peppers, some salt and black pepper. Stir and fry for 5 minutes. Cool the mixture and remove the bay leaves.

3. Stuff the turkey with half of the mixture and add 2 lines of eggs, four on each side, pressed into the stuffing. Cover this with the remainder of the stuffing. Do not neglect to stuff the leg and wing portions. Sew up the bird.

4. Wrap the turkey firmly in a cotton kitchen towel and tie up the ends and middle of the bundle tightly.

5. Put the turkey in a large roasting pan with a cover. Prepare the herb-flavored bath by mixing all ingredients. Pour the herb-flavored bath over the turkey bundle. Cover and bring the liquid to a boil. Simmer over low heat for 2 hours.

6. Remove the turkey and place it between 2 wooden or plastic cutting boards. Weigh down the top board with a heavy stone or metal object. I use a village stone mortar and pestle which serves well for this purpose. Press and cool for 8 hours. This may be done in or

(recipe continues)

out of the refrigerator but logically in a cool spot. At the end of this period the turkey should be refrigerated for several hours.

7. When ready to serve, remove the cloth towel and slice the turkey into generous portions. Serve cold. The *prensado* is traditionally served with a variety of salads plus a Guatemalan rice.

SERVES 12 GENEROUSLY

PINOL DE CHUMPIPE

TURKEY WITH TOASTED CORNMEAL

JACALTENANGO, GUATEMALA

Jacaltenango is a small mountainous town in the Department of Huehuetenango. For some years, until recent times, one would go there on horseback or in a jeep with double transmission over an extremely dubious rocky road. It is not much better today but the road is wider to allow bus service from a major town. The women of the town weave and embroider beautiful headbands and belts and wear their traditional *huipil* (overblouse) with a rather funky, Colonial frilly collar.

The *pinol* is the corn that is toasted and ground to a powder and used throughout Indian villages to provide bulk and flavor for meat dishes and to thicken sauces. The turkey would be a village or free-range turkey. This dish exhibits pre-Hispanic origin by its very simplicity.

1 turkey, 6 pounds
6 cups water
1 tablespoon salt, or to taste
3 pounds dried corn kernels

1. Cut the turkey into serving pieces; discard loose skin and fat. Put the turkey in the water with the salt and bring to a boil. Simmer over moderate heat for about 1½ hours.

2. During this process, toast the whole corn kernels on a *comal* (clay dish) or dry skillet until the corn has turned light brown and emits a fragrant toasted aroma. Grind the corn to a fine powder and add this to the turkey.

3. Cook the mixture until the turkey is tender and the mixture has thickened to a gruel.

4. Serve the turkey pieces and gruel in bowls with tamalitos and/or rice as side dishes.

SERVES 8

CHUMPÉ SUDADO EN MANZANA

TURKEY STUFFED WITH APPLES

EL SALVADOR

This is a very old recipe from the more sophisticated people in the major cities of El Salvador. It is reputed to have been devised by elderly spinster ladies whose preoccupation was good food and ingenious recipes.

Turkey gizzard, heart and liver
Lightly salted water
¼ pound (1 stick) butter, at room temperature
2 teaspoons salt
½ teaspoon pepper
½ teaspoon thyme
1 tablespoon prepared mustard
1 turkey, 10 pounds

Stuffing

2 cups unpeeled firm, tart apple cubes
1 cup sliced onion
1 cup sliced sweet red pepper
1 cup sliced carrot
1 cup cubed French bread, lightly moistened

Sauce

1 cup chopped onion
½ cup chopped sweet red pepper
½ cup chopped tomato
1 tablespoon chopped parsley
1 cup chopped celery with leaves and ribs
2 cups water
1 cup white table wine

20 capers
20 green stuffed olives

1. Cook the gizzard and heart in lightly salted water for about 1 hour, or until tender; add the liver about 10 minutes before end of cooking time. Set aside.

2. Mix the butter, salt, pepper, thyme and mustard together. Rub the mixture on the inside and outside of the turkey.

3. Make the stuffing: Mix the apple cubes with the sliced onion, sweet pepper, carrot and bread. Stuff the neck end firmly with this mixture and put the remainder in the cavity. It is probably not necessary to sew up the openings.

4. Without additional butter, brown the turkey on all sides in a roaster over moderate heat for about 10 minutes. Add all the sauce ingredients except capers and olives and bring to a boil on top of the stove.

5. Put the turkey into a preheated 350°F. oven and bake for 3 hours or more, until the turkey is done. Baste frequently.

6. Make the gravy: Remove all the pan gravy from the turkey roaster. There should be about 2 cups or more. Grind the gizzard, heart and liver quite fine with the capers and their liquid and add to the gravy. Bring it to a boil with the olives and let it simmer slowly for 5 minutes.

7. To serve, slice the white and dark meat. Put the dark meat on the bottom of a large serving platter and cover it with the white meat. Pour the warm sauce over all.

SERVES 12 GENEROUSLY

PAVO EN ESPECIAS

TURKEY AND SPICES

EL SALVADOR

This is a popular recipe of the countryside, farm country and agricultural areas in El Salvador.

¾ cup sesame seeds
3 tablespoons squash seeds
6 bay leaves
1 teaspoon peppercorns
1 teaspoon thyme
4 whole cloves
½ teaspoon ground cinnamon
1 teaspoon orégano
½ cup French bread crumbs
2 medium-size onions, whole
2 medium-size tomatoes
4 garlic cloves, whole
¼ cup prepared mustard, at room temperature
¼ pound (1 stick) butter
1 tablespoon Worcestershire sauce
1 chile pasa (pasilla), seeds and stem removed, soaked in water
10 cups water
1 turkey, 10 pounds, whole

1. Toast the sesame seeds, squash seeds, bay leaves, peppercorns, thyme, cloves, cinnamon and orégano in a dry skillet until they are lightly colored and release their aromas.

2. Toast the bread and moisten it with water. Char the onions, tomatoes and garlic in a dry skillet over moderate heat for about 5 minutes. Peel the tomatoes.

3. Mix together the mustard, butter and Worcestershire sauce.

4. Grind the seeds, spices and chile pasa in a blender with 2 cups water. Grind the bread, onions and tomatoes separately to a smooth *recado* (sauce). Mix the seed and tomato sauces together with 8 cups water and strain it through a metal sieve.

5. Now rub the turkey inside and out with the mustard/butter mixture, pushing some into the neck and skin cavity. Brown the turkey all over in a large roasting pan over moderate heat for about 10 minutes. Add the strained sauce.

6. Roast in a 375°F. oven, basting frequently, for about 3 hours, or until tender. Cut the turkey into pieces and serve with plenty of sauce.

SERVES 12

PULIQUÉ DE CHUMPIPE

TURKEY POT-AU-FEU
SAN ANTONIO PALOPÓ,
GUATEMALA

San Antonio Palopó is one of the fourteen Indian villages that perch around the perimeter of the visually spectacular Lake Atitlán in the Mayan highlands. This *puliqué* is one of their ceremonial dishes, prepared on special occasions connected with religious observances.

1 turkey, 10 pounds
10 cups water
2 teaspoons salt, or to taste
1 cup sliced ripe tomato
1 cup sliced onion
½ cup cilantro
1 tablespoon fresh hot green chile pepper, or to taste
½ cup masa (tortilla flour moistened with water)
1 pound small whole potatoes, peeled
1 pound small carrots
4 chayote (huisquil), peeled and quartered
1 pound cabbage, cut into chunks

1. Cook the whole turkey in the water with the salt over moderate heat for about 2 hours, or until it is tender.

2. Meanwhile, prepare a sauce in the processor with the tomato, onion, cilantro and chile pepper. Add this to the turkey broth with the *masa* for thickening and simmer for 5 minutes.

3. As the turkey approaches the doneness stage, add the potatoes and carrots and simmer for about 10 minutes. Add the chayote and cabbage, which are softer vegetables, and cook the entire preparation until soft and thickened.

4. Remove the turkey and cut it into serving pieces.

5. Serve the turkey separately at room temperature. The sauce and vegetables are served in separate bowls. The diner can mix them all together in his own soup bowl (which is my preference) or consider them as three separate items in the dinner.

SERVES 12 GENEROUSLY

PULIQUÉ

TURKEY IN THICK SAUCE

SAN JORGE LA LAGUNA, GUATEMALA

This relatively simple recipe comes from one of the Indian villages on Lake Atitlán. San Jorge is an attractive and quiet village with a sixteenth-century church and not much more. The village women weave beautiful traditional costumes for both men and women and wear them daily. The *puliqué* is a ceremonial and fiesta preparation that is a favorite in the village but, since turkey is expensive, would only be served on special occasions.

1 turkey, 10 pounds, whole with the giblets
10 cups water
2 teaspoons salt, or to taste
1 cup chopped onion
½ cup coarsely chopped cilantro
1 cup tortilla flour (masa harina)
½ teaspoon achiote

1. Cook the turkey in the water with the salt, onion and cilantro in a large covered saucepan or roaster over moderate heat for about 2 hours, or until the turkey is tender. Turn several times during this process. Remove the turkey and set aside. Leave the broth in the pan.

2. Mix 1 cup of the broth with the tortilla flour and achiote into a moist ball. Bring the broth to a boil, add the cornmeal ball, and mix it well. Simmer the mixture over low heat for 15 minutes, stirring frequently. The seasoned broth should be lightly thickened by the cornmeal and of a pale, pinkish color.

3. Cut the turkey into moderate-size pieces. Traditionally, broth and turkey are served separately, but I prefer to pour the sauce (or soup) over the turkey into individual bowls. Eat with tamalitos.

SERVES 12

PULIQUÉ DE PATO

DUCK STEW

PANAJACHEL, GUATEMALA

This duck stew from Panajachel is thickened in the same way as the turkey *puliqué*, but is much more highly seasoned.

1 duck, 4 to 4½ pounds, cut into serving pieces
6 cups water
1 teaspoon salt
1 cup chopped tomato
¼ cup chopped onion
1 garlic clove, chopped
2 teaspoons orégano
¼ teaspoon whole cloves
½ teaspoon freshly ground black pepper
½ teaspoon thyme
¼ teaspoon achiote
2 bay leaves
½ cup masa (tortilla flour moistened with water)

1. Cook the duck in the water with the salt over moderate heat until soft, about 1½ hours.

2. Make a smooth sauce in a processor with 1 cup of the broth and the tomato, onion, garlic, orégano, cloves, black pepper, thyme and achiote. Add this sauce and the bay leaves to the duck. Add *masa* to thicken the sauce.

3. Simmer over low heat for 30 minutes longer, until the sauce is reduced and thickened. The sauce should not be gummy. Serve warm.

SERVES 6

Note: All of these duck recipes are enhanced by cooking the day before and allowing the flavors to become intensified overnight. The fat may then be skimmed off the dish more easily.

PATO EN PIÑA

DUCK AND PINEAPPLE
EL SALVADOR

From El Salvador comes this more sophisticated duck recipe, with the pineapple and wine adding a sweet note to the otherwise spicy sauce.

1 duck, 4½ pounds, with giblets
3 cups water
1 cup chopped onion
½ cup chopped tomato
1 teaspoon salt
½ teaspoon freshly ground black pepper
3 garlic cloves, chopped
2 tablespoons corn oil
1 cup crushed pineapple, fresh or canned
2 teaspoons Worcestershire sauce
2 teaspoons prepared mustard
½ cup sliced sweet green pepper
1 cup white table wine

1. Cook the giblets in the 3 cups of water with ½ cup onion, the tomato, salt, pepper and garlic until soft. Add the liver for the last 15 minutes. Strain and reserve the liquid. Reserve the giblets for another use.

2. Fry the other ½ cup onion in 2 teaspoons oil until translucent. Mix with the crushed pineapple.

3. In a flameproof casserole, brown the duck in the rest of the oil over moderate heat for 5 minutes, or until the color changes. Add the reserved giblet broth, the pineapple and onion mixtures, Worcestershire sauce, mustard, green pepper and wine. Bring to a boil, cover the casserole, and cook until the duck is tender, about 1½ hours.

4. Remove the cover toward the end of the cooking time to allow

some of the liquid to evaporate. Turn the duck several times during the cooking. Skim off as much fat as possible prior to serving.

SERVES 6

Variation: A 3-pound chicken is prepared in essentially the same way, except it is cut into serving pieces before cooking. Discard the loose skin and fat. Follow the same system of preparation except that all the quantities should be reduced by half.

PATO EN JUGO DE NARANJA

DUCK IN ORANGE-JUICE SAUCE

GUATEMALA CITY

1 duck, 4 to 4½ pounds, cut into serving pieces
½ cup sliced onion
2 tablespoons corn oil
1 cup chopped ripe tomato
2 garlic cloves, chopped
2 bay leaves
½ teaspoon thyme
1 cinnamon stick, 1 inch
2 whole cloves
¼ teaspoon freshly ground black pepper
1 cup fresh orange juice
1 cup water

1. In a flameproof casserole, brown the duck and onion in the oil over moderate heat. Add the tomato, garlic, bay leaves, thyme, cinnamon, cloves and black pepper. Stir and fry for 5 minutes to mix everything together.

2. Add the orange juice and water, bring to a boil, and continue to simmer over moderate heat for 1½ hours, or until the duck is tender and the sauce reduced by half. Serve warm.

SERVES 6

PATO GUISADO

DUCK STEW WITH POTATOES

LIVINGSTON, GUATEMALA

The people of Livingston are not really duck eaters, but ducks wander around in the town's grassy lanes nibbling on everything around them, and some people do keep them for sale. I suppose that all their lives the townspeople see aquatic birds and wild ducks in the estuaries of this port town on the Caribbean and are indifferent to the taste since their basic diet is fish.

This duck stew is especially good because of the seasonings of the region. Since the ducks are a bit muscular from their meandering, there is very little fat and the meat is exemplary, unlike American ducks which have a preponderance of fat. In preparing the *guisado*, remove loose skin and fat from the duck before cooking, and remember that the fat in the duck may be removed more easily by cooking the duck ahead of time and refrigerating it so that the fat congeals.

1 duck, 4 to 4½ pounds, cut into serving pieces
4 cups water
2 tablespoons white or cider vinegar
1 teaspoon salt
1½ cups chopped ripe tomatoes
½ cup chopped onion
3 garlic cloves, chopped
1 teaspoon thyme
½ teaspoon orégano
4 bay leaves
¼ teaspoon achiote
3 cups ½-inch cubes of peeled potatoes

1. Simmer the duck in the water with the vinegar and salt in a large saucepan or flameproof casserole over moderate heat.

2. Meanwhile, prepare a smooth sauce in a processor with the tomatoes, onion, garlic and 1 cup of broth from the duck. Add the sauce

to the duck with the thyme, orégano, bay leaves and achiote. Continue to simmer over moderate heat until the duck is nearly soft, about 1½ hours.

3. Add the potato cubes and simmer for 15 minutes more. The sauce will be reduced and the potatoes will be softened. Serve warm with rice and tortillas.

SERVES 6

PATO EN LECHE DE COCO

DUCK IN COCONUT MILK

LIVINGSTON, GUATEMALA

Another duck recipe from Livingston; this is a smooth, rich dish because of the coconut milk.

1 duck, 4 to 4½ pounds, cut into serving pieces
1 cup chopped ripe tomato
½ cup chopped onion
3 garlic cloves, chopped fine
1 teaspoon thyme
3 bay leaves
1 teaspoon salt, or to taste
¼ teaspoon achiote
4 cups Rich Coconut Milk (see Index)

1. Put everything together into a large heavy saucepan or flame-proof casserole and bring to a boil over moderate heat. Baste continuously for 10 minutes so the coconut milk does not separate or curdle.

2. Continue to cook in an uncovered pan, basting frequently, for 1½ hours or until the duck is tender and the sauce is reduced by about half. Serve warm.

SERVES 6

PATO EN COCO

DUCK IN COCONUT MILK SAUCE

LIVINGSTON, GUATEMALA

Much like the preceding recipe, this one adds piquancy with the vinegar, and uses the *puliqué* method of cooking.

1 duck, 4 to 4½ pounds, cut into serving pieces
½ cup chopped tomato
¼ cup chopped onion
2 garlic cloves, chopped
2 tablespoons corn oil
½ teaspoon freshly ground black pepper
1 teaspoon thyme
3 bay leaves
1 teaspoon salt, or to taste
2 tablespoons white or cider vinegar
4 cups Rich Coconut Milk (see Index)
¼ teaspoon achiote

1. Lightly brown the duck, tomato, onion and garlic in the oil over moderate heat for 10 minutes.

2. Add the black pepper, thyme, bay leaves, salt and vinegar, and stir well.

3. Bring the coconut milk to a boil in another pan with the achiote and pour it over the duck. Simmer over low heat, uncovered, for 5 minutes, basting continuously. Cover the pan and simmer for about 1½ hours, until the duck is tender and the sauce reduced and thickened. Serve warm.

SERVES 6

Note: This, like all other duck recipes, can be made the day before and refrigerated. The fat will then congeal and can be removed easily.

PALOMITAS GUISADAS

BRAISED PIGEONS
GUATEMALA CITY

Pigeons are not always easy to come by, but I have found that Rock Cornish hens are perfectly good substitutes. They should be about 1 pound each or a bit more.

4 pigeons, each 1 pound
½ cup sour orange juice
1 teaspoon salt
1 tablespoon corn oil
¾ cup chopped ripe tomato
¼ cup chopped onion
1 garlic clove, chopped
2 bay leaves
½ teaspoon thyme
¼ teaspoon freshly ground black pepper
¼ teaspoon orégano
1 cinnamon stick, 1 inch
1 slice of fresh gingerroot, ½ teaspoon (optional)
½ cup chicken broth

1. Soak the pigeons in the sour orange juice with the salt for 1 hour. Turn several times. Remove pigeons and reserve the marinade.

2. Heat the oil in a heavy saucepan over moderate heat and brown the pigeons for 5 minutes, turning several times. Add the tomato, onion, garlic, bay leaves, thyme, black pepper, orégano, cinnamon and gingerroot. Stir and fry for 5 minutes.

3. Add the chicken broth and the orange-juice marinade. Cover the pan and simmer over moderate to low heat for about 40 minutes, or until pigeons are tender. Serve warm.

SERVES 4

GUISO PARA PATO, PALOMITAS Y POLLO

A STANDARD FRICASSEE OF DUCK, PIGEONS OR CHICKEN

GUATEMALA

This is a standard recipe for pigeons and chickens as well as duck. In one old family recipe, the instructions were to take small strips of bacon and *sew* it with strong thread to the backs of the pigeons. Poultry in Guatemala is generally lean, so adding fat strips was common. Poultry in the United States, on the other hand, is overly fat and no additional oil is needed.

Guiso describes the cooking technique in which the poultry (or meat) is browned in oil first and liquid is added afterward to complete the cooking process—the same as a *guisado.*

1 duck, 4½ pounds, cut into frying pieces, loose skin and fat
    discarded
2 tablespoons corn oil
1 teaspoon salt, or to taste
¼ teaspoon freshly ground black pepper
3 bay leaves
½ teaspoon thyme
3 garlic cloves, sliced
½ cup sliced onion
½ cup white table wine
½ cup sliced ripe tomato
½ cup water

1. Brown the duck pieces in the oil in a large heavy pan over moderate heat. Sprinkle with salt and pepper. Add the bay leaves, thyme, garlic and onion, and mix well. Continue to brown for 10 minutes.

2. Add the wine and tomato. Cover the pan and simmer over moderate to low heat until the duck is tender, about 1½ hours. Add the water if the liquid evaporates too quickly.

3. Serve warm. Remove as much melted fat as possible.

SERVES 6

BEEF

Beef may be considered a comparatively modern meat, which was incorporated into the cuisine after the Spanish conquest. It is eaten more in the city than in the countryside and is used in traditional dishes such as the Pepián (Spicy Beef, see Index). The beef in Guatemala is range fed and tough but has great flavor. Simmering for hours is a common practice in making soups and stews, but pressure cookers, as a means of reducing the cooking time, have become popular in cities and towns. Wood is often expensive and must be bought or gathered.

Tender steaks are rarities, so recipes for their preparation do not appear. The popular Carne Asado, which shows up as an item on a typical menu assortment, is nothing more than a thin piece of fillet, rib or rump steak (in various degrees of firmness), seasoned with salt and pepper and broiled quickly over charcoal (see Index for menu for Plato Chapín).

None of this will influence the preparation of the Mayan beef recipes in the American kitchen since their seasonings are admirable and our beef is superb.

CARNE DE RES EN LECHE DE COCO

STEAK IN COCONUT MILK

LIVINGSTON, GUATEMALA

1 pound beefsteak, flank, rump or sirloin, cut into ¼-inch-thick
   slices
2 tablespoons corn oil
½ cup chopped tomato
½ cup chopped onion
½ cup chopped sweet green pepper
1 teaspoon salt, or to taste
½ teaspoon freshly ground black pepper
1 cup coconut milk

1. Fry the beef in the oil in a large skillet over moderate heat until
the color changes, about 2 minutes. Add the tomato, onion, sweet
green pepper, salt and black pepper. Stir-fry rapidly for 3 minutes
more.

2. Add the coconut milk, bring to a boil, and simmer over moderate
heat, basting frequently, for 10 minutes. Note that the oil from the
coconut milk rises to the top as the sauce thickens.

3. Serve warm with rice or rice and beans, tortillas and hot sauce. A
proper Livingston combination.

SERVES 4

Variation: This recipe works very well with breast of chicken. Use
1 pound breast of chicken cut into ½-inch-wide slices. Use the same
ingredients and proportions as for steak.

CARNE A LA PARILLA

STEAK GRILLED OVER CHARCOAL

NICARAGUA

The *chimichuri* is a typical marinade for beefsteaks, introduced from Argentina into Nicaragua where it has become a standard fixture on the culinary scene.

Rancho Parado is the name given to the usual country platter consisting of the steak grilled over charcoal, accompanied with rice and red beans and a cabbage salad. Three compatible foods and served everywhere.

6 beefsteaks, 6 to 8 ounces each, cut thin
1 teaspoon salt
½ teaspoon freshly ground black pepper
1 cup Chimichuri (recipe follows)

1. Rub the steaks with the salt and pepper. Marinate them in *chimichuri* from 1 to 4 hours, the longer the better.

2. Broil over charcoal to rare, medium or well done. Baste generously with the marinade during this process. Serve hot with the marinade.

SERVES 6

CHIMICHURI

MARINADE, ARGENTINE STYLE

NICARAGUA

1 cup chopped parsley
6 garlic cloves, chopped
¼ cup sliced onion

2 tablespoons sour orange juice
¼ teaspoon salt
¼ teaspoon freshly ground black pepper
1 cup corn oil

1. Blend everything together into a fine purée. Use with Carne a la Parilla.

CARNES DESMENUZADAS

BEEF THREADS IN SOUR ORANGE

NICARAGUA

1½ pounds boneless beef chuck
5 cups water
1 teaspoon salt
3 tablespoons corn oil
⅓ cup sliced onion
⅓ cup sliced tomato
½ cup thin-sliced sweet red pepper
¼ teaspoon freshly ground black pepper
2 tablespoons sour orange juice

1. Cook the beef in the water with the salt over moderate heat for about 1 hour, or until tender. Remove the beef, cool it, and pull the meat into 2- or 3-inch-long shreds.

2. Heat the oil in a skillet and over moderate heat fry the onion, tomato and sweet red pepper for 2 minutes.

3. Add the beef shreds and black pepper and continue to fry for 3 minutes more. Add the sour orange juice and mix well. Fry for 2 minutes more. Serve warm with tortillas.

SERVES 6

RONDÓN

BEEF IN COCONUT MILK
NICARAGUA

Rondón is a specialty of the Miskito Indians of the Atlantic Coast of Nicaragua. Cassava, bananas, plantain and coconut milk are the tropical staples, and their combination reflects the tradition of the tropical coast.

Coconut milk has a tendency to separate if not stirred during the cooking process. To prevent this and have a whole milk sauce, it is brought to a boil separately and added to an already simmering pot.

1 pound boneless beef chuck, cut into 2-inch pieces
4 garlic cloves
2 cups water
2 tablespoons prepared mustard
1 tablespoon cider vinegar
½ pound cassava, peeled and cut into 4 pieces
2 green bananas, peeled and cut vertically into halves
1 green plantain, peeled and cut vertically into halves
3 cups coconut milk
1 teaspoon salt, or to taste
¼ teaspoon freshly ground black pepper

1. Cook the beef and garlic in the water over moderate heat until soft, about 1 hour.

2. Add the mustard and vinegar, then add the cassava, bananas and plantain, and continue to simmer.

3. In a separate pan, bring the coconut milk to a boil and add it to the simmering beef pot. Add the salt and black pepper and continue to simmer, uncovered, over low heat for 20 minutes. The beef, cassava, bananas and plantain should have softened and the sauce should be somewhat reduced. Serve warm with tortillas.

SERVES 6

HILACHAS

THREADS

GUATEMALA
CITY

2 pounds beef chuck or similar cut
5 cups water
1 teaspoon salt, or to taste
2 tablespoons sliced onion
2 garlic cloves, sliced
1 cup sliced ripe tomato
1 cup sliced tomatillos (mil tomates)
1 cup stale bread cubes
1 chile guaque (guajillo), seeds and stem removed
¼ teaspoon achiote
2 cups cubed raw potatoes

1. Cook the beef in the water with the salt for 1 hour, or until beef is soft. Remove beef and reserve the broth. Shred the beef into 3-inch threads and set aside.

2. Simmer the onion, garlic, tomato, tomatillos, bread cubes, chile and achiote in 2 cups of the beef broth over moderate heat for 10 minutes. Cool the mixture somewhat and process it into a smooth paste.

3. Add an additional 2 cups of the broth to the sauce and simmer the mixture over low heat for 10 minutes to thicken it.

4. Add the potatoes and beef threads and simmer for 20 minutes or so, until the potatoes are soft and the sauce has thickened to the consistency of a soft custard. Serve warm.

SERVES 6

HILACHAS

THREADS

COBÁN, GUATEMALA

2 pounds beef chuck, in one piece
3 cups water
1 teaspoon salt, or to taste
1 cup sliced ripe tomato
¼ cup sliced tomatillos (mil tomates)
2 garlic cloves, sliced
1 chile guaque (guajillo), seeds and stem removed
1 small onion, sliced
1 pound potatoes, about 4 small potatoes
1 tortilla, softened in water
⅛ teaspoon ground allspice
¼ teaspoon freshly ground black pepper
⅛ teaspoon achiote

1. Cook the beef in 2½ cups water with the salt for 1 hour, or until beef is soft. Remove beef and reserve the broth. Pull the meat fibers apart with your fingers into shreds about 2 inches long. Set aside.

2. Cook together the tomato slices, tomatillos, garlic, *chile guaque* and onion in ½ cup water in a covered saucepan for 10 minutes. Set aside.

3. Cook the potatoes in their skins until soft but firm, about 15 minutes. Peel and cut into ½-inch cubes.

4. Prepare a smooth sauce in a food processor with the tomato mixture and the softened tortilla.

5. Put 1½ cups of the reserved beef broth in a pan with the tomato/ tortilla sauce and simmer over low heat for 10 minutes. Add the allspice, black pepper and achiote. Add the potatoes and the beef threads and continue to simmer for 10 minutes more.

6. Serve warm. Traditionally served with white rice and boiled chayote (*huisquil*), cut into 2-inch sticks.

SERVES 6

LOMO EN VINO TINTO

COLD BEEF IN RED WINE

EL SALVADOR

This is an old family recipe with the characteristic seasoning of El Salvador. This dish is customarily included in a buffet.

½ cup fine-chopped onion
3 garlic cloves, chopped fine
½ cup fine-chopped tomato
1 tablespoon fine-chopped parsley
⅓ cup fine-chopped mustard pickles
3 pounds boneless beef chuck, in one thick piece
¼ cup pork fat, cut into 10 ¼-inch cubes
1 tablespoon prepared mustard
2 tablespoons butter, at room temperature
1 teaspoon salt
¼ teaspoon freshly ground black pepper
2 cups red table wine

1. Mix together the onion, garlic, tomato, parsley and mustard pickles.

2. Make 10 incisions in the beef, 1 inch wide and 1 inch deep. Push 1 piece of pork fat and 2 teaspoons of the vegetable mixture into the beef incisions.

3. Mix the mustard, butter, salt and pepper together and rub it all around the beef. Brown the beef on all sides in a heavy pan over moderate heat.

4. Add the wine, cover the pan, and cook for 2 hours, or until beef is soft. If the sauce dries out too quickly, add about ½ cup water.

5. Remove the beef, wrap it in aluminum foil, and chill it in the refrigerator overnight. Strain the sauce and refrigerate it overnight.

6. Remove and discard the fat from the sauce. Serve the beef cold, in generous slices. Reheat the sauce and serve it separately.

SERVES 8

SALÓN RELLENO

STUFFED BEEF

EL SALVADOR

This recipe was described to me as an antique. The *salón* is a particular cut of meat in El Salvador, probably the rump. For our purpose boneless chuck may be used although it has a softer texture than the rump.

3 pounds beef chuck or rump steak, in one piece
3 tablespoons corn oil

Stuffing

¼ cup fine-chopped carrot
2 tablespoons fine-chopped parsley
¼ cup fine-chopped onion
¼ cup fine-chopped sweet green pepper
¼ cup fine-chopped tomato, seeds removed
¼ teaspoon Worcestershire sauce
¼ teaspoon freshly ground black pepper
1 teaspoon salt
1 tablespoon cider vinegar

Sauce

2 cups tomatoes, fresh or canned
2 tablespoons sliced onion
½ cup sliced sweet red pepper
¼ teaspoon thyme
1 teaspoon salt
2 cups water
3 bay leaves

1. Cut a long incision into the center of the beef, not all the way through, to make a pocket.

2. Mix all the stuffing ingredients together and stuff the mixture into the pocket in the beef. Sew up the incision.

3. Process all the sauce ingredients except the bay leaves, to make a smooth sauce.

4. Heat the oil in a large heavy pan and brown the beef on all sides, just enough to change the color. Add the blended sauce mixture and the 3 bay leaves and bring to a boil over moderate heat. Cover the pan and cook for about 2 hours, or until beef is soft. Turn beef several times during this process. Add ½ cup water if the sauce evaporates too fast.

5. Remove the beef from the sauce and refrigerate it for 24 hours. Refrigerate the sauce separately and remove any congealed fat.

6. When ready to serve, heat the sauce and serve with cold meat slices.

SERVES 8

CARNE DE RES CON CAFÉ

BEEF COOKED IN COFFEE

EL SALVADOR

3 pounds beef chuck, cut into 2-inch cubes
3 tablespoons corn oil
3 cups sliced onions
1½ cups sliced sweet green peppers
4 garlic cloves, sliced
2 cups chopped ripe tomatoes
2 cups prepared strong coffee
¼ cup tomato catsup
6 small carrots, halved

1. Brown the meat well in oil over moderate heat. Add the onions, green peppers, garlic and tomatoes. Mix and bring to a boil.

2. Add the coffee and catsup, and continue cooking in a covered pan until soft, about 1½ hours.

3. Add the carrots for the last 20 minutes. The sauce will be reduced and thickened. Serve warm with rice.

SERVES 8

ESTOFADO

BRAISED BEEF

SAN PEDRO AYAMPUC, GUATEMALA

This *estofado* is a popular dish in San Pedro Ayampuc, especially during fiesta when nearly all the houses have it simmering in clay or metal pots in their simple village kitchens.

2 pounds beef chuck, cut into 2-inch cubes
4 cups water
1 teaspoon salt, or to taste
½ cup raw rice, soaked in 1 cup water for 1 hour
1 tablespoon flour
½ cup French bread cubes, moistened with water
¼ teaspoon achiote
¼ cup white or cider vinegar
1 teaspoon thyme
¼ cup sliced onion
½ teaspoon freshly ground black pepper
2 garlic cloves, sliced
1 cup sliced ripe tomato
2 whole cloves
1 cinnamon stick, 2 inches
2 bay leaves

1. Cook the beef in the water with the salt over moderate heat until nearly soft, about 1 hour. Remove the beef and reserve 3 cups of broth.

2. Prepare a smooth sauce in the processor with the soaked rice, flour, French bread cubes, achiote, vinegar, thyme, onion, black pepper, garlic and tomato.

3. Add sauce to the beef with the cloves, cinnamon and bay leaves. Add the reserved 3 cups broth and simmer over low heat for 1 hour. The rich, red sauce will thicken and the seasonings blend. If you prefer a stronger red color, add ⅛ teaspoon more of the achiote.

4. Serve warm with tortillas and rice.

SERVES 6

Variation: Boneless pork cubes (2 pounds) or a 3-pound chicken cut into serving pieces may be substituted for the beef. Beef and pork are the most typical meats used.

CARNE DE RES EN CHICHA

BEEF IN SWEET-SOUR SAUCE

TAXISCO, GUATEMALA

¼ cup lemon juice
¼ cup brown sugar
¼ cup white rum or venado (see Note)
2 pounds beef chuck, cut into 3-inch pieces
2 garlic cloves, chopped
½ teaspoon salt, or to taste
½ teaspoon freshly ground black pepper
2 tablespoons corn oil
¼ cup tomato paste
1 cup sliced sweet red pepper
2 whole small onions; cut a crisscross ¼ inch deep in root ends
½ cup water

1. Mix together the lemon juice, sugar and rum or *venado*. This is the *chicha*.

2. Fry the beef, garlic, salt and black pepper in the oil over moderate heat for 10 minutes, until beef is browned.

3. Add the lemon juice mixture (*chicha*), cover the pan, and simmer over low heat for 15 minutes.

4. Add the tomato paste, sweet pepper, onions and water. Simmer over low heat until the meat is soft and almost all the liquid has evaporated, about 45 minutes. Serve warm.

SERVES 6

Note: *Venado*, also known as *aguardiente*, is a colorless alcohol made from cane sugar, perhaps similar to vodka, and is a popular drink mixed, straight or in cooking.

CARNE GUISADA

SPICY BEEF STEW

JALAPA, GUATEMALA

2 tablespoons corn oil
2 pounds beef chuck, cut into 1-inch cubes
½ teaspoon salt, or to taste
½ teaspoon freshly ground black pepper
3 bay leaves
¼ teaspoon thyme
1 chile guaque (guajillo), seeds and stem removed, cut into strips
1 cinnamon stick, 1 inch
2 whole cloves
3 cups water
¼ cup sour orange juice
½ cup sliced ripe tomato
2 tablespoons sliced onion
1 garlic clove, sliced
¼ cup toasted bread crumbs

1. Heat the oil in a saucepan over moderate heat and brown the beef for 5 minutes. Sprinkle with salt, pepper, bay leaves, thyme, *chile guaque* strips, cinnamon and cloves. Stir well, add the water and orange juice, and bring to a boil.

2. Prepare a smooth sauce in a processor with the tomato, onion and garlic. Add this to the beef and continue to simmer for about 1 hour, or until beef is soft.

3. Add the crumbs to thicken the sauce, and simmer over low heat for 10 minutes more. If the sauce has thickened too much, add ¼ cup more water. Serve warm.

SERVES 6

Variation: Two pounds of cubed pork can be used instead of the beef.

PULIQUÉ

BEEF STEW IN THICK SAUCE
SANTO DOMINGO XENACOJ, GUATEMALA

2 pounds beef chuck or similar cut
3 cups water
1 teaspoon salt, or to taste
1 cup chopped tomato
4 scallions, chopped
1 cup raw rice
2 chayotes (huisquil), quartered
¼ cup toasted cornmeal, moistened with water
¼ teaspoon achiote
1 tablespoon chopped cilantro

1. Cook the beef in the water with the salt in a covered pan for 1 hour, or until soft. Remove the meat and reserve the liquid, which should be about 2 cups.

2. Cook the tomato and scallions together in another pan for 5 minutes. Set aside.

3. Cook the rice and chayotes in the beef broth over moderate heat for 10 minutes. Add the tomato/scallion mixture, the toasted cornmeal, the achiote and cilantro, and continue to cook over low heat for 20 minutes.

4. Slice the beef into serving pieces, add them to the sauce, and simmer over low heat for 10 minutes more. Serve warm.

SERVES 6

Note: The old method of making *puliqué* was to toast the dry, ripe corn kernels in a clay *comal* over a wood fire until the corn turned a light tan color. (The *comal* is a large clay plate about 20 inches in diameter of pre-Hispanic origin, upon which the Maya had traditionally cooked their tortillas. It is today a common artifact of the kitchen in Indian homes throughout Guatemala.)

The toasted corn was ground into meal and used for several purposes as well as for the *puliqué*. The beef was cooked in water and salt until tender. The cornmeal was moistened with water into a mush and shaped into a ball, then added to the beef and broth. It was this thick, simply seasoned beef that was the old-style *puliqué*. Now, more ingredients and seasonings have been added.

CARNE DE RES GUISADA

BEEF STEW WITH TOMATO

PANAJACHEL, GUATEMALA

The *guisada* is a party dish prepared when one wishes to invite guests among the Cakchiquel of Panajachel. The rich, red sauce, not too thick but with dimension, is a popular beef preparation of this tribal and tourist village on the northern shore of Lake Atitlán.

2 pounds beef chuck or similar cut, cut into 2-inch pieces
3 cups water
1 teaspoon salt, or to taste
1 pound whole small tomatoes
2 small onions, peeled
1 garlic clove, peeled
1 sweet red pepper, halved, seeds and stem removed
½ cup French bread crumbs
½ teaspoon thyme
1 teaspoon sugar
3 bay leaves

1. Cook the beef in the water with the salt over moderate heat until soft, about 1 hour.

2. Toast the tomatoes, onions, garlic, sweet pepper and bread crumbs in a dry skillet over low heat until slightly charred, about 10 minutes.

3. Prepare a smooth sauce in the processor with the tomato mixture, thyme and sugar, with 1 cup of the beef broth. Add this sauce to the beef with the bay leaves.

4. Simmer over moderate to low heat for about 1½ hours, which should be the total cooking time. Add ¼ cup water if the sauce appears to be too thick. Serve warm.

SERVES 6

CARNE GUISADA

SPICED BEEF STEW

CHIQUIMULILLA,
GUATEMALA

2 pounds beef chuck, cut into 2-inch pieces
1 tablespoon corn oil
½ teaspoon thyme
3 bay leaves
1 cup sliced tomato
¼ cup sliced onion
1 garlic clove, sliced
1 chile guaque (guajillo), seeds and stem removed, sliced
½ chile pasa (pasilla), seeds and stem removed, sliced
1 cup sliced sweet red pepper
1 teaspoon salt, or to taste
2 cups water
¼ cup moistened bread cubes, processed into a smooth paste

1. Fry the beef in the oil over moderate heat for 5 minutes. Add the thyme and bay leaves, and fry for 1 minute more.

2. Process into a smooth paste the tomato, onion, garlic, *chile guaque* and *chile pasa*, sweet red pepper, salt and water. Add this to the beef and simmer over moderate heat for about 1 hour or until beef is soft.

3. Finally add the bread and simmer for 10 minutes more to thicken the sauce. Serve warm.

SERVES 6

Variation: Two pounds boneless pork or a 3-pound chicken, cut into serving pieces, may be used in place of the beef. The chicken will take less cooking time.

CARNE PICADO

CHOPPED BEEF FRY

CHIQUIMULA, GUATEMALA

I often enjoyed sitting on a street corner with a pretty Chiquimul-teca street vendor who was selling her homecooked foods. The large woven basket contained *tostados* (crisp fried tortillas), guacamole, shredded cabbage, several sauces pungent with chile, vegetable and beef *picado* and a black bean spread. For 5 or 10 cents per tortilla with some sort of topping, one could have a tasty and nourishing snack. It was a busy corner.

1 pound beef chuck
2 cups water
2 tablespoons corn oil
2 tablespoons chopped onion
½ cup whole green peas
½ cup diced potato
½ cup diced carrot
½ cup sliced green snap beans
1 tablespoon chopped parsley
1 tablespoon chopped celery
1 tablespoon chopped sweet red pepper
1 teaspoon salt, or to taste
½ teaspoon pepper
⅛ teaspoon achiote, dissolved in 1 teaspoon water

1. Cook the beef in the water over moderate heat until it is soft, about 1 hour. Drain. Chop the beef coarsely in a food processor. Set aside.

2. Heat the oil in a large skillet. Fry the onion over moderate heat for 2 minutes, then add all the other ingredients at once, including the beef. Mix well, cover the skillet, and fry the *picado* for 15 minutes.

3. Serve warm or at room temperature on tortillas or *tostados* as an appetizer.

SERVES 4 TO 6

Variation: *Verdura Picada—Vegetable Fry:* Omit the beef for a completely vegetarian *picado* to be served as an appetizer or as a vegetable dish with poultry or beef.

SALPICÓN

CHOPPED BEEF APPETIZER
QUEZALTENANGO, GUATEMALA

I was taught this recipe in Quezaltenango when my hostess stepped into her garden and picked a sour orange (*naranja agria*) to make the juice. Since this is not always possible in our northern regions, I suggest you add ½ teaspoon cider vinegar to the orange juice to reinforce the slightly acid flavor of the *salpicón*.

1 pound round steak or similar cut of beef
2 cups water
¼ cup fine-chopped fresh mint
¼ cup fine-chopped onion
½ teaspoon salt, or to taste
½ teaspoon pepper
3 tablespoons sour orange juice

1. Cook the beef in the water over moderate heat for 1 hour, or until soft. Drain and chop the beef fine in a food processor.
2. Add the mint, onion, salt, pepper and orange juice. Mix well. Refrigerate for 1 hour before dining.
3. Serve chilled or at room temperature, with tortilla crisps, toast or fresh tortillas, as an appetizer. It makes an excellent luncheon dish as well.

SERVES 4

LOMO MECHADO

POKED BEEF

GUAZACAPÁN, GUATEMALA

3 to 4 pounds beef chuck or round steak, in one piece
½ cup chopped sweet red pepper
2 garlic cloves, chopped
¼ cup chopped onion
2 slices of bacon, chopped
2 teaspoons prepared mustard
1 teaspoon salt, or to taste

1. Poke a knife into the beef to make about 10 incisions 1 inch deep and 1 inch wide.

2. Mix together the sweet pepper, garlic, onion, bacon, mustard and salt into a paste. Fill the incisions with this mixture.

3. Put the beef in a roasting pan and cover it tightly. Roast in a 350° F. oven for about 2 hours, depending upon what degree of doneness you prefer. This beef tastes better if it is medium/well done. Baste from time to time during the roasting. Serve warm or at room temperature.

SERVES 8

CARNE DE RES GUISADA

SPICED BEEF STEW

PALÍN, GUATEMALA

Palín is that rare thing, a village of Pokomam Indians wearing their tribal costumes. The village is in a fertile valley at a lower altitude than Guatemala City as one travels toward the Pacific Ocean.

Tropical fruits abound. The giant ceiba tree that commands the tiny plaza in front of the Colonial church is reputed to be more than 500 years old.

2 pounds beef chuck or similar cut, cut into 3-inch pieces
1 tablespoon corn oil
¼ cup white or cider vinegar
4 cups water
1 teaspoon salt, or to taste
¼ cup sliced onion
2 cups sliced ripe tomatoes
½ cup sliced tomatillos (mil tomates)
2 garlic cloves, sliced
1 chile gauque (guajillo), seeds and stem removed, sliced thin
2 teaspoons thyme
¼ teaspoon achiote
2 bay leaves
¼ cup toasted bread crumbs
2 cups sliced potatoes

1. Brown the beef in the oil in a large heavy saucepan over moderate heat for 5 minutes. Add the vinegar, water and salt; stir well and simmer.

2. Prepare a smooth sauce in the processor with the onion, tomatoes, tomatillos, garlic, *chile guaque,* thyme and achiote. Add this to the beef with the bay leaves.

3. Continue to simmer over moderate/low heat for about 1 hour or more, until beef is soft.

4. Add the bread crumbs for thickening and the potato slices. Cook for 20 minutes more, until beef and potatoes are soft and the sauce is thick but fluid. Serve warm with rice.

SERVES 6

PEPIÁN NEGRO DE INDIO

BEEF IN A BROWN SAUCE
GUATEMALA CITY

The flavor of the *pepián* improves if eaten the second day. *Pepián* dishes (and there are many variations) are favorite foods, traditionally eaten throughout Guatemala on Corpus Christi Day, which occurs in June and always on Thursday.

1 small onion, peeled, whole
4 garlic cloves, peeled, whole
½ cup tomatillos (mil tomates), fresh or canned
1 small ripe tomato
2 tortillas
2 pounds beef chuck, cut into 2-inch cubes
5 cups water
1 teaspoon salt, or to taste
¼ cup raw rice
1 dried chile guaque (guajillo), seeds and stem removed
1 dried chile zambo
½ cup chopped cilantro
1 cup sliced carrot
2 cups potato cubes
2 cups 2-inch pieces of green snap beans

1. In a dry skillet over low heat toast the onion, garlic, tomatillos and ripe tomato for 10 to 15 minutes, until the skins are charred.

2. Toast the tortillas in the oven or toaster until they are lightly charred.

3. Cook the beef in the water with the salt for about 1 hour, until soft. Add the tortillas during this time and cook them for 5 minutes to soften. Remove tortillas and set aside.

4. Toast the rice in a dry skillet until dark brown. Grind it to a fine powder in a food processor. Set aside. Toast the *chile guaque* and *chile zambo* until lightly charred. Set aside.

5. Prepare a smooth sauce in a food processor with the toasted onion, garlic, tomatillos, ripe tomato, moistened tortillas, *chile guaque, chile zambo,* cilantro and 1 cup of the beef broth. Set aside.

6. When the beef is almost tender, add the carrot, potatoes and green beans to the pot and simmer over moderate heat for 10 minutes. Add the sauce and ground rice, and simmer slowly for 10 minutes more. The *pepián* should have about 3 cups thick, brown and spicy sauce remaining. Serve warm.

SERVES 8

Note: The three vegetables may be reduced by half if you prefer a meatier dish.

PEPIÁN

SPICY BEEF

GUATEMALA CITY

1 chile guaque (guajillo)
1 chile zambo, or ½ teaspoon dried hot red chile flakes
½ cup tomatillos (mil tomates)
2 small ripe tomatoes
2 small onions, peeled
10 whole black peppercorns
3 garlic cloves, peeled
1 stalk of cilantro, 6 inches long
1 tablespoon raw rice
2 pounds beef chuck or similar cut, cut into 2-inch cubes
3 cups water
1 teaspoon salt, or to taste
¼ teaspoon achiote
1 chayote (huisquil), cut into ½-inch cubes
½ pound green snap beans, cut into 2-inch pieces
½ cup potato cubes

1. In a dry skillet over moderate to low heat, toast the *chile guaque, chile zambo,* tomatillos, tomatoes, onions, peppercorns, garlic and cilantro for 10 minutes, or until everything changes color and becomes dry.

2. Toast the rice in a dry skillet over low heat until light brown.

3. Cook the beef in the water with the salt over moderate heat for about 1 hour, or until soft.

4. Prepare a smooth sauce in a processor with the toasted ingredients and the rice, with 1 cup of the liquid from the beef.

5. When the meat has softened, add the sauce and the achiote for color. Simmer this over low heat with the chayote, green beans and potatoes for 15 minutes more, until vegetables are soft and the sauce has thickened. Serve warm.

SERVES 6

Variation: The *pepián* can be made with 2 pounds of boneless pork or 1 pound pork and 1 pound beef.

PISTO

MONEY-BEEF AND VEGETABLES
GUATEMALA CITY

This makes an admirable luncheon dish and lends itself to variation. Chayote (*huisquil*) and cauliflower are two other vegetables that do well in the *pisto*. Any combination of three vegetables plus the potato may be used. The word *pisto* is slang for money.

1 pound beef chuck or similar cut
3 cups water
½ teaspoon salt
1 cup diagonally sliced carrot
1 cup 1-inch diagonal pieces of green snap beans
1 cup peas, fresh or frozen
1 cup potato cubes
½ cup tomato cubes
2 tablespoons chopped onion
1 garlic clove, chopped
2 tablespoons corn oil
2 teaspoons white or cider vinegar

1. Cook the beef in the water with the salt until soft, 1 to 1½ hours. Remove beef and reserve the liquid. Chop the beef into coarse pieces.

2. Cook the carrot, green beans, peas and potatoes in the beef liquid until soft. This can be done all together or separately. Drain well.

3. Fry the tomato, onion and garlic in the oil in a skillet over moderate heat for 3 minutes. Add the beef, cooked vegetables, salt to taste and the vinegar. Stir and fry the mixture for 5 minutes until well heated. Serve warm with tortillas or French bread.

SERVES 4

PINOL (KUJ KATI)

BEEF AND MAIZE

SAN JOSÉ NACAHUIL,
GUATEMALA

Nacahuil, a Cakchiquel Indian region, is one of the forgotten villages in the hills surrounding Guatemala City. It is small, unassuming and primitively simple, and the dirt road to the village is not inviting. Many women of the village weave their beautiful *huipiles* (over-blouses) and embroider their *fajas* (long thick belts) for their own use or for sale.

This *pinol* is an important dish that is cooked for ceremonial purposes, marriages, church festivals and fiestas in general.

2 pounds beef chuck, cut into 2-inch cubes
4 cups water
1 teaspoon salt, or to taste
½ cup sliced onion
½ cup sliced ripe tomato
6 branches of cilantro, leaves and stems
2 cups tortilla flour (masa harina)

1. Cook the beef in the water with the salt in a saucepan over moderate heat until soft, about 1½ hours.

2. In a processor grind the onion, tomato and cilantro with 1 cup of beef broth into a paste. Add this to the beef; stir well.

3. Toast the tortilla flour in a dry skillet over low heat for 5 to 10 minutes, until the color becomes a light tan. Add to the beef. Simmer over low heat for 20 minutes, stirring constantly, until the gruel is thick and smooth.

4. Serve warm, the meat and gruel together.

SERVES 6

COMIDA AMARILLA

YELLOW FOOD—A BEEF STEW

SAN PEDRO AYAMPUC, GUATEMALA

San Pedro Ayampuc is about 45 minutes from Guatemala City by car but several centuries in time as far as the way of life is concerned. In this village the women still wear their *huipiles,* but very little weaving is done. Also, here hot chile is seldom added to the food. However, hot sauces are made and served separately for those who have a tolerance for chiles.

2 pounds beef chuck or similar cut, cut into 2-inch cubes
3 cups water
1 teaspoon salt, or to taste
2 cups sliced ripe tomatoes
¼ cup sliced onion
¼ teaspoon achiote
½ teaspoon thyme
1 cup French bread, soaked in water
4 bay leaves

1. Cook the beef in the water with the salt over moderate heat until soft, about 1½ hours. Remove the meat and set aside. Reserve 2 cups broth.

2. Prepare a sauce in the processor with the tomatoes, onion, achiote, thyme and bread. Add this to the meat with the reserved broth and the bay leaves. Simmer over moderate to low heat for 20 minutes, until the sauce is thickened and the flavors are distributed. Serve warm with tortillas.

SERVES 6

Variations: A 3-pound chicken or 2 pounds of boneless pork can be substituted for the beef, but the cooking time of the different meats should be adjusted somewhat.

TLHOLAC—CARNE DE LOS DIOSES—CARNE MAYA

BEEF IN ANCIENT MAYA STYLE

GUATEMALA

This recipe was recovered from an early sixteenth-century book of Colonial recipes. I have adapted it, using present-day Guatemalan spices and seasonings. I believe it is a reasonable facsimile of an ancient method of preparing beef.

2 cups sour orange juice
2 tablespoons salt
1 teaspoon pepper
5 pounds beef, rump steak or similar cut, in one piece
¼ cup chopped dried beef
1 garlic clove, chopped
¼ cup chopped onion
2 slices of bacon, chopped
3 tablespoons corn oil
4 bay leaves
1 teaspoon minced fresh gingerroot
1 chile guaque (guajillo), chopped
½ teaspoon thyme
2 whole cloves
1 cup beef broth
2 cups water

1. Mix the orange juice, salt and pepper together and marinate the beef in this for 24 hours.

2. The next day remove the beef and reserve the marinade. Cut 8 incisions 1 inch deep into the beef. Chop the dried beef, garlic, onion and bacon together, mix well, and fill the incisions with this mixture.

3. Brown the beef in the oil in a large pot over moderate heat for 10 minutes. Add the reserved marinade, the bay leaves, gingerroot, *chile guaque*, thyme, cloves, beef broth and water. Bring to a boil and then simmer *slowly* over low heat on top of the stove for 4 to 5 hours. Or bake in a 250° F. oven for the same time.

4. Cool and slice the beef. Serve cold or at room temperature.

SERVES 10 TO 12

PINOL DE CARNE DE RES

BEEF IN TOASTED CORNMEAL GRUEL

SAN PEDRO SACATEPÉQUEZ, GUATEMALA

2 pounds beef chuck or similar cut
5 cups water
1 teaspoon salt, or to taste
1 cup tortilla flour (masa harina)
1 cup sliced ripe tomato
¼ cup sliced onion
1 sweet red pepper, sliced
2 branches of cilantro

1. Cook the beef in the water with the salt for 1½ hours, or until tender.

2. Toast the tortilla flour in a dry skillet over low heat for about 5 minutes or more, until the aroma is released and the color has changed to light tan. Add this to the beef and continue to simmer over low heat, stirring continuously to avoid lumps.

3. Prepare a sauce in the processor with the tomato, onion, sweet pepper and 1 cup of the beef broth. Add the sauce to the beef with the cilantro and simmer slowly for 15 minutes more.

4. Remove the beef and cut into serving pieces. Serve beef and gruel separately or all together in bowls. Accompany with tortillas.

SERVES 6

ROPA VIEJA

OLD CLOTHES

GUATEMALA CITY

Ingredients such as wine, olives and capers are of Spanish origin but have been so thoroughly integrated into the Guatemala cuisine that they have become, by adoption, national ingredients. The *ropa vieja* is a preparation of modern approach.

¼ cup corn oil
1 pound beef flank steak, sliced thin across the grain
¼ cup chopped onion
3 garlic cloves, chopped
1 cup chopped ripe tomato
½ cup cubed carrot
½ teaspoon salt, or to taste
¼ teaspoon freshly ground black pepper
½ cup potato cubes
¼ cup whole stuffed olives
¼ cup cubed sweet red pepper
½ cup red wine, Burgundy or Bordeaux

1. Heat the oil in a large skillet over moderate heat. Add the steak and stir-fry rapidly for 1 minute. Add the onion and garlic and continue to fry for 2 minutes.

2. Add the tomato, carrot, salt, black pepper, potato cubes, olives and sweet red pepper, and stir-fry for 5 minutes.

3. Pour in the wine and stir-fry until the liquid has evaporated and the vegetables are cooked through. During this process, cover the skillet for a few minutes so that the firmer vegetables are cooked. Then uncover and let liquid evaporate. Serve warm.

SERVES 6

PULIQUÉ

A STEW OF MIXED MEATS
ANTIGUA, GUATEMALA

2 pounds boneless beef or pork, or a 3-pound chicken
4 cups water
1 teaspoon salt, or to taste
1 cup sliced ripe tomato
½ cup sliced tomatillos (mil tomates)
1 garlic clove, sliced
¼ cup sliced onion
½ cup cilantro, leaves and stems, or ¼ cup sliced epazote
3 tablespoons tortilla flour (masa harina), moistened

1. Cook the beef, pork or chicken in the water with the salt for about 1 hour, or until soft. Remove the meat and cut into 2-inch cubes. Reserve the broth.

2. Prepare a smooth sauce (recado) in a processor with the tomato, tomatillos, garlic, onion, cilantro or epazote and ½ cup beef broth. Force the sauce through a metal strainer to remove coarse bits.

3. Mix the meat, the balance of the broth and the sauce together in a large saucepan. Bring to a boil and add the tortilla flour thickener. Simmer over low heat for 20 minutes to distribute the seasonings and thicken the sauce.

4. Serve warm with white rice.

SERVES 6

Note: The *puliqué* can be made with one or more meats according to one's personal preference. My own inclination is a combination of beef and chicken in more or less equal amounts. The two meats can be cooked together and the chicken, which has been cut into serving pieces, can be removed at the appropriate time while the beef continues to cook until ready.

Epazote can be substituted for the cilantro. It has a pleasant medicinal flavor and is popular in the *puliqué* of Quezaltenango.

COSHON (COXON)

DRIED SMOKED DEER IN SAUCE

QUICHÉ, GUATEMALA

This is a very old recipe from the Department of Quiché where deer were plentiful and a common source of meat prior to the Spanish Conquest. Nowadays, one can find deer meat in some mountain villages, but the *coshon* is now prepared with beef. Not a recipe one would cook very often, it is of historic and cultural interest, and perhaps a challenge to the cook who is sometimes given a venison roast.

2 pounds beef or venison fillet, flank steak or boneless chuck
½ cup sour orange juice
1 teaspoon salt
¼ cup ½-inch slices of green scallion leaves
½ cup sliced ripe tomato
¼ cup sliced tomatillos (mil tomates)
2 garlic cloves, sliced
¼ cup sliced onion
½ teaspoon dried hot red chile flakes
1 cup beef broth
1 teaspoon corn oil
1 fresh chile guaque (guajillo), cut into thin strips

1. Prepare the *cecina* (dried beef or deer) in this manner: Soak the meat in the orange juice, salt and scallions for 24 hours.

2. Remove the meat from the marinade and dry it in the sun for 2 or 3 days. Choose a sunny corner outdoors. At the end of that time rinse the meat in cold water and dry it.

3. Broil the meat over charcoal or in a gas broiler, but preferably charcoal, for 5 minutes on each side. Cool the meat and cut it into ½-inch cubes.

4. Grind the tomato, tomatillo, garlic, onion, chile flakes and beef broth into a smooth sauce. Fry it in the oil for 2 minutes. Then add

the meat cubes and simmer slowly over low heat for 30 minutes, until the meat is soft and the sauce is thickened.

5. Serve warm, decorated with the strips of the fresh chile. The *coshon* has a modest amount of sauce; accompany with tortillas.

SERVES 4

PICADILLO

CHOPPED BEEF AND VEGETABLES

CHIQUIMULILLA, GUATEMALA

½ cup green peas, fresh or frozen
½ cup ¼-inch cubes of carrot
½ cup ¼-inch slices of green snap beans
1 potato, peeled
2 tablespoons corn oil
¼ cup chopped onion
¼ cup chopped ripe tomato
1 garlic clove, chopped
2 bay leaves
¼ teaspoon thyme
¼ teaspoon freshly ground black pepper
½ pound ground beef
½ teaspoon salt, or to taste

1. Drop the peas, carrots and green beans into boiling water for 1 minute and drain well. Cook the whole potato until nearly soft, drain, and cut into ¼-inch cubes.

2. Heat the oil in a skillet and fry the onion, tomato, garlic, bay leaves, thyme and black pepper over moderate heat for 2 minutes. Add the beef and salt and fry for 3 minutes more.

3. Add all the vegetables and stir-fry for 3 minutes to distribute the seasonings.

4. Serve warm, as a lunch or dinner dish with other foods, or as an appetizer with crispy fried tortillas, fresh tortillas or toast.

SERVES 4

GUISO DE CARNE

BASIC CHOPPED BEEF

COSTA RICA

1 tablespoon corn oil
½ pound ground beef
¼ cup chopped sweet red pepper
2 tablespoons chopped fresh cilantro
¼ cup chopped onion
½ teaspoon salt
¼ teaspoon freshly ground black pepper

1. Heat the oil in a skillet over moderate heat. Add all the ingredients and stir-fry for 3 minutes.
2. Use as a quick luncheon dish, served with tortillas or toast, or as a filling in other recipes.

SERVES 2

Variation: Add 1 cup cubed chayote and the mixture becomes the filling for Empanadas con Plátano Verde (Green Plantain Turnovers, see Index).

TORTAS DE CARNE

BEEF PATTIES

COSTA RICA

1 pound ground beef
2 garlic cloves, put through a garlic press
½ cup white bread, soaked in 2 tablespoons milk
3 tablespoons chopped celery
½ teaspoon salt, or to taste
¼ teaspoon pepper
¼ cup corn oil

1. Mix everything together except the oil.

2. Prepare patties 3 inches in diameter and ½ inch thick. Brown them in the hot oil over moderate heat until rare to well done, according to taste.

3. Drain briefly on paper towels and serve warm.

SERVES 6

CARNE ACHORIZADA

GROUND BEEF FRY
HONDURAS

1 pound ground beef
½ teaspoon salt
¼ teaspoon pepper
1 tablespoon cider vinegar
2 tablespoons corn oil
½ teaspoon dissolved achiote
3 garlic cloves, put through a garlic press
2 tablespoons chopped onion
¼ cup chopped sweet red pepper
1 tablespoon chopped cilantro

1. Mix the beef, salt, pepper and vinegar together. Heat the oil in a skillet and over moderate heat stir-fry the beef.

2. Add the achiote, garlic, onion, sweet pepper and cilantro. Continue to stir-fry until the ingredients are cooked, 5 to 8 minutes, and the liquid has evaporated. This is a dry fry.

3. Serve warm with tortillas, *tostados* or French bread as an appetizer. Or serve as a main dish.

SERVES 4

TORTITAS DE CARNE DE RES

SPICED BEEF PATTIES

GUATEMALA CITY

The patties can be eaten with a number of other dishes at lunch or dinner. They are also popular as an appetizer; in that case, prepare the patties half the size indicated.

2 garlic cloves, chopped
2 tablespoons chopped onion
¼ cup chopped peeled ripe tomato
3 tablespoons corn oil
½ teaspoon salt, or to taste
¼ teaspoon freshly ground black pepper
1 pound ground beef
2 eggs, beaten
¼ cup toasted bread crumbs
1 tablespoon chopped fresh mint (optional)
Flour

1. Fry the garlic, onion and tomato in 1 tablespoon corn oil. Add the salt and black pepper. Cool and process into a smooth paste. Add this to the beef with the eggs, bread crumbs, and mint if used. Mix well.

2. Prepare round meatballs with 2 heaping tablespoons of the beef mixture. Dust them with flour and flatten them out into patties about 3 inches in diameter and ½ inch thick.

3. Heat 2 tablespoons oil in a skillet over moderate heat and fry the patties rare, medium or well done as you wish—better well done. Drain briefly on paper towels. Serve warm.

SERVES 4 TO 6

TORTITAS DE CARNE CON VERDURAS

BEEF AND VEGETABLE PATTIES

LIVINGSTON, GUATEMALA

Livingston is a bread and sweet pepper country rather than the tortilla and hot chile country of the Mayan highlands.

1 pound ground beef
2 eggs, beaten
3 tablespoons flour
¼ cup fine-chopped carrot
¼ cup fine-chopped potato
2 tablespoons chopped sweet red or green pepper
2 tablespoons chopped celery
¼ cup chopped ripe tomato
¼ cup chopped onion
1 garlic clove, chopped
1 teaspoon salt, or to taste
½ teaspoon pepper
¼ cup corn oil

1. Mix together everything except the oil to make a well-distributed mixture. Make patties 3 inches in diameter and ½ inch thick.

2. Heat the oil in a skillet over moderate heat. Brown the patties on each side for about 5 minutes.

3. Drain on paper towels and serve warm. Serve with Pan de Coco (Coconut Bread, see Index).

SERVES 4

LENGUA FINGIDA

FALSE TONGUES, GROUND BEEF LOAF

GUATEMALA

The title "False Tongues" is given to this dish because it is prepared in the same way as one might prepare beef or veal tongues, and the ground beef is shaped more or less like tongues. Occasionally, hard-cooked eggs are also included and pushed into the center of the loaves. When sliced, the additional adornment of the white and yolk of the eggs changes the name of the dish to "Eye of the Deer."

False Tongues

1½ pounds lean ground beef
1 large egg
2 tablespoons capers, chopped
¼ cup chopped sweet red pepper
½ cup toasted bread crumbs
1 teaspoon salt, or to taste
¼ teaspoon freshly ground black pepper
¼ cup chopped onion
12 stuffed olives
6 cups water

Sauce

2 cups sliced ripe tomatoes
Reserved broth from cooking the meat
¼ cup thin-sliced scallion, green part only
2 tablespoons chopped sweet red pepper
1 teaspoon chopped capers

1. Mix the beef, egg, 2 tablespoons capers, ¼ cup sweet pepper, bread crumbs, ½ teaspoon of the salt, the pepper and onion together. Divide the mixture into 2 equal parts. Push 6 olives into each half and shape them into 2 oval footballs.

2. Bring the water and remaining ½ teaspoon salt to a boil in a large pan over moderate heat. Add the loaves, cover the pan and cook the 2 loaves over moderate to low heat for 30 minutes. The liquid will reduce somewhat. Remove the loaves and set aside. Reserve the broth.

3. Process the tomatoes and 2 cups of the broth into a smooth sauce. Add this to the balance of the reserved broth (2 cups or more) and bring it to a boil over moderate heat. Add the scallion, sweet pepper and capers. Simmer the mixture over moderate to low heat for 20 minutes to thicken the sauce.

4. To serve, slice the cooled beef loaves into ½-inch-thick slices. Serve the warm sauce separately.

SERVES 4 TO 6

LENGUA FINGIDA

FALSE TONGUE, AN IMITATION
GUATEMALA CITY

1 pound ground beef
½ cup chopped sweet red pepper
½ cup chopped chayote (huisquil)
¼ cup chopped stuffed olives
¼ cup capers, drained and chopped
½ cup shredded carrot
¼ teaspoon freshly ground black pepper
1 egg, beaten
¼ cup toasted bread crumbs
2 teaspoons white or cider vinegar
¼ cup chopped onion
1 teaspoon salt, or to taste
4 cups water
¼ teaspoon thyme
3 bay leaves

1. Mix the beef, sweet pepper, chayote, olives, capers, carrot, black pepper, beaten egg, bread crumbs, vinegar, onion and salt together rather well. Shape it into a longish football and put in a flameproof dish.

2. Steam over the water with the thyme and bay leaves in a Chinese-style steamer over moderate to low heat for 1 hour. Remove and cool.

3. Slice the loaf into generous slices and serve with a Chirmol (Simple Tomato Sauce, see Index). Serve warm.

SERVES 6

Note: Traditionally the recipe calls for the False Tongue to be wrapped and tied in green corn leaves torn from a fresh ear of corn. Then the loaf is cooked in water seasoned with salt, thyme and bay leaves. The corn leaves also add their fresh, green flavor to the meat.

TACOS DE REPOLLO RELLENO

STUFFED CABBAGE ROLLS

NICARAGUA

The tacos are also called *Niños Dormidos*, sleeping children, since they are reputed to look somewhat like children wrapped in blankets and asleep.

10 cabbage leaves, large and small
¼ cup plus 2 teaspoons corn oil
½ pound ground beef, chicken or pork
1 cup plain cooked rice
¼ cup fine-chopped onion
1 garlic clove, chopped fine
½ teaspoon salt
½ teaspoon freshly ground black pepper
2 tablespoons chopped tomato
1 egg, separated
2 teaspoons flour

1. Cut the thick center veins from the cabbage leaves and discard them. Cut the large leaves into halves but use the entire small leaves. Cook the leaves in water over moderate heat for 2 minutes. Drain well and set aside.

2. Heat 2 teaspoons oil in a skillet and fry the meat and rice together for 3 minutes. If pork is used, fry for 5 minutes. Add the onion, garlic, salt, black pepper and tomato, and stir-fry for 1 minute more.

3. Beat the egg white until stiff, fold in the lightly beaten yolk, sift the flour over all, and fold it in.

4. Heat ¼ cup oil in a skillet over moderate heat. Place 1 tablespoon of the rice mixture on a cabbage leaf. Fold the leaf over diagonally to prepare a taco about 4 inches long and ½ inch thick. Dip the taco into the egg mixture and brown it on both sides in the oil for 2 to 3 minutes. Continue with all the leaves.

5. Drain on paper towels. Serve warm as an appetizer or as a luncheon dish.

MAKES 6 TO 8

RECADO DE COSTILLA DE RES

SHORT RIBS OF BEEF

COATEPEQUE, GUATEMALA

Coatepeque is in the Department of Quezaltenango and being at a lower altitude than the highland villages is warmer. The diet is different, with more vegetables and less meat eaten. The *recado* (sauce) is one of the typical dishes of this region.

2 pounds short ribs, cut into 3-inch cubes including bones
4 cups water
1 teaspoon salt, or to taste
1 cup sliced tomato
2 garlic cloves, sliced
¼ cup sliced onion
½ teaspoon freshly ground black pepper
¼ cup tortilla flour (masa harina) moistened with water into a
    ball
¼ teaspoon achiote
1 stalk of epazote

1. Cook the beef in the water with the salt over moderate heat for about 1 hour, or until meat is soft.

2. Prepare a smooth sauce in the processor with the tomato, garlic, onion and black pepper. Add the sauce to the meat and simmer over low heat for 10 minutes.

3. Now add the tortilla flour ball and the achiote to thicken and color the sauce. Mix well and simmer for 5 minutes.

4. Last, add the epazote stalk and simmer for 5 minutes more to bring out the aroma and flavor of this herb.

5. Serve warm with rice, tamalitos and green beans in a butter sauce.

SERVES 6

SESOS EN HUEVO

BEEF BRAIN IN EGG BATTER

GUATEMALA CITY

2 cups water
1 teaspoon salt
¼ teaspoon thyme
2 bay leaves
1 beef brain, about ¾ pound
2 eggs, separated
¼ cup corn oil
Flour for coating

1. Bring the water to a boil in a saucepan with the salt, thyme and bay leaves, and simmer for 2 minutes. Add the brain, cover the pan, and simmer over moderate heat for 15 minutes. Drain and cool the brain well. Then cut it into ⅜-inch-thick slices.

2. Beat the egg whites until stiff. Fold in the lightly beaten yolks and mix.

3. Heat the oil in a skillet over moderate heat. Dip the brain slices into the flour and then into the egg. Brown the slices on both sides for about 3 minutes. Drain briefly on paper towels.

4. Serve warm with a Chirmol (Simple Tomato Sauce, see Index).

SERVES 4

MOLDE DE SESOS CON COLIFLOR

BAKED BEEF BRAIN WITH CAULIFLOWER

EL SALVADOR

This unusual combination of brain and cauliflower is another one of the surprisingly original recipes found in El Salvador; it is part of their culinary culture.

4 tablespoons butter
4 tablespoons flour
3 cups hot milk
⅛ teaspoon freshly ground black pepper
1 teaspoon salt
¼ cup heavy cream
3 tablespoons grated Parmesan-style cheese
1 beef brain, cooked and cut in ½-inch cubes (see Note)
1½ pounds cauliflower, cut into small florets
1 tablespoon toasted bread crumbs

1. Melt the butter in a large skillet and over moderate to low heat add the flour and stir well. Make a béchamel sauce by adding the milk in a steady stream, stirring continuously, and then adding the pepper and salt. Stir for about 3 minutes until the sauce thickens. Remove from heat and set aside.

2. Mix together the cream and cheese. Mix the brain cubes and cauliflowerets together.

3. Pour half of the sauce into a greased baking dish. Add the brain cubes and cauliflowerets. Pour the balance of the sauce over all. Spread the cream and cheese mixture over that, and sprinkle with the bread crumbs.

4. Bake in a 350° F. oven for 30 minutes, until a light brown crust has formed. Serve warm.

SERVES 6

Note: *How to Prepare Brains:* Put 1 beef brain, 1 cup milk, 1 garlic clove, chopped, 2 tablespoons chopped onion, ½ teaspoon salt and ⅛ teaspoon black pepper in a saucepan. Cover and cook over moderate to low heat for 15 minutes. Drain well, remove the large membranes, and cut brain into ½-inch cubes.

LENGUA SALITRADA

PICKLED TONGUES

EL SALVADOR

6 tablespoons coarse salt
2 teaspoons saltpeter
1 teaspoon black pepper
12 garlic cloves, peeled, whole
6 bay leaves
1 cup sliced onion
1 teaspoon thyme
2 whole cloves
1 chile gauque (guajillo), seeds and stem removed, cut into halves
2 beef tongues, 3 pounds each, rinsed and dried

1. Mix all the pickling ingredients together. Place the tongues in a glass container or stone crock and cover with the pickling mixture. Cover tightly and refrigerate for 4 days. Turn the tongues over each day. They will produce their own liquid.
2. Cook the tongues in a pressure cooker for 1 hour, or in a conventional pan for 2 hours or more, with the liquid and pickling ingredients. If there is not enough liquid, add water up to half the depth of the pan.
3. Peel the tongues while still warm. Wrap them in aluminum foil and refrigerate for several hours. Serve cold, sliced.

SERVES 8 TO 10

LENGUA EN SALSA

VEAL TONGUE IN SAUCE

JALAPA, GUATEMALA

1 or 2 fresh veal tongues, 2 to 2½ pounds altogether
3 cups water
½ teaspoon salt
2 cups sliced ripe tomatoes
½ cup sliced onion
¼ teaspoon thyme
¼ teaspoon freshly ground black pepper
½ cup sliced sweet red pepper
1 tablespoon white or cider vinegar
1 tablespoon corn oil
1 bay leaf
6 capers
6 stuffed green olives

1. Cook the tongue in the water with the salt for 1½ to 2 hours, or until soft. Cool and skin the tongue. Cut the tongue into ½-inch-thick slices. Reserve the liquid.

2. Prepare a sauce in the processor with the tomatoes, onion, thyme, black pepper, sweet red pepper, vinegar and 1 cup of the tongue liquid.

3. Heat the oil in a skillet over moderate heat and fry the sauce with the bay leaf for 10 minutes. Add the capers, olives and tongue slices and simmer over low heat for 10 minutes more. Serve warm.

SERVES 6

Variation: Beef tongue can be substituted for veal. Since a beef tongue is much larger, it will require a longer time to cook. Use 6 cups water and 2 teaspoons salt, and cook the tongue for probably 3 hours, or until soft. Skin the tongue and cut it into slices. Reserve the liquid to prepare the sauce but add half again more of the other ingredients.

LENGUA EN SALSA VEGETALES

TONGUE IN VEGETABLE SAUCE

NICARAGUA

1 beef tongue, 2 to 2½ pounds
6 cups water
6 garlic cloves, sliced
½ pound potatoes, peeled
1 chayote (huisquil), peeled
1 cup peeled and seeded green papaya
1 cup green peas, fresh or frozen
¼ cup sliced onion
¼ cup sliced tomato
¼ cup sliced sweet red pepper
½ teaspoon achiote, dissolved
1 tablespoon cider vinegar
1 teaspoon sugar
1 teaspoon salt, or to taste
¼ teaspoon freshly ground black pepper

1. Cook the tongue in the water with the garlic until it is soft, about 1½ hours. Peel off and discard the skin. Cut the tongue into ¼-inch-thick slices. Set aside. Reserve the liquid.

2. Cut the potatoes in ½-inch cubes, the chayote into 2-inch pieces, the papaya into ½-inch cubes. Add these to the green peas, onion, tomato, sweet pepper, achiote, vinegar, sugar, salt and black pepper. Add 2 cups of the reserved tongue liquid and bring the mixture to a boil over moderate heat. Add the tongue slices.

3. Cook everything together until the vegetables are soft and the liquid has reduced by half, about 20 minutes. Serve warm with rice or tortillas.

SERVES 6

LENGUA EN PEPIÁN DULCE

TONGUE IN SWEET PEPIÁN SAUCE

GUATEMALA CITY

1 veal tongue, about 2 pounds
4 cups water
1 teaspoon salt
1 medium-size tomato
1 chile pasa (pasilla)
1 tablespoon sesame seeds
2 tablespoons squash seeds
1 cinnamon stick, 1 inch, broken up
2 scallions, sliced
1 whole allspice
¼ teaspoon freshly ground black pepper
2 teaspoons sugar
1 tablespoon toasted bread crumbs
1 tablespoon corn oil
1 tablespoon raisins
1 tablespoon blanched almonds, split

1. Boil the tongue in the water with 1 teaspoon salt over moderate heat for 1½ hours, or until tongue is soft. Remove the tongue and peel off the skin. Cut the tongue into generous slices. Reserve the broth.

2. In a dry skillet over moderate to low heat toast the whole tomato, the *chile pasa,* sesame seeds and squash seeds until they are lightly brown, about 10 minutes.

3. Remove the seeds and stem of the chile pasa, cut it into strips, and soak it in 1 cup tongue broth.

4. Process into a smooth sauce the tomato, *chile pasa* in the soaking liquid, the sesame and squash seeds, cinnamon stick, scallions, allspice, black pepper and 1 cup of tongue broth. Push this through a metal sieve and discard the coarse particles in the sieve. Add the sugar and toasted bread crumbs.

5. Heat the oil in a saucepan and over moderate heat fry the sauce for 2 minutes. Add the sliced tongue, raisins and almonds, and simmer over low heat for 15 minutes. If the sauce is too thick, add ½ cup more tongue broth. Serve warm.

SERVES 6

Variation: The same process can be used to prepare a 3½-pound chicken cut into serving pieces. Discard loose skin and fat. Also, omit the raisins and almonds from the sauce and sprinkle them over all when serving.

LENGUA EN SALSA

TONGUE IN SAUCE
ZACAPA, GUATEMALA

1 veal or small beef tongue, about 2 pounds
5 cups water
2 small onions, whole
2 garlic cloves, whole, peeled
1 teaspoon salt
1 pound ripe tomatoes, about 4
¼ cup tomatillos (mil tomates)
¼ cup chopped sweet red pepper
1 tablespoon sliced onion
2 teaspoons corn oil
⅛ teaspoon achiote
½ teaspoon sugar
¼ cup chopped parsley
2 tablespoons toasted bread crumbs

1. Simmer the tongue in the water with 1 onion, 1 garlic clove and 1 teaspoon salt in a covered pan over moderate heat for about 1½ hours, or until tongue is soft. Remove the tongue, peel it, and cut it into ¼-inch-thick slices. Reserve the broth.

2. Toast the tomatoes, tomatillos, sweet pepper, 1 onion and 1 garlic clove in a dry skillet over moderate heat until they are lightly charred, about 10 minutes. Process these into a smooth paste with ½ cup of reserved tongue broth. Rub the paste through a metal sieve and discard the pulp.

3. Fry the sliced onion in the oil for 2 minutes. Add 1 cup of tongue broth, the achiote, sugar, tomato sauce, parsley and bread crumbs. Simmer and stir for 5 minutes.

4. Add the tongue and simmer over low heat for 10 minutes more. Serve warm with rice and Berenjena Frita (Fried Eggplant, see Index).

SERVES 6

LENGUA ENVUELTA EN HUEVO

TONGUE SLICES IN BATTER

ZACAPA, GUATEMALA

1 veal tongue, 1½ to 2 pounds
5 cups water
1 teaspoon salt
¼ cup sliced tomato
¼ cup sliced onion
2 garlic cloves, sliced
3 eggs, separated
1 teaspoon flour
¼ cup corn oil

1. Cook the tongue in the water with the salt, tomato, onion and garlic over moderate heat for 1½ hours, or until soft. Remove the tongue and peel off and discard the skin. Cool the tongue and cut into ½-inch-thick slices. Discard the liquid.

2. Beat the egg whites until stiff. Fold in the beaten yolks and the flour.

3. Heat the oil in a skillet over moderate heat. Dip each slice of tongue into the batter and brown in the oil for 2 minutes on each side.

4. Drain on paper towels and serve warm with a Chirmol (Simple Tomato Sauce, see Index).

SERVES 6

ENSALADA DE PANZA DE RES

TRIPE SALAD, AN APPETIZER

PALENCIA, GUATEMALA

Tripe is prepared in several ways. This salad, with a variety of textures and flavors, is one of my favorites. It goes well with drinks and can double as a luncheon salad.

1 pound cooked beef tripe, cut into slices 2 inches long and ¼ inch wide
½ cup chopped ripe tomato
¼ cup coarse-chopped celery leaves and tender ribs
¼ cup thin-sliced onion rings
½ cup thin-sliced sweet green pepper
2 tablespoons olive oil
½ teaspoon salt, or to taste
¼ cup lemon or lime juice

1. Mix everything together and refrigerate for 2 hours or more.
2. Serve as an appetizer with hot tortillas, tortilla chips or toasted breads.

SERVES 4 TO 6

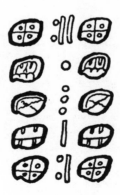

TIRAS

TRIPE IN SAUCE

CHIQUIMULILLA, GUATEMALA

2 pounds cooked beef tripe
2 tablespoons lemon or lime juice
2 cups water
1 cup sliced ripe tomato
½ cup sliced tomatillos (mil tomates)
1 garlic clove, sliced
2 tablespoons sliced onion
½ teaspoon salt, or to taste

1. Cook the tripe in water until it is tender, about an hour. Drain well and cut it into 2-inch diamond-shaped pieces. Mix the tripe with the lemon juice and 1 cup of water, and let it stand for 1 hour.

2. Prepare a smooth sauce in the processor with 1 cup of water, the tomato, tomatillos, garlic and onion. Put this in a saucepan with the salt and bring it to a boil. Simmer over moderate heat for 10 minutes.

3. Drain the tripe and add the pieces to the sauce. Simmer in an uncovered pan over low heat for 15 minutes.

4. Serve warm with rice, French bread (*pan Français*) or tortillas.

SERVES 6 TO 8

Note: The *tiras* does have ample sauce and should be slightly acid because of the tomatillos. However, as a substitute for these, which might not always be available, add 1 tablespoon lemon juice to the sauce as it simmers.

RABO EN CHICHA

OXTAIL IN FRUIT WINE
JALAPA, GUATEMALA

The people of Jalapa are of a different racial type from the Maya in the highlands. This southeast region of Guatemala, near the border of El Salvador, was settled by the early Spaniards and there is no real admixture with Guatemalans from other regions. Blessed with a comfortable climate, hardworking peasants have developed the rich valleys in tobacco, dairy products and beef cattle. The *rabo* exhibits the best of two worlds—the original recipe of the Colonial Spaniard and the spices of the Mayan highlands.

2 to 3 pounds oxtail, divided into serving pieces
3 cups water
1 teaspoon salt, or to taste
1 cup Chicha (see Index)
½ cup chile gauque (guajillo), seeds removed
½ chile pasa (pasilla), seeds removed
1 cup sliced ripe tomato
¼ cup sliced onion
3 garlic cloves, sliced
1 tablespoon corn oil
¼ teaspoon freshly ground black pepper
2 whole allspice berries, or ¼ teaspoon ground
1 cinnamon stick, 1 inch
¼ teaspoon grated nutmeg
⅛ teaspoon ground aniseed
¼ teaspoon thyme
2 bay leaves
1 tablespoon raisins
6 capers
6 green olives
¼ cup toasted bread crumbs

1. Cook the oxtail in the water with the salt over moderate heat for about 2 hours, or until almost soft. Add the *chicha* and simmer over low heat.

2. Toast the *chile guaque* and *chile pasa* in a dry skillet over low heat for 10 minutes. Slice or tear into pieces.

3. Prepare a sauce in the processor with the tomato slices, onion, garlic and chiles, and fry this in the oil in a skillet with the black pepper, allspice, cinnamon, nutmeg, aniseed and thyme for 2 minutes. Add this to the oxtail.

4. Then add the bay leaves, raisins, capers and olives. Stir well, then add the crumbs for thickening. Simmer over low heat for 20 minutes.

5. The *rabo* does have ample sauce. Serve warm with rice.

SERVES 6

PORK
AND
OTHER
MEATS

When the Spanish introduced the pig into Central America after the Conquest of 1524, it must have created an enormous amount of interest. This has not diminished to this day. Pork in the highlands is popular, cheap and available. Many dishes were created around this strange new creature—so fertile, so prolific—that was introduced along with the cow, sheep and goat. It is the common denominator of all the animal meats of Guatemala.

One of the most amusing sights on market days is to see mature pigs moving to market under the loudest vocal protest, screaming with rage and frustration. Or at another time, to see 20 or 30 small piglets tied with a small rope around their necks moving along the road with some sort of magician who keeps them all moving at a good pace like a puppeteer with his puppets on a string.

ESTOFADO DE MARRANO

PORK STEW

GUAZACAPÁN, GUATEMALA

This is a popular regional dish for family reunions, wedding parties, birthdays or any other festive occasion in Guazacapán. It is always cooked over a wood fire in the peasant kitchen, which is situated away from the sleeping quarters. The smoke of the wood fire lends an exotic flavor to an already well-seasoned preparation.

2 pounds boneless pork, cut into 2-inch cubes
Several bones for stock
½ cup fine-chopped onion
½ cup fine-chopped ripe tomato
3 garlic cloves, chopped fine
½ teaspoon thyme
1 bay leaf
2 tablespoons chopped tomatillo (mil tomate), optional
2 tablespoons cider vinegar
¼ teaspoon achiote
2 cups water
3 tablespoons toasted bread crumbs

1. Put everything except the bread crumbs together in a saucepan. Mix well. Simmer over moderate heat for 1½ hours, until the meat is soft.

2. Add the bread crumbs to thicken the sauce, and simmer for 5 minutes more, stirring the stew to mix in the crumbs.

3. Remove and discard the bones. Serve the stew warm.

SERVES 8

PULIQUÉ DE MARRANO

PORK AND SPICE

SANTIAGO SACATEPÉQUEZ, GUATEMALA

Santiago Sacatepéquez is a large village not too far from Guatemala City, yet retaining an important weaving tradition. Many of the village women weave their tribal costumes in several different styles. On the Day of the Dead, November 2, giant kites are flown in the cemetery to propitiate the spirits of the dead. A *puliqué* is prepared in the homes and marketplace at this time.

2 pounds boneless pork, cut into 2-inch cubes
4 cups water
1 teaspoon salt, or to taste
2 cups sliced ripe tomatoes
1 cup sliced tomatillos (mil tomates)
2 chiles guaque (guajillo), seeds and stems removed
¼ cup sliced onion
½ teaspoon black pepper
¼ teaspoon achiote
¼ cup all-purpose flour, dissolved in ½ cup water
4 whole cloves
6 stalks of epazote

1. Cook the pork in the water with the salt over moderate heat for about 1 hour, or until nearly soft.

2. Meanwhile, prepare a sauce in the processor with the tomatoes, tomatillos, chiles, onion, black pepper, achiote and the flour paste. Add this to the pork with the cloves and the epazote.

3. Simmer over moderate heat until the pork is soft and the sauce is reduced and thickened. Total cooking time is about 2 hours. Serve warm with rice and tortillas.

SERVES 6

Variation: Boneless beef chuck, a 3½-pound chicken or an equal amount of turkey, cut into serving pieces, can be prepared in the same manner. The cooking time must be adjusted downward for the poultry.

ADOBADO DE CARNE DE MARRANO

PICKLED PORK

MERCADO AT FLORIDA, GUATEMALA

Pork *adobado* is often prepared by the butchers in the town municipal markets (*mercados*) and so is relatively easy to obtain. However, some prefer their own family combination of spices.

½ cup sliced tomatillos (mil tomates)
4 garlic cloves, sliced
1 teaspoon ground cuminseed
1 teaspoon thyme
1 teaspoon orégano
½ teaspoon achiote
½ teaspoon freshly ground black pepper
1 teaspoon salt, or to taste
¾ cup vinegar
¼ cup corn oil
2 pounds boneless pork, sliced into 6 ½-inch-thick steaks

1. Prepare a smooth sauce in the processor with all the ingredients except the pork and oil. Rub this thick, red sauce into the pork and marinate in the refrigerator for 1 or 2 days.
2. Heat the oil in a skillet and fry the steaks over moderate heat until they are well done. Cover the skillet now and then to cook the pork through to the center. Total cooking time is about 15 minutes. Serve warm.

SERVES 6

FRIJOL BLANCO CON MARRANO

WHITE BEANS AND MEAT

JOYABAJ, GUATEMALA

Joyabaj is one of the weaving towns in the Quiché, where the women wear their national tribal costumes and lead simple agricultural lives. The region is known for its cinnamon and *ayote* (squash) production. This bean dish is one of the region's favorites since large quantities can be prepared at very little cost in a region where there isn't a lot of money moving around.

½ pound dried white beans
4 cups water
½ teaspoon salt, or to taste
1 medium-size onion, chopped (½ cup)
2 medium-size ripe tomatoes, chopped (1 cup)
2 garlic cloves
½ teaspoon orégano
1 chile guaque (guajillo), seeds and stem removed
⅛ teaspoon achiote
½ pound boneless pork, cut into 2-inch pieces
1 cinnamon stick, 1 inch

1. Soak the beans in salted water overnight.

2. Next day, cook beans over moderate heat until soft, about 1½ hours.

3. Toast the onion and whole tomatoes in a dry skillet over low heat for 10 minutes, or until they appear slightly charred.

4. Prepare a smooth sauce in the processor with the onion, garlic, tomatoes, orégano, *chile guaque*, 1 cup bean liquid and the achiote. Add this to the beans with the pork and cinnamon stick.

5. Simmer everything together over low heat for 30 minutes, or until the meat is tender. If the mixture seems a bit too thick, add ½ cup water. Serve warm with tortillas.

SERVES 6

Variation: Boneless beef chuck can be substituted for the pork.

FRIJOLES CON CARNE

PORK AND BEANS

HUEHUETENANGO, GUATEMALA

1 pound dried small red beans (frijoles colorados)
6 cups water
1 teaspoon salt, or to taste
½ cup whole tomatillos (mil tomates)
2 small ripe tomatoes, whole
2 garlic cloves, peeled, whole
1 medium-size onion, peeled, whole
1 pound pork, cut into 1-inch cubes

1. Soak the beans in 3 cups water with ½ teaspoon salt for 4 hours. Cook until beans are soft but not mushy, about 1 hour.

2. Toast the tomatillos, tomatoes, garlic and onion in a dry skillet over moderate to low heat until lightly charred, 5 to 8 minutes. Process these into a smooth paste with 2 tablespoons cooked beans.

3. Cook the pork in 3 cups water with ½ teaspoon salt over moderate heat until soft, about 1 hour. Drain. In the same saucepan fry the meat in its own oil for 5 minutes, to brown lightly.

4. Add the sauce and simmer over moderate heat for 5 minutes. Add the beans, stir well, and simmer the mixture over low heat for 15 minutes. Serve warm.

SERVES 6 TO 8

REVOLCADO

A STEW OF PORK

GUATEMALA CITY

The word *revolcado* actually means "the mixture," which it is. Traditionally, the entire head of the pig is used and cooked together with the other internal parts, the head providing a stronger broth.

Pork

2 tongues
2 kidneys
2 hearts
1 pound boneless pork
1 pound liver (optional)
1 ear (optional)
10 cups water
1 teaspoon salt

Sauce

2 cups sliced ripe tomatoes
¼ cup sliced onion
3 garlic cloves, sliced
½ cup sliced sweet red pepper
2 teaspoons dried hot red chile flakes
¼ teaspoon achiote
3 tortillas, halved
½ cup toasted bread crumbs

1. Cook the meats together in the water with the salt over moderate heat for 1 hour or a bit more, until it is all tender.

2. Trim the skin from the tongues and cut all the meat into ½-inch cubes. There will be about 5 cups meat. Reserve the broth, about 8 cups.

3. Cook the sauce ingredients in 2 cups of reserved pork broth over moderate heat for 15 minutes. Process the mixture into a smooth sauce. Add it to the balance of the reserved broth, which is now about 6 cups.

4. In a large saucepan, combine the broth and sauce and cubed meats. Simmer over moderate to low heat for 30 minutes, stirring frequently. The rich, red sauce will thicken. Adjust the salt. Serve warm with white rice.

SERVES 8

Variation: Also used, although not nearly so popular, is the *revolcado* made with veal or beef tongue, meat, heart, kidney and liver in place of the pork mixture.

PEPENA

FRIED PORK CUBES

NICARAGUA

This is an easily prepared dish, which provides a good luncheon platter, but can also serve as an appetizer with drinks.

2 pounds boneless pork with a little fat
1 cup water
2 teaspoons corn oil
1 teaspoon salt, or to taste

1. Cut the pork into 1-inch cubes. Put them in a pan with the water and bring the mixture to a boil over moderate heat. Cook for 30 minutes, stirring frequently.
2. Add the oil and salt and continue to cook until the pork is browned and the water has evaporated, about 20 minutes more.
3. Serve warm with the traditional accompaniments such as cooked cassava slices and cabbage salad.

SERVES 6

PULIQUÉ

PORK STEAKS IN SAUCE

SAN MIGUEL CHICAJ,
GUATEMALA

Puliqué is a traditional dish of San Miguel, served at marriage parties, fiestas and the ceremonials of the church *cofradías* (elders). It is an important food for the holidays of this small village in the middle of nowhere. The handwoven women's costumes of this village are spectacular and are still worn from time to time. But traditional recipes, like handweaving, disappear or fall into disfavor; it is a pleasure, therefore, to record this very tasty concoction for posterity.

3 tablespoons corn oil
2 pounds boneless pork, cut into small steaks 3 inches long, 2
    inches wide and ½ inch thick
3 cups water
½ cup sliced onion
1 cup toasted sesame seeds
½ teaspoon freshly ground black pepper
1 teaspoon salt, or to taste
1 teaspoon ground cuminseed
¼ teaspoon achiote
2 medium-size ripe tomatoes, sliced
3 medium-size potatoes, cut into ½-inch-thick slices
½ cup all-purpose flour, moistened with ½ cup water

1. Heat the oil in a skillet over moderate heat and fry the pork
steaks for 5 minutes, or until lightly browned. Add the water and
bring to a boil.

2. Prepare a smooth sauce in a processor with the onion, sesame
seeds, black pepper, salt, cuminseed, achiote and tomatoes. Add this
to the pork and simmer over moderate heat for 45 minutes, or until
the pork is softening.

3. Add the potato slices and simmer slowly for 10 minutes. Then
add the moistened flour and stir well to thicken the sauce. Simmer
slowly for 15 minutes. Total cooking time is about 1½ hours. Serve
warm.

SERVES 6

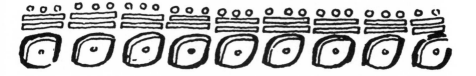

CHILIMAL

PORK IN A THICK SAUCE
NEBAJ, GUATEMALA

Nebaj is a magnificent village of the Ixil Indians with a remarkable weaving tradition. The women's costume is celebrated throughout Guatemala for its beauty and incomparable weaving technique. This recipe for their *chilimal* is in the old style of preparation. Nowadays, additional seasonings have crept in, such as cloves and coriander, which give it another dimension.

1½ pounds boneless pork shoulder, cut into 2 pieces
4 cups water
1 teaspoon salt, or to taste
1 cup chayote (huisquil), cut into ½-inch cubes
2 cups ½-inch cubes of potatoes
¼ cup sliced onion
2 garlic cloves, sliced
1 cup sliced ripe tomatoes
1 teaspoon dried hot red chile flakes
¼ teaspoon achiote
¼ cup masa (tortilla flour, moistened)

1. Cook the pork in the water with the salt for about 1 hour, or until it is soft. Remove the meat and cut it into strips 2 inches × ½ inch. Set meat aside and reserve the pork liquid.

2. Cook the chayote and potatoes in the pork liquid for 10 minutes, until softened but still firm. Remove and set aside.

3. Prepare a sauce in the processor with the onion, garlic, tomatoes, hot chile and achiote with 2 cups of the pork liquid. Bring the sauce to a boil in a saucepan over moderate heat.

4. Add the *masa* to thicken the sauce and simmer slowly for 10 minutes, stirring frequently. Add the pork and vegetables. Simmer for 10 minutes more.

5. The sauce should be thick without being gummy. If it appears too thick, add more pork liquid and salt to taste. Serve warm with plain, boiled rice.

SERVES 6

CARNE ADOBADO

PORK IN SPICY SAUCE
COBÁN, GUATEMALA

2 pounds boneless pork, cut into 3-inch pieces
2 medium-size ripe tomatoes
1 cup tomatillos (mil tomates)
¼ teaspoon ground cloves
1 teaspoon black pepper
½ teaspoon ground cinnamon
4 garlic cloves, sliced
½ cup sliced onion
¼ teaspoon achiote, dissolved in 1 cup water
½ cup vinegar
1 teaspoon salt, or to taste
3 tablespoons corn oil

1. Cook the pork in a dry saucepan over moderate heat until the color changes, about 5 minutes. Set aside.

2. Make a smooth sauce in the processor with the tomatoes, tomatillos, cloves, black pepper, cinnamon, garlic, onion, achiote and water, vinegar and salt. Pour the sauce over the pork and marinate it overnight.

3. The next day, remove the pork from the sauce. Heat the oil in a skillet over moderate heat and brown the pork for 10 minutes. Then return pork to the sauce.

4. Cook the pork in the sauce in a covered saucepan for about 1½ hours, or until tender. There should be about 1 cup sauce remaining. Serve warm with rice and tortillas.

SERVES 6

LOMO DE MARRANO RELLENO PRENSADO

PRESSED STUFFED BONELESS PORK

GUATEMALA CITY

The *lomo relleno* is an elegant preparation, worth every moment necessary to assemble and cook it. It can be prepared several days in advance of that special occasion and refrigerated until you are ready to serve.

Meat

3 to 4 pounds pork fillet or loin
2 teaspoons prepared mustard
1 teaspoon paprika
1 teaspoon white pepper
1½ teaspoons salt

Stuffing

½ cup raw carrot cubes
½ cup raw green snap bean slices
½ cup green peas, fresh or frozen
20 stuffed olives, sliced
1 tablespoon capers, chopped
2 tablespoons chopped sweet red and green pepper
1 pound ground beef
1 teaspoon salt, or to taste
1 teaspoon prepared mustard
2 tablespoons fine-chopped onion
1 garlic clove, chopped fine
½ pound thin-sliced ham

Cooking Broth (Court Bouillon)

2½ quarts water
4 leeks, white part only
6 scallions, cut into halves
1 tablespoon thyme
3 tablespoons salt, or to taste
6 bay leaves
10 peppercorns

1. Cut the fillet or loin open, butterfly fashion, into a rectangular shape. Mix the mustard, paprika, white pepper and salt together and spread the inside of the meat with the paste. Refrigerate for 2 or more hours.

2. Make the stuffing mixtures: Mix carrot, green beans, peas, olives, capers and chopped sweet pepper together. Mix the beef, salt, mustard, onion and garlic together.

3. Open out the pork completely. Cover the inside from end to end with the thin-sliced ham. Spread the beef mixture over the ham from end to end. Cover the beef with the vegetable mixture.

4. Roll the stuffed pork away from yourself to form a log or *lomo*. Sew the seam up across the log with 8 or 9 widely spaced stitches to hold it all together.

5. Wrap the *lomo* in a cotton kitchen towel and tie it tightly with string. Tie a knot at one end and continue to circle the *lomo* to the other end, where it should be firmly tied.

6. Prepare the cooking broth in a large roasting pan with a tight-fitting cover. Pour the water into the pan and add the other broth ingredients. Place the wrapped *lomo* in the broth and cook in the covered pan over moderate heat for 2½ hours. Turn the *lomo* over once in middle of cooking time.

7. After the *lomo* is done, but while still wrapped, put it between 2 wooden cutting boards to press it into a more or less flattened shape. Top the boards with a heavy weight and press the *lomo* for 8 hours. As soon as it has cooled, after 2 hours, it can be refrigerated for remaining 6 hours.

(recipe continues)·

8. At the end of this time, unwrap the *lomo*, but continue to refrigerate it until ready to serve cold. Cut it into 1-inch-wide slices and serve with traditional Guatemalan salads plus a Green Sauce and a Red Sauce (recipes follow).

Green Sauce

1 cup fine-chopped tomatillos (mil tomates)
1 teaspoon fine-chopped fresh hot green chile pepper

1. Mix tomatillos and chile together and serve cold. A pungent, acid sauce.

Red Sauce

1 tablespoon chopped onion
1 teaspoon corn oil
1 medium-size ripe tomato, chopped
1 bay leaf
¼ teaspoon thyme
¼ teaspoon freshly ground black pepper

1. Fry the onion in the oil for a minute and add everything else. Fry together for 2 minutes more.

2. Remove the bay leaf and process the rest into a smooth, red sauce. Chill. Serve cold.

SERVES 8 TO 10

MARANITO A LA BARBACOA

BARBECUED ROAST PIGLET

EL SALVADOR

This is a traditional recipe of the Indian village of Izalco. Originally, the piglet was wrapped in banana leaves and put into a wood fire made in a hollow in the ground. Piglet and all were then covered with earth. The piglets were baked in this fashion for about 5 hours. One can always find a small piglet in a Central American village, but here you may have to accept a much larger animal; in that case, just double the other ingredients and the cooking time. It may also be possible to buy half a piglet.

2 medium-size tomatoes, charred over a barbecue or under a
     broiler
2 medium-size onions, charred
1 tablespoon sesame seeds, toasted in a dry skillet
1 tablespoon squash seeds, toasted in a dry skillet
½ cup French bread, toasted
½ teaspoon freshly ground black pepper
2 teaspoons salt
½ teaspoon sliced fresh gingerroot
½ pound pork liver, or the small liver of the piglet
1 piglet, 4 pounds, dressed

1. Grind together everything except the piglet, to prepare a rich, thick sauce. This includes the liver.

2. Cover the piglet all over inside and out with the sauce. Wrap it in aluminum foil and bake it in a 375°F. oven for 3 hours.

3. Unwrap the foil and test the piglet for tenderness. If it is not done, wrap again and roast for another 15 to 20 minutes, or until well done.

4. Unwrap the piglet and serve warm, cut into sections or sliced. The liver provides a sort of pâté that envelops the piglet.

SERVES 4

PIERNA DE CERDO

STUFFED LEG OF PORK

EL SALVADOR

This is one of those recipes that originate in the cities for city folk. Countryside cooking is more basic and less complicated. One should not be astonished at the use of a cola drink and canned peaches in this dish; it exhibits how a recipe evolves. Beginning with a recipe from Colonial times, ingredients and techniques change to mirror changes in the culture. In this case, these two ingredients were added at the time they were first available in El Salvador and were considered a luxury. Now the taste of them in this dish would be missed, if they were omitted.

7 to 8 pounds fresh leg of pork
40 stuffed green olives
2 tablespoons capers
8 ounces dried prunes, pitted
2 cups fine-chopped tomatoes
½ cup fine-chopped onion
4 ounces sliced bacon, chopped fine
2 garlic cloves, chopped fine
3 tablespoons prepared mustard
1 teaspoon sugar
8 ounces cola drink (Coke or Pepsi)
12 ounces beer
1 cup canned peach halves

1. Remove any fat or skin from the pork. Rinse with cold water and wipe dry.

2. Chop fine half of the stuffed olives, half of the capers and half of the pitted prunes. Set aside the whole olives, capers and prunes. Mix all the chopped ingredients together to make a stuffing.

3. Cut 10 incisions all around the pork, 1 inch wide and 2 inches deep. With your fingers push about 2 teaspoons of the stuffing into each incision. Push in firmly so the stuffing will not fall out.

4. Mix together the mustard and sugar and rub the mixture all over the pork.

5. Put the pork in a large roasting pan and add the cola and the beer. Add the reserved whole olives, capers and prunes. Refrigerate the pork overnight; or prepare everything early in the morning and let it marinate until ready to roast in the afternoon.

6. Roast the pork, covered, in a 350°F. oven for 3 hours. Baste it now and then with pan juices. Toward the end of the roasting time, when the pork appears to be tender, add the canned peaches and their liquid. Bake and baste for 20 minutes more.

7. Slice the pork and serve warm, with the sauce and the fruits.

SERVES 12 TO 14

CHORIZOS TÍPICOS

TYPICAL SAUSAGE FRY
NICARAGUA

This is a popular method of preparing ground pork, not as a stuffed sausage but as a dish with a light vinaigrette sauce.

1 pound boneless pork, cubed
2 slices of bacon, cut up
4 garlic cloves, sliced
½ teaspoon achiote, dissolved
½ cup sliced onion
½ teaspoon salt, or to taste
¼ teaspoon freshly ground black pepper
1 tablespoon vinegar, diluted with ¼ cup water

1. Grind together the pork, bacon, garlic, achiote, onion, salt and black pepper to make a coarse mixture. Add the vinegar and water and mix well.

2. Fry the mixture in a skillet over moderate heat for 10 to 12 minutes, until it is lightly browned and cooked through. The *chorizo* should be moist with a bit of sauce.

3. Serve hot with tortillas or plain boiled green or ripe plantain.

SERVES 4

CHORIZO

RED SAUSAGE

HUEHUETENANGO, GUATEMALA

The *chorizos* of Huehuetenango are considered to be some of the best made. The lady vendors sell strings of these red sausages in marketplaces wherever one goes. Your local butcher may have pork sausage skins.

½ cup tomatillos (mil tomates)
½ teaspoon freshly ground black pepper
¼ teaspoon ground cuminseed
1 garlic clove, sliced
¼ teaspoon orégano
½ teaspoon achiote
1 teaspoon salt, or to taste
1 pound pork, ground fine
Pork sausage skins

1. Grind together into a paste the tomatillos, black pepper, cuminseed, garlic, orégano, achiote and salt. Add this to the pork and mix thoroughly. This can all be done in a food processor.

2. Stuff the mixture into sausage skins to make 1-inch round balls or 2-inch egg-shaped ovals.

3. Fry the sausages in very little oil in a skillet, until crisp. Drain on paper towels.

MAKES 8 TO 10 SAUSAGES

Variation: The *chorizo* mixture can be prepared in patties 2 inches in diameter and ¼ inch thick; fry them in a small amount of oil until well done and crisp.

LONGANIZA

SPICY SAUSAGE

HUEHUETENANGO,
GUATEMALA

¼ cup sliced onion
2 teaspoons sliced hot green chile
2 tablespoons parsley
¼ cup sour orange juice
4 tablespoons white or cider vinegar
½ teaspoon freshly ground black pepper
1 teaspoon salt, or to taste
2 pounds pork, ground fine but with very little fat
Pork sausage skins
Corn oil

1. Grind the onion, chile, parsley, orange juice, vinegar, black pepper and salt to a smooth paste. Add this to the pork and mix it well in the processor.

2. Stuff the mixture into sausage skins to make 2-inch egg-shaped ovals.

3. Fry the *longanizas* in very little oil in a skillet until crisp. Drain on paper towels.

MAKES 20 SAUSAGES

Variation: Prepare patties from the pork mixture 2 inches in diameter and ¼ inch thick. Fry in very little oil until crisp. Drain on paper towels.

BUTIFARRA

ANISE-FLAVORED SAUSAGE

ZACAPA, GUATEMALA

The *venado* mentioned in this recipe is the country liquor of Guatemala, the *aguardiente* or colorless liquor that is used in cocktails or straight. It is a drink similar to vodka, made from cane sugar, and the variety purchased in liquor stores or bars (*cantinas*) is refined and bottled in the industrial manner. The alcohol used in the *butifarras* partially "cooks" the meat as it marinates overnight. Rum or vodka are perfectly acceptable substitutes.

1½ pounds pork, ground
½ teaspoon ground aniseed
3 teaspoons salt
¾ teaspoon freshly ground black pepper
½ teaspoon ground cloves
¾ cup white rum, vodka or venado
Pork casing

1. Mix everything except the casing together and refrigerate for 24 hours.

2. Stuff the meat into a casing to fill the entire length, then with a string tie off individual sausages 2 inches in length and 1 inch wide.

3. Bring a large pan of water to a boil and simmer the entire sausage length over moderate heat for 15 minutes. Remove and dry the length over a line or clothes hanger for 2 hours.

4. Serve the *butifarra* cold in salads, sandwiches or as an hors d'oeuvre. It is also used as one of the sausages in the Fiambre (see Index).

MAKES 20 SAUSAGES

Variation: The seasoned meat can be prepared in thin patties 3 inches in diameter and ¼ inch thick; brown them in a small amount of oil.

MOLE DE CONEJO

MOUNTAIN RABBIT

SAN MARCOS, GUATEMALA

The municipality of San Lorenzo is in the Department of San Marcos, which has an altitude of about 8,000 feet. It is cold country but rich in agriculture. Driving through the countryside on dirt roads one sees panoramas of one green valley after another spotted with houses and small villages.

The people of this region are Quiché Indians and both men and women still wear various parts of their tribal costume, so one assumes that they will also hold to culinary tradition. This turns out to be the case.

Rabbit is a popular meat and families in San Lorenzo, where this recipe originated, raise rabbits as other tribal families might raise chickens or turkeys. The hills are full of wild rabbits, too, and the family man or boy might bag 4 or 5 fat ones, pursuing them with the house dog and a good strong *palo* (stick), which is used to kill the rabbit.

This rabbit *mole* contains olives, a puzzle in the dish of an isolated mountain township. Someone from Spain left his mark.

1 rabbit, 4 pounds, cut into serving pieces
4 cups water
1 teaspoon salt, or to taste
1 cup sliced ripe tomato
1 tablespoon sliced tomatillo (mil tomate)
2 teaspoons orégano
¼ teaspoon achiote
¼ cup chopped onion
6 green olives, pitted
2 cups masa (tortilla flour moistened with water)

1. Cook the rabbit in the water with the salt in a large saucepan over moderate heat until soft, about 1 hour.

2. Prepare a smooth sauce in the processor with the tomato, tomatillo, orégano, achiote, onion, olives, 1 cup rabbit liquid and the *masa*.

3. Mix the sauce with the rabbit and simmer over low heat for 20 minutes. The total cooking time of rabbit and sauce is about 1½ hours.

4. Serve warm with tamalitos, tortillas and boiled potatoes.

SERVES 6

FISH
AND
SEAFOOD

G uatemalans are not by nature, inclination or historical back-
ground fish eaters. I am referring to the highland Maya and
others in the major cities, not those living in the Pacific and Caribbean coastal regions.

The Maya in the highlands are near enough to rivers, but they
do not fish. The staggeringly beautiful Lake Atitlán is surrounded by
tribal villages where there are many fishermen, but much of their
catch is sold and their principal diet is still based on meat. There are
always exceptions, but the nomadic tribes that finally settled in the
Guatemala highlands were agriculturalists. No tradition of fishing
was established. This is confirmed by the absence of calligraphic
references to fish, fishermen or the gods who protected them, in the
ancient Codices.

The exception, a vivid one, is the emphasis on seafood in the
cooking of the Guatemala Caribbean town of Livingston. Most of

the recipes are from this mixed culture of Indians, Africans, Spaniards and even Chinese, people who came and settled down to work and developed a cuisine.

In recent years, fish has been brought from the Pacific Coast to the highland Indians and is sold on market days. These fish have been roasted over charcoal on the coast and then brought inland for sale. I witnessed an extraordinary sight in the village of San Pedro Sacatepéquez recently (1982). A village woman was selling a well-roasted alligator *(lagarto)* with a charcoal-blackened skin, which had been brought up from the coast. The white, cooked flesh looked reasonably edible and she was selling small pieces in banana leaves to knowledgeable villagers. To me it was a bizarre sight, but when one considers that an alligator is just a very large iguana, a source of protein since pre-Hispanic times, I suppose it was only natural.

CALDO DE PESCADO

FISH SOUP

LIVINGSTON, GUATEMALA

This *caldo* is made with small whole fish, large fish cut into 1-inch-thick slices, and fillets. We have a choice here, and my own inclination is to use the fillets as well as slices from a large fish to strengthen the soup.

4 cups water
1 teaspoon salt, or to taste
2 pounds fish—red snapper, sea bass, palometa, flounder, scrod or
    similar fish
¼ cup sliced tomato
¼ cup sliced onion
2 garlic cloves, crushed
2 tablespoons chopped cilantro
¼ cup thin-sliced celery
½ teaspoon freshly ground black pepper
⅛ teaspoon achiote
¼ cup thin-sliced carrots
¼ cup cubed chayote (huisquil), optional

1. Bring the water to a boil with the salt. Add the fish and all the other ingredients. Cover the pan and simmer over moderate to low heat for 20 minutes. Baste several times during this process.

2. Serve warm with corn or white tortillas.

SERVES 6

PACHAY

STEAMED FISH

LIVINGSTON, GUATEMALA

The Kekchi Indians have come down to Livingston from Cobán and have their own community at the port. They are an essentially highland people but have opened small shops, fished in their *cayucos* (dugout canoes), and blended into the port activities. The women wear their *huipiles* and traditional skirts and with their small features are identifiable everywhere.

This *pachay* is a Kekchi dish prepared with the cheap and abundant fish of the port.

1 small garlic clove, chopped
2 tablespoons chopped onion
1 tablespoon chopped tomato
1 tablespoon chopped cilantro
½ teaspoon salt, or to taste
⅛ teaspoon freshly ground black pepper
⅛ teaspoon achiote, dissolved in 1 teaspoon water
1 pound whole fish—sea bass, scrod, red snapper, mackerel
Banana leaf or aluminum foil

1. Mix the garlic, onion, tomato, cilantro, salt, black pepper and achiote together. Put half of the sauce in the center of a banana leaf or sheet of foil, place the fish on top, and pour the rest of the sauce over it. Fold it all into a package.
2. Bake or roast the package in a *comal* or a dry skillet for 20 minutes. Turn the package over several times during the roasting process. Unfold and serve warm.

SERVES 2

SUDADO

FISH SAUTÉ

PUERTO SAN
JOSÉ,
GUATEMALA

San José is a typical small seaport on the Pacific Ocean side of Guatemala—slightly seedy and reminiscent of a Somerset Maugham setting. Fish is plentiful and cheap and is eaten daily by everyone. The name of this typical dish is *sudado*, which is slang of the port and means "underdone," implying that the fish should not be overcooked. I would frequently drive down from the heights of Guatemala City to swim at the port's black sand beaches and sample their fish preparations.

1 cup chopped tomato
¼ cup chopped onion
3 garlic cloves, chopped
3 bay leaves
1 teaspoon thyme
½ teaspoon orégano
½ teaspoon salt, or to taste
2 tablespoons corn oil
¼ cup water
2 pounds fish—the whole fish or fillets such as scrod, sea bass,
    flounder

1. Fry the tomato, onion, garlic, bay leaves, thyme, orégano and salt in the oil in a large skillet over moderate heat for 3 minutes. Add the water and simmer for 2 minutes more.

2. Add the whole fish or fillets, cover the pan, and simmer for 15 minutes, turning the fish over once. If too much liquid has accumulated, remove the cover and simmer for a minute or two more to thicken the sauce. Serve warm.

SERVES 4

PESCADO GUISADO CON COCO

FISH SAUTÉ IN COCONUT MILK

LIVINGSTON, GUATEMALA

This is the simple, classic style of cooking fish in Livingston.

1 pound whole sea bass, red snapper, mackerel or similar fish
1 cup Rich Coconut Milk (see Index)
½ teaspoon salt, or to taste
½ teaspoon freshly ground black pepper
¼ cup thin-sliced sweet green pepper
¼ cup sliced tomato
¼ cup chopped celery

1. Score the whole fish 3 times diagonally on each side.
2. Bring the coconut milk to a boil in a skillet over moderate heat. Add the fish and baste for 3 minutes. Then add the salt, black pepper, sweet green pepper, tomato and celery. Continue to baste for 5 minutes.
3. Simmer the fish in an uncovered skillet over low heat, turning the fish over once, for 10 minutes. Serve warm.

SERVES 2

PESCADO A LA TIPITAPA

FISH FROM TIPITAPA

NICARAGUA

Not too far from the Nicaraguan capital, Managua, is the little town of Tipitapa where this famous fish dish originated. With the fish kept whole but relieved of the worst of its bones, this becomes a toothsome but easy-to-eat treat. Because it is the boning of the fish that gives this dish its special character, we have included the necessary instructions. It's easy for anyone who's ever dressed a fish.

1½ pounds sea bass, red snapper or similar fish
½ cup sliced onion
¼ cup sliced tomato
½ cup thin-sliced sweet red pepper
1 teaspoon Worcestershire sauce
½ teaspoon sugar
½ cup water
¼ cup white table wine
2 teaspoons corn oil
1 bay leaf
3 tablespoons cornmeal
¼ cup corn oil

1. Bone the fish as described.

2. Cook the onion, tomato, sweet pepper, Worcestershire sauce, sugar and water together over moderate heat for 10 minutes. Add the wine, oil and bay leaf and cook for 5 minutes more. Set this sauce aside and keep warm.

3. Toast the cornmeal in a dry skillet for about 2 minutes, or until the aroma is released and the color changes.

4. Heat the oil in a skillet over moderate heat. Roll the fish liberally in the cornmeal and fry in the oil until slightly crisp, about 5 minutes on each side. Turn the fish only once. Remove and drain on paper towels for a moment.

5. Pour the warm sauce over the fish. Serve warm.

SERVES 4

How to Bone a Fish

1. Remove the gills and the interior membranes in the head and discard them. Cut along the stomach and remove the viscera.

2. Insert the points of a sharp kitchen shears into the back just in front of the back fin until you reach the spine. Cut the spine through at that point. Reverse the fish to the tail end. Insert the shears into the end of the back fin and cut through the spine at that end.

3. Now with a sharp knife cut along the length of the back fin well into the fish on both sides of the fin, cutting the meat away from the bone. Pull the fin out, along with any loose bones. Rub the fish inside and out with 1 teaspoon salt and ½ teaspoon pepper. Now the fish is ready.

CAMARONES AL AJO

GARLIC SHRIMPS
LIVINGSTON, GUATEMALA

1 pound medium shrimps, whole, not peeled
½ teaspoon salt
½ teaspoon freshly ground black pepper
3 tablespoons butter
2 garlic cloves, minced
1 tablespoon Worcestershire sauce
1 tablespoon water
2 teaspoons cornstarch

1. Mix the shrimps, salt and pepper together. Fry them in the butter in a skillet over moderate heat until shrimps turn pink, about 2 minutes.

2. Mix the garlic, Worcestershire sauce, water and cornstarch into a paste.

3. Add the paste to the shrimps and continue to stir-fry over high heat for 3 minutes. The sauce will be reduced but not dried out. Serve warm with rice and beans.

SERVES 4

CAMARONES EMPANISADO

SHRIMPS IN WHITE BATTER
LIVINGSTON, GUATEMALA

½ pound medium or large shrimps
½ teaspoon salt
½ teaspoon freshly ground black pepper
2 egg whites
2 teaspoons flour
¼ cup corn oil

1. Peel and devein the shrimps and split them open in butterfly style.

2. Mix the shrimps with salt and black pepper and let them stand for 10 minutes.

3. Beat the egg whites until frothy but not stiff. Fold in the flour. Heat the oil in a skillet over moderate heat.

4. Dip the shrimps into the batter and fry them until lightly brown.

5. Drain briefly on paper towels and serve warm. Serve with Frijoles con Arroz (Rice and Beans) and Puré (Fried Plantain Mash, see Index for recipes).

SERVES 2

TIBURÓN ENCURTIDO FRITO

SHARK STEAKS
PUERTO SAN JOSÉ, GUATEMALA

There are several varieties of edible shark available, and the fishermen at the Pacific port of San José pull them in frequently. The lemon or lime juice partially "cooks" the steaks, and the brief frying in hot oil brings out their best qualities.

1 pound or more of edible shark fillet, cut into ¼-inch-thick
　　steaks
¼ cup lime or lemon juice, or more
1 teaspoon salt, or to taste
¼ cup corn oil

1. Marinate the shark in the lime juice and salt for not less than 1 hour.

2. Heat the oil in a skillet over moderate heat. Drain the shark steaks well and fry them for 1 minute on each side. Serve warm.

SERVES 4

TIBURONCITO HELEN MARGOTH

BABY SHARK FRY

LIVINGSTON, GUATEMALA

Shark is a throwaway fish in the profligate ambience of Livingston. The rich and clear waters of the Río Dulce (Sweet River) flow through Guatemala and empty into the Caribbean at Livingston. The fishing grounds teem with every type of tropical fish and seafood. Dolphins are seen from the town pursuing shoals of sardines, and clouds of aquatic birds gorge themselves on an apparently unlimited supply of small fish. Pelicans are the scavengers of the harbor and clean up the refuse when the fishermen harvest their catches in family netting operations, diving with open beaks like animated vacuum cleaners and scooping up all around them. With so many other fish available, shark is not in much demand and the soft, tender veal-like baby shark have yet to be included in the traditional cuisine of Livingston. But in the meantime, one can buy them for 50 cents each (or even get them free) and relish the infinitely delicious flavors of the shark fry.

1 baby shark, 2 to 2½ pounds
¼ cup fine-chopped tomato
¼ cup minced onion
1 teaspoon and 3 tablespoons corn oil
2 tablespoons flour
1 egg, beaten

1. Fillet the shark, remove the rather leathery skin, and divide the fish into 4 pieces, or buy shark steaks, ready to cook.
2. Fry the tomato and onion in 1 teaspoon oil for 3 minutes to prepare a simple sauce.
3. In another skillet, heat 3 tablespoons oil over moderate heat. Dip the shark pieces into the flour and then coat them with beaten egg. Brown in the oil for 3 minutes on each side. Drain briefly on a paper towel.
4. Serve warm, pouring the sauce over the pieces.

SERVES 4

PATÍN

DRIED BABY FISH IN A SAUCE— AN APPETIZER

SANTIAGO ATITLÁN, GUATEMALA

Patín is the typical popular dish of this village on the southern shore of Lake Atitlán. The various inlets of the shoreline are breeding places of the local lake fish, and these are caught and dried in quantities. The women of Santiago prepare the *patín* and sell it to the other lake villagers who do not catch the minnows and therefore cannot make the *patín*.

4 ounces dried freshwater minnows, each 1 inch long
½ pound ripe tomatoes
½ teaspoon hot chile, dried or fresh
½ teaspoon salt, or to taste

1. Toast the fish in a dry skillet until dry and lightly tan.

2. Process the tomatoes, chile and salt into a smooth paste. Simmer this over low heat until hot and thick. Add the toasted fish and stir several times.

3. Serve warm or at room temperature with fresh or toasted tortillas.

SERVES 2 TO 4

TASHMUL DE PESCADO

STEAMED FISH PACKAGE

SANTA BÁRBARA
SUCHITEPÉQUEZ, GUATEMALA

Santa Bárbara is near the Pacific Coast, and its tropical rivers are full of fish and especially freshwater shrimps. The people are fish eaters here, and this *tashmul* is justifiably popular because of its sealed-in flavors.

1 to 1½ pounds freshwater fish—perch, bass, trout—diced
½ cup sliced tomato
¼ cup thin-sliced onion
½ teaspoon freshly ground black pepper
½ teaspoon salt, or to taste
½ teaspoon thyme
2 bay leaves
2 mashan leaves or 2 sheets of aluminum foil

1. Mix the diced fish, tomato, onion, black pepper, salt, thyme and bay leaves together. Put the mixture in the middle of the leaves or foil, fold over each half to the center, then fold over each end toward the middle.

2. Stean the packages in a Chinese-style steamer over hot water over moderate heat for 30 minutes. Unwrap and serve hot in the wrappers.

SERVES 2

Variation: This procedure works very well if you substitute a 1-pound fillet of an ocean fish such as scrod, sea bass, mackerel, or whatever is one's personal preference.

Note: Since the green mashan leaf is not available, aluminum foil is a serviceable substitute in all of these recipes. Fold the foil over the fish mixture envelope-style and twist the ends to seal the contents.

SAVALO

TARPON HASH
LIVINGSTON, GUATEMALA

Potatoes cooked but still firm may be substituted for the chayote. Mackerel, snook, red snapper and especially shark are excellent substitutes for the tarpon. Tarpon, known in Livingston as *savalo*, is found in the daily fish catches there and is a rather dry fish with dark flesh. In this regard it is reminiscent of tuna, another delicious substitute for the tarpon.

Perhaps it was the open wood fire in the simple brick stove that gave this particular *savalo* a characteristic country seaport aroma and flavor that I shall never forget.

2 pounds tarpon, sliced
2 cups water
½ teaspoon salt
1 cup diced carrots
1 cup diced chayote (huisquil)
¼ cup tomato paste, homemade or canned
¼ teaspoon freshly ground black pepper
⅓ cup chopped onion
2 tablespoons white or cider vinegar
2 tablespoons corn oil
¼ teaspoon achiote

1. Cook the tarpon in the water with very little salt over moderate heat for 15 minutes. Cool and flake the fish. There should be about 3 cups.

2. Cook the carrots and chayote in boiling water with a little salt for 3 minutes. Drain well.

3. Combine the fish, carrots, chayote, tomato paste, black pepper, onion and vinegar and mix well.

4. Heat the oil in a large skillet over moderate heat and add the achiote, stirring well to dissolve it. Add the fish/vegetable mixture to the skillet and stir-fry over low heat for 10 minutes. Serve warm.

SERVES 6

TORTITAS DE SAVALO

FISH PATTIES

LIVINGSTON, GUATEMALA

Although made with tarpon here, these patties can be made with any fish fillet that is available. Meatier fish is closer to the original idea.

½ cup raw potato cubes
½ cup raw carrot slices
¼ cup sliced leek, white and tender green parts
¼ cup chopped celery
2 tablespoons chopped tomato
2 tablespoons chopped onion
½ teaspoon salt, or to taste
½ teaspoon freshly ground black pepper
½ cup flour
1 pound fish fillet—tarpon, shark, swordfish, scrod, tuna,
    flounder—chopped coarse
¼ cup vegetable oil

1. Process the potato, carrot, leek, celery, tomato and onion to a relatively smooth paste. Add the salt, black pepper and flour and mix well. Add the chopped fish and mix well.

2. Heat the oil in a skillet over moderate heat. Shape the patties about 3 inches in diameter and ½ inch thick. Brown them in the oil on both sides for about 10 minutes. Drain on paper towels. Serve warm or at room temperature.

SERVES 6

SEVICHE DE PESCADO

LEMON FISH APPETIZER

LIVINGSTON, GUATEMALA

The seviche is also prepared with shellfish. In food stalls in the marketplaces in Livingston it is made with shellfish, shrimps and occasionally small squids. It is prepared while you wait and served immediately to hungry customers. My own preference is to refrigerate the seviche for a while to allow the lemon juice to "cook" the fish. Also, it is more palatable to my taste when chilled.

½ pound scrod, flounder or sole fillet, cut into very thin slivers
¼ cup lemon juice, or more
1 cup fine-chopped ripe tomato
¼ cup fine-chopped onion
1 tablespoon fine-chopped parsley
1 tablespoon fine-chopped mint
½ teaspoon fine-chopped fresh hot chile
1 tablespoon Worcestershire sauce
½ teaspoon salt
⅛ teaspoon pepper

1. Mix everything together and refrigerate for a minimum of 30 minutes, more if you wish. Serve chilled.

SERVES 4

CHIRIN (CALDO DE MARISCOS)

SIMPLE SEAFOOD SOUP

MONTERRICO, GUATEMALA

This soup comes from Monterrico Island, part of the Chiquimulilla Canal complex that runs along the Pacific Coast of Guatemala. This tropical canal is hardly used now for commercial activities, but it is used by launches to take the inhabitants of Monterrico back and forth to the mainland. The island itself is small and almost self-contained by the people who grow corn, make cheese in their palm-leaf huts, grow tamarind and citrus. Seafood is abundant and the black sand beach is first-rate for good swimmers. Shark is also eaten and vice versa!

4 scallions, sliced
½ cup chopped tomato
1 tablespoon corn oil
4 cups hot water
2 garlic cloves, whole, unpeeled
2 small whole fish, about ½ pound each—sea bass, mackerel or
    similar fish—dressed
½ pound fish roe, when available
1 pound medium or large shrimps, whole in their shells
6 or 8 clams or mussels (optional, but recommended)

1. Fry the scallions and tomato in the oil in a large saucepan over moderate heat for 1 minute. Add the hot water and garlic and bring to a boil.

2. Add the fish, fish roe, shrimps, and clams if used, and simmer over low heat for 15 minutes.

3. Serve warm with ample lemon or lime slices, tortillas and any sort of salad.

SERVES 4

TAPADO

SEAFOOD SOUP IN COCONUT MILK
LIVINGSTON, GUATEMALA

This *tapado* is a popular seafood preparation in Livingston, where it is difficult to find a badly prepared traditional dish that uses coconut milk. Most of the restaurants in the town are frontier-style shacks or a bit better, but the quality of the food makes one forget all that. The okra in town were extraordinary, 6 inches long and 1 inch thick, with a pale green skin, very tender and not at all gummy.

2 pounds whole fish—red snapper, sea bass, mackerel or similar
    fish
2 tablespoons corn oil
4 cups Rich Coconut Milk (see Index)
⅛ teaspoon achiote
4 whole blue crabs
½ pound medium or large shrimps
1 teaspoon dried orégano, or 5 fresh leaves
2 tablespoons chopped cilantro
¼ cup sliced onion
¼ teaspoon freshly ground black pepper
½ teaspoon salt, or to taste
¼ cup sliced sweet red or green pepper
6 whole okra, fresh or frozen
1 small ripe plantain with a black skin, peeled and cut into
    ¼-inch-thick diagonal slices
1 green banana, peeled and quartered (optional)

1. Score the whole fish diagonally twice on each side. Heat the oil in a skillet and fry the fish over moderate heat for 3 minutes. Remove fish and set aside.

2. Bring the coconut milk to a boil with the achiote in a large saucepan over moderate heat. Add to the coconut milk the crabs, shrimps, orégano, cilantro, onion, black pepper, salt, sweet pepper, okra, plantain and banana. Simmer uncovered over low heat for 20 minutes, basting frequently.

3. Add the fried fish and simmer for 10 minutes more. Serve warm. Serve with white rice, bread or any type of tortilla.

SERVES 6

CALDO DE PESCADO SIMPLE

SIMPLE FISH SOUP

PUERTO SAN JOSÉ, GUATEMALA

2 tablespoons corn oil
½ cup chopped onion
1 garlic clove, chopped
1 cup chopped tomato
3 cups water
1 teaspoon dried orégano, or 5 fresh leaves
1 almost ripe plantain with a yellow skin, or 1 green banana,
    peeled and cut into ¼-inch-thick diagonal slices
1 to 1½ pounds whole fish, sea bass or similar fish, cut into
    2-inch-wide slices
½ teaspoon salt, or to taste

1. Heat the oil in a skillet and over moderate heat fry the onion, garlic and tomato for 3 minutes. Add the water, orégano and plantain or banana slices. Simmer over low heat for 15 minutes to soften the quite firm plantain.

2. Add the fish and salt, cover the skillet, and simmer for 15 minutes more to cook the fish. Baste several times during this process. Serve warm.

SERVES 4

TAPADO

SEAFOOD STEW
PUERTO BARRIOS,
GUATEMALA

There are many types of *tapado* that one can sample on the banana coast of the Caribbean. This version is my favorite since it features, along with the seafood, ripe plaintain and banana.

½ pound shrimps in the shell
2 or 3 whole crabs
½ cup boiling water
½ cup sliced tomato
½ cup sliced onion
½ cup sliced sweet green pepper
1 ripe plantain, peeled and cut into 1-inch pieces
1 firm ripe banana, peeled and cut into 1-inch pieces
½ teaspoon salt, or to taste
¼ teaspoon achiote
½ pound fillet of any fish such as halibut, sole, flounder
1 tablespoon corn oil
1 cup Rich Coconut Milk (see Index)

1. Cook the shrimps and crabs in the boiling water for 3 minutes. Add the tomato, onion, sweet pepper, plantain, banana, salt and achiote.

2. Meanwhile, fry the fish in the oil for 2 minutes on each side. Cut the fillet into 3-inch pieces and add it to the stew with the coconut milk.

3. Simmer everything together over moderate heat for 10 minutes, basting frequently. Do not cover the pan or skillet. Serve warm.

SERVES 6

VEGETABLES, SALADS AND PICKLES

The richness of the volcanic soils of Guatemala produces matchless vegetables tasting of their own intrinsic flavors. No one driving through the countryside in the highlands can fail to see the brilliant green fields of cabbage and cauliflower like moving waves in the folds of the mountains. The land is not flat, but every inch is used regardless of the physical difficulty in planting and harvesting. Mountain people utilizing the mountains.

European vegetables such as cabbage, beets and carrots compete brilliantly with the *huisquil* (chayote), squash and pumpkin of Central America. Watercress, chard, lettuce and spinach are eaten raw or cooked.

Onion, garlic and leek, brought by the Spanish, are used to flavor tomatoes, sweet peppers and green beans, which the Spanish found on arrival in Guatemala. The blending of cultures was at work establishing a new cuisine.

The list of vegetables available in Guatemala reads like a compendium of a botanical dictionary. During the rainy season (July, August and September) I have combed the Indian markets for the orange *anacate* mushroom (a chanterelle), cepe or any others lying in a basket. The village women would eat one in front of me, proving that they were not poisonous, and for a few dimes one could buy handfuls.

Along the tropical coasts green bananas and plantains are cooked and eaten as vegetables with meat or fish as well as prepared as desserts. There is an eclectic approach to vegetables, and occasionally the line is thin between a savory or dessert preparation.

Pickled vegetables, sometimes chile hot, are standard in the home. They are used in sandwiches, as a sort of chutney, or as an important ingredient in appetizers with fresh or toasted tortillas.

ALBÓNDIGAS DE BANANA

GREEN BANANA DUMPLINGS
LIVINGSTON, GUATEMALA

4 green bananas
½ teaspoon salt
3 cups Rich Coconut Milk (see Index)
1 tablespoon tomato paste, canned or homemade
1 bay leaf
¼ cup sliced sweet green pepper

1. Grate the bananas by hand or in a processor with the salt to make a smooth paste, about 2 cups.

2. Bring the coconut milk to a boil with the tomato paste and bay leaf in a skillet over moderate heat.

3. Drop 1 heaping tablespoon of the banana purée into the simmering coconut milk, basting several times. Continue with the rest of the purée in the same fashion. Cover the skillet and simmer over low heat for 10 minutes. Turn the dumplings over, add the sweet pepper at this time, and simmer for 5 minutes more.

4. Serve warm as an accompaniment to meat or fish dishes. Very compatible with Frijoles con Arroz (Rice and Beans, see Index).

SERVES 4

GARBANZOS PETRONILA

CHICK-PEAS AND SAUSAGE

GUATEMALA

A traditional recipe from a Guatemalan family cook, Petronila. The chick-pea and sausage combination is of Spanish origin, like so many of the Guatemala foods eaten in the capital. This dish is a non-Mayan Indian preparation of the city rather than the countryside.

3 thin slices of bacon
2 Spanish chorizos or hot Italian-style sausage, cut into ½-inch-
    thick slices
½ cup chopped onion
2 garlic cloves, chopped
½ cup chopped tomato
1 full cup of watercress, spinach or Swiss chard
½ cup water
1 pound canned chick-peas, drained

1. Fry the bacon and sausage in a skillet until browned. Remove them, drain well on paper towels, and set aside. Reserve 1 tablespoon of the melted fat.

2. Fry the onion, garlic and tomato in the reserved fat in the same skillet for 5 minutes. Stir-fry well.

3. Cook the greens in the water in a covered pan over high heat for 3 minutes to wilt them. Squeeze them dry and add to the tomato fry.

4. Add the chick-peas and fried sausage and bacon. Stir-fry over moderate heat for 5 minutes, until all is well mixed.

5. Serve warm as a one-dish lunch with rice, French bread and salad.

SERVES 4 TO 6

GARBANZOS EN TOMATE

CHICK-PEAS IN TOMATO

GUATEMALA CITY

Canned chick-peas are the easy way out and can be used with confidence. Reserve ½ cup of the liquid from the can. Spanish-style chorizo can be used instead of the Italian sausage.

½ pound Italian-style sweet sausage, sliced
3 slices of bacon, cut into ¼-inch-wide pieces (optional)
½ cup chopped onion
3 garlic cloves, chopped
3 bay leaves
¼ teaspoon thyme
1 cup coarse-chopped sweet red peppers
1 tablespoon corn oil
1 pound cooked chick-peas, canned or dry
6 ounces canned tomato paste
½ cup liquid reserved from the chick-peas

1. Fry the sausage and bacon in a skillet over moderate heat until the fat has been rendered and the meats are crisp. Remove the sausage and bacon and drain on paper towels. Discard the fat.

2. In another skillet, fry the onion, garlic, bay leaves, thyme and sweet peppers in the oil over moderate heat for 3 minutes. Add the chick-peas, sausage and bacon and stir-fry for 2 minutes.

3. Add the tomato paste and the reserved chick-pea liquid. Simmer the mixture over low heat for 15 minutes. Serve warm.

SERVES 6

TORTILLA DE COLIFLOR

CAULIFLOWER FRITTERS
GUATEMALA CITY

These are the typical fritters sold in the food stalls in the municipal market in back of the principal cathedral in Guatemala City. It is the everyday fare of the luncheon shoppers who make their meat, fruit and vegetable purchases in the green market rather than in the more antiseptic city supermarket.

1 small head cauliflower, about 1 pound
2 cups water
½ teaspoon salt, or to taste
3 eggs, separated
⅛ teaspoon achiote
1 tablespoon flour
¼ cup corn oil

1. Cut the cauliflower into 2-inch florets and cook them in the water with the salt for 3 minutes, until soft but still firm. Pour off the water.

2. Beat the whites of the eggs until stiff. Mix together the lightly beaten yolks and the achiote and combine this with the whites. Fold in the flour.

3. Heat the oil in a skillet over moderate heat. Dip 2 or 3 pieces of cauliflower into the egg batter and fry the fritter until brown on both sides. Drain on paper towels briefly. Serve warm.

SERVES 4 TO 6

EJOTES EN IGUAXTE

GREEN BEANS IN SQUASH-SEED SAUCE

COBÁN, GUATEMALA

½ pound whole green snap beans
2 cups water
½ teaspoon salt
1 cup shelled squash seeds
¼ cup chopped tomato
¼ cup chopped onion
2 teaspoons corn oil
1 cup beef broth

1. Cook the whole green beans in the water with the salt until soft, but with a crunch. Drain well and set aside.

2. Toast the squash seeds in a dry skillet over low heat until light brown, about 10 minutes. Grind the seeds into a powder and sift them through a metal sieve.

3. Fry the tomato and onion in the oil in a skillet over moderate heat for 5 minutes. Add the beef broth and the ground squash seeds. Stir well and simmer over low heat for 5 minutes. Add ¼ cup more broth if the sauce becomes too thick.

4. Pour the sauce over the green beans. Serve with meat and poultry dishes.

SERVES 4

EJOTES REVUELTOS CON HUEVO

SCRAMBLED GREEN BEANS

CHIQUIMULA, GUATEMALA

Chiquimula is a charming place of one- or two-story houses painted in a variety of pastel colors. Surrounded by mountains in a fertile but hot valley on the road to El Salvador, it is a center of agricultural activities. Some of the best clay pottery used as cooking utensils in Guatemala is made in the region. Besides the green beans and tomatoes, the market is filled with eggplant, a popular vegetable, which is sliced, salted, dried and dipped into a beaten egg batter, then fried in oil to make the popular fritters. Tomatoes are exemplary and of two varieties, the *ciruela* (plum), the Italian variety, and the *mandarina*, round, flat and scalloped and probably of pre-Hispanic origin.

2 cups ¼-inch diagonal slices of green snap beans
1 cup water, lightly salted
2 tablespoons corn oil
¼ cup chopped onion
¼ cup chopped ripe tomato
5 eggs, beaten
Salt

1. Cook the green beans in the salted water for 3 minutes. Drain well.

2. Heat the oil in a large skillet over moderate heat and fry the onion and tomato for 2 minutes. Add the beans and fry for 2 minutes more.

3. Add the eggs and salt to taste, and scramble everything together until the eggs have set as you like them—moist or firm and dry. Serve warm at any meal of the day.

SERVES 4

EJOTES ENVUELTOS EN HUEVO

GREEN BEAN FRITTERS

COBÁN, GUATEMALA

This recipe is also called *Indie Calzado*, or Indian Shoes, since at one time the beans apparently resembled the leather-thonged sandals of the Indians in the Cobán region. I have always failed to see the resemblance.

2 cups 3-inch pieces of green snap beans
1 cup water
½ teaspoon salt, or to taste
3 tablespoons corn oil
¼ cup chopped onion
½ cup chopped tomato
½ teaspoon freshly ground black peppei
2 eggs, beaten

1. Cook the green beans in water with the salt over moderate heat until soft but still crunchy, about 3 minutes. Drain and reserve ¼ cup liquid.

2. Heat 1 tablespoon oil in a skillet over moderate heat and fry the onion, tomato and black pepper together to prepare a simple sauce, for 2 minutes. Add the reserved bean liquid and simmer slowly for 10 minutes. Set aside.

3. Heat 2 tablespoons of oil in a skillet over moderate heat. Using a large spoon and a fork, dip 5 or 6 beans into the beaten eggs, coating them well. Carefully transfer them to the hot oil and cook them in bundles. Brown lightly on both sides. The egg coating should cook almost immediately and hold the bundles together.

4. Pour the sauce over the fritters, or serve the sauce separately. Serve warm.

SERVES 4

TORTAS DE YUCA

CASSAVA PANCAKES

COSTA RICA

The *tortas* are served for lunch to accompany meat and poultry dishes. They are also served with fish in the coastal areas. Wherever they may be served, these lightly sweetened crisp pancakes are the food of the country.

2 pounds cassava, peeled and grated
½ cup grated mild cheese or farmer cheese
1 teaspoon salt
3 tablespoons sugar
2 tablespoons butter, melted
1 tablespoon flour
1 egg, beaten
¼ cup corn oil

1. Mix everything together except the oil. Heat the oil in a skillet over moderate heat.

2. Prepare pancakes 4 inches in diameter and about ½ inch thick. Brown on both sides. Drain briefly on paper towels. Serve warm.

SERVES 6

ZANAHORIAS RELLENAS

STUFFED CARROTS

HONDURAS

8 large thick carrots, about 1½ inches in diameter at the top
3 cups water
1 teaspoon salt
1 cup farmer cheese
1 tablespoon chopped parsley
1 tablespoon chopped onion
4 tablespoons butter

1. Peel the carrots and trim off a little of the bottom and top. Cook them in the water with the salt over moderate heat until soft but not overdone. Drain well.

2. Scoop out the center core of the carrots for about 3 inches in depth. Process the carrot cores and the farmer cheese into a purée. Stuff the carrots with the purée.

3. Fry the parsley and onion lightly in the butter and spread the mixture in a baking dish large enough to hold the carrots in one layer. Roll them around in the butter. Bake in a 350°F. oven for 15 minutes. Serve warm.

SERVES 4 TO 6

RECADO DE PACAYA

PACAYA FRITTERS IN PINK SAUCE

COBÁN, GUATEMALA

½ cup chopped onion
5 tablespoons corn oil
⅛ teaspoon ground cloves
½ teaspoon ground cinnamon
1 teaspoon freshly ground black pepper
1 cup sliced tomato
¼ teaspoon achiote, dissolved in 1 cup water
2 cups rice flour, mixed into 3 cups cold water
3 pounds pacaya buds, or 2 pounds canned hearts of palm
4 eggs, separated
1 tablespoon flour
1 teaspoon salt

1. Fry the onion in 2 tablespoons oil in a saucepan or large skillet over moderate heat for 2 minutes.

2. Combine into a smooth sauce, in a processor, the cloves, cinnamon, black pepper, tomato and achiote. Add the sauce to the onion. Simmer the mixture over low heat for 5 minutes.

3. Add the rice flour mixture and stir well. Simmer for 15 minutes, stirring frequently. The mixture will thicken considerably.

4. Peel the pacaya buds, cover them with hot water, bring them to a boil, and drain immediately. Do this 3 times to remove the slightly bitter taste that is characteristic of the buds. Set aside.

5. Beat the egg whites until stiff but still moist. Add the beaten yolks and fold them into the whites with the tablespoon of flour and the salt.

6. Heat the other 3 tablespoons oil in a skillet over moderate heat. Dip the pacaya buds into the batter and brown in the oil on both sides for 2 to 3 minutes. Drain briefly on paper towels.

7. Serve the fritters by pouring the warm sauce over all. Or you may prefer to serve the fritter and sauce separately, which is my own inclination.

SERVES 8

Variations: The buds of the pacaya palm are not available in the United States. Canned hearts of palm, well drained, are a good substitute since the flavor, texture and appearance are similar to the pacaya.

Also, slices of raw eggplant, zucchini, cauliflower, lightly cooked, or cabbage leaves, blanched in hot water and drained dry, can be used in the same manner as the *pacaya*. Dip the vegetables into the egg batter, fry in oil, and serve with the pink sauce.

REPOLLO EN RECADO FRITO

SHREDDED CABBAGE IN SAUCE

GUATEMALA CITY

2 pounds shredded cabbage
1 teaspoon salt
2 tablespoons corn oil
2 tablespoons chopped onion
1 garlic clove, chopped
¼ cup chopped tomato
2 tablespoons water
2 tablespoons grated Parmesan-style cheese

1. Sprinkle salt over the cabbage and pour boiling water over it. Let it stand for 5 minutes. Drain well and press out excess liquid.

2. Prepare the sauce: Heat the oil in a skillet over moderate heat. Brown the onion and garlic slightly; add the tomato and water. Simmer and stir for 5 minutes.

3. Add the cabbage and mix well. Fry for 5 minutes more. Serve warm, sprinkled with the grated cheese.

SERVES 6

REMOLACHAS EN CREMA

CREAMED BEETS

HONDURAS

1½ pounds fresh beets, cooked in their skins until soft
3 hard-cooked egg yolks, chopped
1 cup thick cream
1 teaspoon salt
½ teaspoon freshly ground black pepper
1 tablespoon chopped onion

1. Peel the beets and cut into quarters. Add all the other ingredients, mix well, and warm lightly for serving.

SERVES 6

Note: Canned whole beets may be used—a 1-pound can, well drained. Quarter the beets.

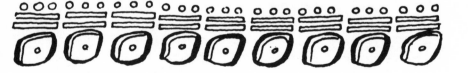

CHILES RELLENOS

STUFFED PEPPERS

GUATEMALA

1 pound boneless pork or beef chuck
4 cups water
½ teaspoon salt, or to taste
1½ cups sliced carrots
1½ cups sliced green snap beans
½ cup green peas, fresh or frozen
2 tablespoons corn oil, plus ¼ cup or more
½ cup chopped onion
½ cup chopped tomato
½ teaspoon thyme
2 bay leaves

3 tablespoons cider or white vinegar
24 small sweet peppers
Flour
4 large eggs, separated

1. Cook the meat in 3 cups water with the salt for 1½ hours, or until soft. Remove the meat and chop it coarse in a food processor.

2. Cook the carrots, green beans and peas together in 1 cup of water for 5 minutes. Drain. Chop the carrots and green beans (the peas remain whole), and add them to the meat.

3. Heat 2 tablespoons oil in a skillet over moderate heat and fry the onion, tomato, thyme and bay leaves for 3 minutes. Add this to the meat and vegetables. Add the vinegar and mix well. Remove and discard the bay leaves.

4. Prepare the sweet peppers by broiling them for 2 or 3 minutes until lightly charred. Wrap them quickly in a towel and let them stand for 30 minutes to soften the skins. Peel the skins as much as possible, open the peppers on one side, and remove the seeds.

5. Stuff the peppers firmly with about 2 tablespoons of the meat stuffing each and sprinkle them on both sides with flour. If the pepper does not completely cover the stuffing it will not matter since the flour and later the egg will seal everything together.

6. Beat the whites of the eggs until stiff and dry. Add the yolks and mix well.

7. Heat the remaining oil in a skillet over medium heat. Very carefully dip the peppers into the egg mixture and brown them in the oil on each side for about 3 minutes. Drain on paper towels.

8. Serve warm or at room temperature with a Chirmol (Simple Tomato Sauce, see Index).

SERVES 8 TO 10

Note: The reason for removing the skin, as recounted to me by a Guatemalan home cook, is because the egg batter will not stick to the glossy skin of the pepper. Removing the skin by charring it, and then steaming in a towel, partially tenderizes the flesh of the peppers as well as preparing the surface for the egg batter.

GUISO DE ELOTE CON CHAYOTE

SAUTÉ OF CORN AND CHAYOTE

COSTA RICA

4 ears of corn
¼ cup chopped onion
3 garlic cloves, crushed
2 tablespoons butter
3 chayotes, peeled, cut into ¼-inch cubes (3 cups)
½ teaspoon salt
1 teaspoon sugar
1 cup milk
1 tablespoon chopped fresh cilantro

1. Scrape the kernels off the cobs to make about 2 cups. Fry the onion and garlic in butter in a skillet over moderate heat for 2 minutes. Add the corn kernels and the chayotes, stir-fry for 1 minute, and cover the skillet. Cook for 5 minutes to soften the vegetables.

2. Add the salt, sugar, milk and cilantro. Simmer this over low heat for about 8 minutes to ensure that the flavors have been combined and the chayote is soft.

3. Serve warm in a bowl, since there will be some sauce. Serve with other dishes, such as meat and poultry.

SERVES 6

Note: One 12-ounce can of corn kernels may be used instead of the fresh corn on the cob.

BERENJENA FRITA

FRIED EGGPLANT

ZACAPA, GUATEMALA

1 pound eggplant, not peeled, cut into ½-inch-thick slices
1 teaspoon salt
3 tablespoons water
¼ cup corn oil

1. Soak the eggplant slices in salt and water in a large shallow dish for 1 hour. Drain well and lightly press out the excess liquid. Dry the slices on a towel.

2. Heat the oil in a skillet over moderate heat and fry the slices in a covered skillet for 5 to 10 minutes, until soft but not mushy. The eggplant has a tendency to soak up oil, therefore it is best to cover the skillet and partially steam the eggplant to cut down on the cooking time. Serve warm.

SERVES 4

BERENJENA GUISADA

EGGPLANT STEW
ANTIGUA, GUATEMALA

2 tablespoons corn oil
¼ cup chopped onion
2 garlic cloves, chopped
½ cup chopped tomato
1 pound eggplant, not peeled, cut into ½-inch cubes
½ teaspoon thyme
2 bay leaves
1 teaspoon vinegar
½ teaspoon salt, or to taste

1. Heat the oil in a skillet over moderate heat and fry the onion, garlic and tomato for 3 minutes.

2. Add the eggplant, thyme, bay leaves, vinegar and salt, and mix well. Cover the skillet and continue to fry, stirring occasionally, for 15 minutes. The eggplant should be cooked but not mushy. Serve warm.

SERVES 4

SOPA DE AJO

GARLIC AND BREAD CASSEROLE

GUATEMALA CITY

This popular and delicious modern dish is reputed to be good for what ails you—a hangover, a stomach problem or the vapors. A cure-all that can stand on its own.

3 garlic cloves, crushed
2 tablespoons corn oil
¼ cup chopped onion
8 slices, 1 inch thick, of 1-day-old French or Italian bread
2 cups beef or chicken broth
Salt

1. Brown the garlic in the oil in a flameproof baking dish. Add the onion and fry lightly over moderate heat for 1 minute. Remove the garlic.
2. Soak the bread in the broth with salt to taste. Add the soaked slices to the oil in the baking dish in a single layer.
3. Bake in a 375°F. oven for 20 minutes to crisp the edges of the bread and evaporate most of the liquid. Serve hot.

SERVES 4

PLÁTANOS

PLANTAINS

GUATEMALA

The fact that there are the four methods, plus variations, of preparing ripe and green plantains, which can be served with any type of Guatemalan, Indian, Indonesian and Mexican foods, is an indication of the versatility of this fruit/vegetable. I have served all four together during a vegetarian dinner without a hint of duplication.

1. Boiled:

1 ripe plantain, with a yellow and black skin
2 cups water
Pinch of salt
2 teaspoons butter

Cut the plantain into 4 equal parts, including the skin. Boil in very lightly salted water over moderate heat for about 10 minutes, or until soft. To serve, peel, discard the skin, and serve as a vegetable, with melted butter.

2. Mashed:

Prepare the plantain as for boiling but mash in a processor with butter and a teaspoon or two of honey.

3. Pan-fried:

1 ripe plantain, with a yellow and black skin
2 tablespoons corn oil

Peel the plantain. Cut it into ½-inch-thick diagonal slices about 3 inches long. Heat the oil in a skillet and over moderate heat fry the slices for several minutes on each side until golden brown. Drain briefly on paper towels.

4. Chips, deep-fried:

1 green plantain
½ cup corn oil

Peel the green plantain by pulling off the firm skin in sections. Cut the plantain horizontally into very thin slices in a processor or with a razor-sharp knife. Heat the oil in a wok or skillet and over moderate heat fry the slices until crisp. Drain them briefly on paper towels and sprinkle them with salt if you desire. Serve them as an appetizer or with meat, poultry or fish dishes.

At country fairs or in the baskets of street vendors in Guatemala, one sees the plantains cut into long thin vertical slices with a hand-held slicer. This is a bit difficult to manage, but it is a traditional method.

TAJALAS VERDES FRITAS

CRISP-FRIED PLANTAIN STRIPS

NICARAGUA

1 green plantain, peeled
½ teaspoon salt
1 cup corn oil for deep-frying

1. Cut the plantain lengthwise into long strips (tongues). Sprinkle them lightly with salt.
2. Heat the oil in a skillet or wok over moderate heat. Drop in 3 or 4 plantain strips at a time. Fry them until golden crisp, remove with a slotted spoon, and drain the strips on paper towels.
3. Serve at room temperature as an appetizer with drinks.

Note: The plantain can also be cut horizontally into thin slices and fried in the hot oil.

Small hand slicers are found in the central markets. They have one blade set diagonally into a firm wood frame. The plantains are sliced on this into long, thin strips. A most popular snack, sold for 10 cents a bag at country fairs and fiestas.

EMPANADAS CON PLÁTANO VERDE

GREEN PLANTAIN TURNOVERS

COSTA RICA

This popular luncheon dish uses plantain and chayote, two of the most available foods found in Costa Rica. You may also prepare small cocktail turnovers by halving the amounts of plantain mash and stuffing in each turnover.

3 green plantains
2 cups water
1 teaspoon salt
2 tablespoons butter or margarine
½ teaspoon freshly ground black pepper
½ cup milk
1 egg, beaten
1 recipe of the Variation of Guiso de Carne (Basic Chopped Beef, see Index)
½ cup corn oil

1. Cut the plantains into 4 pieces including the skin. Cook in the water with ½ teaspoon salt until soft, about 6 minutes. Peel the plantain and mash with the butter, ½ teaspoon salt, the black pepper, milk and egg, and process to a smooth paste.

2. Prepare the turnovers by putting ½ cup of the plantain mixture on a sheet of plastic wrap (originally banana leaves were used) and press it out into a round pancake 6 inches in diameter and ⅜ inch thick. Put 1 heaping tablespoon of the Guiso de Carne variation mixture in the center. Continue until all turnovers are formed.

3. Using the plastic wrap, fold each turnover in half and press it around in a half-moon shape; seal the edges with a little pressure.

4. Heat the oil in a skillet and, over moderate heat, brown the turnovers on both sides for about 5 minutes. Serve warm.

MAKES 6 TURNOVERS

PURÉE

FRIED PLANTAIN MASH

LIVINGSTON, GUATEMALA

Hana is the wood mortar and pestle used by the Caribbean people to pound various vegetables or roots into a purée or dough. *Hana*, the Caribe word, is *mortero* in Spanish. The one in my collection is 11 inches high and 8 inches wide, hand-carved in native hardwood with the center hollowed out to hold about a gallon of contents. The pestle is shaped like a baseball bat and about the same size and is used to pound the plantain into a dough with a strong up-and-down motion. With a food processor, we no longer need depend on the mortar and pestle originally used.

2 half-ripe plantains
3 cups water
½ teaspoon salt
2 tablespoons butter or corn oil

1. Peel the plantains and slice them into thick pieces. Cook them in the water with the salt over moderate heat until they are soft, not mushy, for about 15 minutes. Drain well.

2. Mash the plantain into a thick dough in a processor and shape it into a log or loaf. Refrigerate the loaf for 1 hour. Then cut it into ½-inch-thick slices.

3. Heat the butter or oil in a skillet and brown the slices on both sides over moderate to low heat. Drain on paper towels. Serve warm or at room temperature.

SERVES 4

Note: Half-ripe plantains will have a smooth yellow skin that has not yet started to turn black.

PLÁTANOS CON SALSA

GREEN PLANTAIN WITH SAUCE

LIVINGSTON, GUATEMALA

In Livingston these firm, chewy slices are eaten as one would eat a vegetable, with any meat or fish dish.

¼ cup corn oil
1 large green plantain, peeled and cut into ¼-inch-thick slices
¼ cup chopped onion
½ cup chopped tomato
2 teaspoons cilantro
½ teaspoon salt
¼ teaspoon freshly ground black pepper
1 teaspoon white or cider vinegar
¼ teaspoon chopped fresh hot chile, or dried hot red chile flakes

1. Heat the oil in a skillet and fry the plantain slices over moderate heat until light brown but not crisp. Remove them from the oil.

2. Remove all but 1 teaspoon oil in the skillet and fry the onion for 1 minute. Add the tomato, cilantro, salt, black pepper, vinegar and chile. Simmer the mixture over moderate heat for 3 minutes.

3. Pour the sauce over the plantain slices. Serve warm.

SERVES 4

SOPA CAPIROTADA

LITTLE SOMBREROS
GUATEMALA CITY

This is an old recipe. The name, Little Sombreros, is derived from the slices of eggs that decorate this interesting noodle dish.

½ pound fine noodles (fideos)
1 tablespoon corn oil
2 small onions, cut crisscross one quarter through
2 garlic cloves, peeled
3 small tomatoes, cut crisscross one quarter through
1½ cups chicken broth
1 teaspoon salt, or to taste
1 cup thin-sliced raw potatoes
6 to 8 slices of French bread, toasted dry
3 hard-cooked eggs, sliced
¼ cup farmer cheese, chopped

1. Fry the noodles lightly in oil in a saucepan over moderate heat for 2 minutes. Add the onions, garlic and tomatoes and fry for 2 minutes more.

2. Add the broth and salt. Top this with layers of the potato slices, the toasted bread and slices of egg, and sprinkle the top with the cheese.

3. Simmer covered over very low heat for 20 to 25 minutes, until all the broth has been absorbed and the potatoes are soft. *Do not stir.*

4. Serve warm in the same pan or casserole in which the dish has been cooked in order not to disturb the layers and the appearance.

SERVES 6

TORTITAS DE PAPA

POTATO FRITTERS
GUATEMALA CITY

1 pound small potatoes, about 5
3 cups water
2 egg yolks
½ cup grated Cheddar-type cheese
½ teaspoon salt, or to taste
3 tablespoons corn oil
2 tablespoons flour

1. Cook the potatoes in their skins in the water over moderate heat until they are soft but not overdone. Cool and peel the potatoes.

2. Purée them in a processor. Add the egg yolks, cheese and salt and mix well into a fairly smooth paste.

3. Heat the oil in a skillet over moderate heat. Dust your hands with flour and shape fritters 3 inches in diameter and ½ inch thick. Brown them in the oil on both sides for about 4 minutes. Drain the fritters on paper towels, if you wish. Serve warm.

MAKES ABOUT 10 FRITTERS

PAPAS A LA PASTORA

OLD-STYLE POTATOES

QUEZALTENANGO, GUATEMALA

1 pound potatoes, 4 medium-size, peeled
2 cups water
½ teaspoon salt, or to taste
¼ cup chopped onion
1 cup chopped tomato
½ teaspoon freshly ground black pepper
½ to 1 teaspoon fresh or dry hot chile, to taste
2 tablespoons corn oil
2 tablespoons grated Parmesan-type cheese

1. Cook the potatoes in the water with the salt until soft but still firm. Drain and mash them for country-style potatoes. Do not purée them.

2. Fry the onion, tomato, black pepper and chile in the oil in a skillet over moderate heat for 3 minutes. Add the potatoes and mix well. Fry for 5 minutes more.

3. Serve warm and sprinkle with the cheese.

SERVES 4

PAPAS EN COLORADO CON CAMARONCILLOS

POTATOES AND DRIED SHRIMPS IN RED SAUCE

GUATEMALA

This attractive dish has the flavor of the shrimps combined with garlic, chile and tomato. The bread is the thickening substance, and the potatoes provide bulk that is both filling and tasteful. Dried shrimps are seen in many highland village markets where they are brought by traders from the ocean ports. Yet few of the villagers have ever seen or been near the Pacific or Caribbean, both of which touch Guatemala. Here the shrimps are available in Oriental food stores.

1 pound potatoes, 4 medium-size
½ cup sliced ripe tomato
2 garlic cloves, sliced
1 chile guaque (guajillo), seeded and sliced (optional)
2 tablespoons sliced onion
2 cups water
¼ cup dried shrimps
¼ teaspoon achiote
½ cup French bread, soaked in 2 tablespoons water
1 tablespoon corn oil

1. Cook the potatoes in their skins until soft. Peel them and cut them into ½-inch cubes.
2. Prepare a sauce in the processor with the tomato, garlic, chile, onion, water, dried shrimps, achiote and the soaked bread. Process to a smooth paste.
3. Heat the oil in a skillet over moderate heat and cook the sauce for 5 minutes. Add the potato cubes and continue to simmer over low heat for 10 minutes. The sauce should be a rose color and not overly thick. Serve warm.

SERVES 4

TORTILLA DE BERRO

WATERCRESS OMELET

FINCA PARRAXE, SAMAYAC,
GUATEMALA

4 eggs, well beaten
1 cup coarse-chopped watercress
¼ teaspoon freshly ground black pepper
½ teaspoon salt, or to taste
1 tablespoon fine-chopped onion
1 tablespoon corn oil

1. Mix the eggs, watercress, pepper, salt and onion together.

2. Heat the oil in a skillet over moderate heat. Add the egg mixture and fry until well set, about 2 minutes. Turn the omelet over and brown lightly on the other side.

3. Serve warm for breakfast or lunch.

SERVES 2 GENEROUSLY

TORTITAS DE BERRO

WATERCRESS FRITTERS

QUEZALTENANGO, GUATEMALA

¾ pound watercress
¼ cup water
2 eggs, beaten
½ teaspoon salt, or to taste
2 tablespoons chopped onion
2 tablespoons chopped ripe tomato
2 tablespoons corn oil

1. Cook the watercress in the water in a covered saucepan for 2 minutes. Let the pan stand off the heat for another 2 minutes to wilt the leaves. Cool the watercress and squeeze it dry. Chop fine.

2. Mix the eggs, watercress, salt, onion and tomato together. Heat the oil in a skillet over moderate heat. For each fritter scoop 2 heaping tablespoons of the mixture and drop it into the oil. Brown the fritters lightly on both sides.

MAKES 4 FRITTERS

FIAMBRE

The making of a *Fiambre* is Guatemala's greatest social and culinary event. It is one that anyone can participate in, regardless of social class or economic status. It is anticipated by all with a great deal of enthusiasm. The dictionary defines *Fiambre* as "cold meat salad," which is a gross understatement that in no way defines the formidable kitchen activities, the hours of preparation necessary to process all the steps in presenting what each family claims is *the* authentic *Fiambre*, the BIG salad. It is always served on All Saints' Day.

The genesis of the *Fiambre* has already become a legend, based on an event alleged to have taken place during some past century in the Convent of the Capuchinas in Antigua, the old Spanish Colonial capital of Guatemala. It seems that on All Saints' Day (November 1), according to one version, guests were expected at the Convent to celebrate the Todos Los Santos. However, the cook, who was a nun, found that there was nothing in the larder to prepare the traditional hot meal. So she proceeded to cut up and cook everything available, especially vegetables, eggs and sausage. The resulting salad delighted the guests. This story is repeated with variations but with an air of veracity, so there is no question that some such event actually occurred and has been embellished over the years. (Does this not resemble the invention of American Chinese chop suey?)

As time went on and each family prepared its own personal *Fiambre*, more ingredients were added and the *Fiambre* developed into the grand ritual that it is today. A charming tradition developed in which families would assemble a decorated platter of *Fiambre* and carry it to a neighbor, friend or family member.

Two styles of *Fiambre* are considered traditional; one is with a sweet-and-sour sauce and the other with a sour sauce, essentially a vinaigrette. Both are included here. Smaller versions of each can be prepared by a mathematical reduction of the quantities. However, the *Fiambre* lends itself to a large fiesta and is at its best when the complete performance is produced. Then, of course, it is just as festive the next day.

FIAMBRE

TRADITIONAL SALAD WITH SWEET-AND-SOUR SAUCE

GUATEMALA

It should be borne in mind that this particular *Fiambre* is a production reserved for large groups of people in clubs, family reunions or wherever 50 people or more gather to celebrate All Saints' Day.

Color is king in the salad. Any aesthetic arrangement of the garnishes is acceptable depending upon the innate taste of the person(s) preparing this ritualistic salad.

Vegetables

5 pounds green peas, fresh or frozen
3 pounds green snap beans, cut into 2-inch pieces
2 pounds carrots, cut into 2-inch-long julienne pieces
3 pounds cauliflower, broken into 1-inch florets
20 radishes, sliced
1 pound cooked beets, fresh or canned, sliced
3 pounds cabbage, shredded

Infusion

1 bunch of scallions, sliced
2 cups chopped parsley
1 cup capers
1 cup red chile pimientos
2-inch piece of fresh gingerroot, chopped fine
1 tablespoon olive oil

Poultry and Meats

2 stewing hens, each 5 to 6 pounds, halved
2 frying chickens, each 3 pounds, halved
2 whole onions

4 celery ribs
12 cups water
2 teaspoons salt
3 pounds pickled beef tongue
2 pounds boneless pork
2 pounds boneless beef chuck
1 cup fresh orange juice
1 tablespoon lemon juice
18 longanizas (2 pounds)
18 chorizos
18 butifarras

Sauce

12 cups homemade chicken broth
1 cup liquid from canned asparagus
4 cups cider vinegar
½ cup sugar, or more (for sweet-and-sour flavor)

Garnishes

Lettuce leaves
3 dozen pacaya pods
20 whole radishes
1 pound salami, sliced thin
1 pound mortadella, sliced
1 pound cooked ham, shredded
12 hard-cooked eggs, sliced
1 cup canned red chile pimientos, sliced
4 cans (20 ounces each) asparagus
6 whole sweet green peppers
1 pound farmer cheese, cut into ½-inch cubes
1 pound grated Parmesan-type cheese
1 pound yellow American cheese, shredded

(recipe continues)

1. Prepare the vegetables: Blanch the peas, beans, carrots and cauliflower separately in boiling water for 5 minutes. Drain well. Mix them with the sliced radishes and beets and shredded cabbage.

2. Process the ingredients for the infusion into a smooth paste. Wrap the paste in several layers of cheesecloth and tie it up. Add this bag to the vegetables and refrigerate overnight. Turn the mixture several times so that the flavors of the infusion permeate the vegetables.

3. Cook the hens and the frying chickens with the onions and celery in the water with the salt. Cook covered over moderate heat for 45 minutes.

4. Remove the frying chickens, cover the pan again, and let the hens stand in the hot broth for 30 minutes more. Remove the hens. Skim off and discard as much fat as possible from the broth. (This may be done the previous day. When the broth is chilled, the fat is easily removed and discarded.)

5. Remove and discard the skin and bones from the hens and chickens. Pull off all the meat. Cut the white breast meat into long strips about ½ inch wide, for the garnish. Shred the dark meat to be mixed with the vegetables.

6. Cook the tongue in lightly salted water for about 2 hours, or until tender. Cool and cut into thin slices.

7. Cook the pork in lightly salted water for about 2 hours. Cool the meat and cut into ½-inch cubes.

8. Prepare the beef in the *cesina* manner: Marinate it in the orange juice and lemon juice (in place of the sour Seville orange) in the refrigerator for 2 days. Turn the meat over several times during this process.

9. Discard all the liquid that accumulates. Cook the beef in lightly salted water for about 1 hour, or until tender. Cool the beef and cut it into ½-inch cubes.

10. Cook the *longanizas* and *chorizos* in water for 30 minutes. Cool the sausages and cut into ½-inch-thick slices. The *butifarra* is usually purchased already cooked and is sliced like the other sausages.

11. Mix the sauce ingredients together. Make sure the sugar is dissolved.

12. Prepare all the garnishes.

13. Assemble the salad for serving: Remove the infusion bag from the vegetables. Mix the sauce into the vegetables; add the shredded dark meat of the chickens and hens, the pork cubes, tongue slices, beef cubes and all the sliced sausages.

14. Line the serving platters (use at least 6 large turkey platters) with lettuce leaves. Heap the salad mixture into the platters. Divide the garnishes into 6 equal parts for each platter. Garnish each platter with the white breast meat from the hens and chickens, the pacaya pods, whole radishes, salami and mortadella slices, shredded ham, egg slices, pimiento slices and asparagus. Place 1 whole green pepper on the top of the salad. Scatter the farmer cheese around the surface, followed by the grated and shredded cheeses.

15. Serve the salad at room temperature, with French bread and rolls. Serve 2 platters at a time. As they are emptied or nearly so, replace them with two more, so the table will be continuously attractive.

SERVES 50 OR MORE

Note: Pacaya is the edible flower pod of the pacaya palm tree. A suitable substitute will be the hearts of palm sold in cans and imported from South America.

FIAMBRE

TRADITIONAL SALAD WITH TART SAUCE

GUATEMALA

This recipe is a small-scale *Fiambre* with a tart (*agria*) sauce. Try serving this remarkable salad (is this the largest salad in the world?) at your next family reunion.

Vegetables

1 pound green peas, fresh or frozen
1 pound green snap beans, cut into 2-inch pieces
1 pound carrots, cut into ¼-inch-thick diagonal slices
1 pound cauliflower, broken into 1-inch florets
2 cups white vinegar

Poultry and Meats

1 stewing hen, 5 to 6 pounds, halved
4 cups water
1 teaspoon salt
2 celery ribs
12 butifarra sausages (1½ pounds), cut into 1-inch pieces
24 longanizas and chorizos (3 pounds), cooked and cut into ½-inch-thick slices
4 pounds pickled beef tongue, cooked and sliced thin

Sauce

3 bunches of scallions, chopped fine
4 cups fine-chopped parsley
¼ cup capers, chopped fine
3 cups red or green sweet pepper slices
2 tablespoons fine-chopped fresh gingerroot
1 tablespoon salt, or to taste

1 tablespoon prepared mustard
2 cups homemade chicken broth
¾ cup olive oil
½ cup white vinegar

Garnishes

1 cup pickled onions
1 cup stuffed green olives
Lettuce leaves
6 hard-cooked eggs, sliced
24 radishes, cut into flower shapes
4 cans (4 ounces each) sardines packed in olive oil or in tomato
  sauce
1 cup sliced cooked beets
½ pound farmer cheese, cut into ½-inch cubes
¼ cup grated Parmesan-type cheese
3 or 4 chiles chamberote (see Note)

1. Blanch each vegetable separately in very hot water for 5 minutes. Mix with 2 cups white vinegar 24 hours in advance of the serving time. Cover and refrigerate.

2. Cook the hen in the water with the salt and celery in a covered pan over moderate heat for 45 minutes. Remove from heat and let the pan stand, covered, for 30 minutes more.

3. Remove all the meat from the hen in large pieces. Discard the skin and bones. Cut the white breast meat into 1-inch-wide long strips. Cut the dark meat into 1-inch cubes, or a bit smaller. Reduce the broth to 2 cups by boiling for as long as necessary. Strain and reserve the broth.

4. Make the sauce: In a food processor, grind to a smooth paste the scallions, parsley, capers, sweet peppers, gingerroot, salt and mustard. Add the chicken broth, olive oil and vinegar. Set aside.

5. Mix the blanched vegetables (green peas, green beans, carrots and cauliflower), which have been marinated in vinegar, with the dark

(recipe continues)

meat of chicken, the *butifarra, longaniza* and *chorizo* sausages, and the tongue slices. Include the pickled onions and stuffed olives from the garnishes.

6. Prepare all the rest of the garnishes.

7. Assemble the salad: Always prepare on several platters for several servings. There is a tendency for a salad platter to look as though it had been overturned once it has been disturbed and the garnished surface picked over. As soon as one platter has been finished, replace it with another so the servings are continuously attractive.

Cover a large oblong turkey platter with lettuce leaves so that they protrude slightly over the edge. Heap a goodly amount of the vegetable and meat mixture over the lettuce. Decorate the surface with the strips of white chicken meat, hard-cooked eggs, radishes and sardines. Place the beets around the edge of the platter so the salad mixture is not discolored. Scatter the farmer cheese over the surface, to be followed by the grated cheese.

The sardines may be used to garnish the platters as described, or may be served on a separate platter, a system that often occurs in Guatemala.

A note of caution: do not forget to reserve some of the garnishes for the other platters to be served. Decide in advance how many platters you wish to use (3 or 4) and divide the garnishes accordingly.

Place a *chile chamberote*, if used, in the center of each platter. It is not usually eaten but is, of course, edible.

Serve the *Fiambre* with French bread and rolls.

SERVES 30

Note: *Chile chamberote* is a red and yellow chile, of rather squat appearance, available only during the weeks of the *Fiambre*. Since I do not know of its existence outside of Guatemala, you may substitute sweet red peppers as a decorative garnish.

The sausages called for (*butifarras, longanizas* and *chorizos*) may be available in Spanish groceries, but recipes are included in this book (see Index). A probable substitute can be sweet and hot Italian sausages; cook in the standard method, drain on paper towels, then mix with the salad.

GUACAMOLE

AVOCADO SALAD
GUATEMALA

½ teaspoon orégano
2 ripe avocados
1 hard-cooked egg, peeled
2 tablespoons chopped onion
2 tablespoons lemon or lime juice, or 1 tablespoon of each
Salt

1. Toast the orégano in a dry skillet over low heat for about ½ minute, or until the aroma is released. Shake the pan vigorously.

2. Scoop out the avocado flesh and mash it with a fork but not so well as to eliminate all texture. Mash the egg with a fork and add it to the avocado with the onion, lemon juice and orégano. Add a little salt. Mix well, but do not whip the salad since this would eliminate any texture.

3. Chill the salad and serve with fresh tortillas or tortilla crisps as an appetizer or as a salad with a lunch or dinner menu.

SERVES 4

Note: The avocados of Guatemala *(Persea americana)* are cheap, about 10 cents each, and full of the most desirable nutty flavor. They are sold everywhere and come from privately owned trees or small orchards. Hybrid varieties are also sold, but the botanical manipulation has improved the appearance with a loss of the natural flavor. Sad to relate, for so valuable a vegetable fruit whose botanical origin was the valleys of Mexico and Guatemala.

GUACAMOLE

AVOCADO SALAD
EL SALVADOR

2 ripe avocados, mashed
1 hard-cooked egg, mashed
½ cup grated mild cheese or farmer cheese
1 tablespoon thick cream (optional)
1 tablespoon chopped onion
⅛ teaspoon freshly ground black pepper
Lettuce leaves
1 hard-cooked egg, sliced

1. Mash the avocado as fine as you wish, either as a purée or a bit coarser. Add the mashed egg, grated cheese, cream if used, onion and pepper. Mix well.

2. Serve cold on lettuce leaves topped with slices of hard-cooked egg.

SERVES 4

Note: Serve the guacamole as an appetizer with crisp fried *tostados* or toast. It can also be served as a proper salad.
    This is a popular menu in El Salvador:

> **Guacamole**
> **Gallo en Chicha (Capon in Fruit Wine)**
> **White rice served with slices of hard-cooked egg**
> **Buñuelos en Miel (Fried Dumplings in Honey)**
> **French bread**

GUACAMOLE

AVOCADO SALAD

HONDURAS

3 large ripe avocados
3 tablespoons chopped onion
¼ teaspoon orégano
½ teaspoon salt
¼ teaspoon pepper
3 hard-cooked eggs, chopped
¼ cup farmer cheese, mashed
3 or 4 tablespoons lime or lemon juice

1. Scoop out the avocado pulp and mash it to a coarse texture. Add all the other ingredients and mix well.

2. Serve with *tostados* or fresh hot tortillas.

SERVES 6

Note: I suggest that guacamole be prepared just before serving. Avocados have a tendency to turn black when exposed to air for any length of time. Preparing and serving quickly avoids this.

306 FALSE TONGUES AND SUNDAY BREAD

PILOYES

RED KIDNEY BEAN SALAD
ANTIGUA, GUATEMALA

1 pound dried red kidney beans
4 cups water
6 bay leaves
1 teaspoon thyme
1 teaspoon salt, or to taste
⅔ cup white or cider vinegar
½ cup chicken broth
1 cup ½-inch cubes of cooked chicken
⅓ cup fine-chopped parsley
⅓ cup ½-inch cubes of ripe tomato
¼ cup thin-sliced or cubed onion
⅓ cup cubed sweet green or red pepper
4 longanizas (optional), sliced thin, cooked in 1 cup water,
    drained (see Note)
2 tablespoons olive oil
⅓ cup Parmesan-type grated cheese

1. Soak the beans in the water overnight.

2. Cook beans over moderate heat with the bay leaves, thyme and salt until they are soft but still retain their shape, about 1 hour. Pour off and reserve 1 cup of the bean liquid.

3. Add to the beans ⅓ cup vinegar and sufficient cold water to cover them. Refrigerate for 4 to 6 hours so the beans can absorb the acid flavor.

4. Drain the beans well and return them to the cup of reserved bean liquid. Add the chicken broth, chicken cubes, parsley, tomato, onion, sweet pepper, and sliced sausage if used.

5. Add the olive oil, the other ⅓ cup vinegar and a very small amount of salt to taste. Stir well and refrigerate for several hours before serving.

6. Serve sprinkled with the grated cheese.

SERVES 8

Note: *Longanizas* are mild Spanish sausages, usually available in Mexican or Puerto Rican markets; also see Index for recipe.

ENSALADA DE REMOLACHAS

BEET SALAD

CHIQUIMULILLA, GUATEMALA

The fresh beets in Guatemala are highly flavorful, sweet and of a bright maroon color. They are incomparable and are one of the most popular vegetables in the country.

3 cups (1½ pounds) sliced cooked beets
¼ cup beet liquid reserved after cooking
½ teaspoon salt, or to taste
3 tablespoons lemon or lime juice
2 tablespoons olive oil
1 small onion, sliced in the round

1. Mix everything together. Serve at room temperature, or refrigerate for 1 hour before serving.

SERVES 6

Variation: Occasionally, the salad dressing is made with the juice of the *naranja agria,* the sour oranges that become available during February/March. The juice is used in place of the lemon or lime. The contrast of the acid orange with the beets is unusually good. Perhaps one of our supermarket oranges, should you chance on a sour one, might be an acceptable substitute, or see chapter on ingredients for a substitute.

ENSALADA PALITOS DE ZANAHORIA Y RÁBANO

CARROT AND RADISH SALAD

GUATEMALA CITY

1 cup julienne strips of raw carrot
1 cup julienne strips of radishes
½ cup thin-sliced onion
2 tablespoons olive oil
¼ cup lemon juice
½ teaspoon salt

1. Mix all the ingredients together. Refrigerate for several hours.

SERVES 4

ENSALADA DE NARANJA

SLICED ORANGE SALAD

COBÁN, GUATEMALA

This is an unusually tasty salad of contrasting flavors. The street vendors of Cobán sell this combination of orange slices sprinkled with salt, chile and *pepitoria* in the public square.

3 large oranges
2 tablespoons squash seeds (pepitoria)
Ground dried hot red chile flakes
Salt

1. Peel the oranges with a serrated blade, removing all the skins and fibers. Cut the oranges in the round to make slices about ¼ inch thick. Refrigerate.

2. Toast the squash seeds in a dry skillet over moderate heat until light brown and crisp. Grind them to a powder in a food processor.

3. Serve by sprinkling the orange slices with as much of the ground squash seeds, chile flakes and salt as you wish.

SERVES 4

PICO DE GALLO

ROOSTER'S BEAK—A FRUIT SALAD
COBÁN, GUATEMALA

Although I learned this recipe in Cobán, it is more likely to have been invented in Guatemala City, much closer to the cocktail circuit. In any event it is a most popular but unconventionally flavored salad, usually served as an appetizer prior to dining. The *pico* is also renowned for its ability to stabilize a hangover.

2 cups orange sections
½ cup diced sweet red pepper
1 tablespoon chopped onion
1 tablespoon chopped parsley
½ teaspoon chopped fresh hot chile, or ½ teaspoon hot red chile
  flakes
1 teaspoon sugar
½ teaspoon salt, or to taste

1. Peel the oranges with a serrated blade, removing all the skins and fibers. Cut the orange sections into ½-inch pieces.

2. Mix all the ingredients together and chill for 1 hour before serving.

SERVES 4

CHOJIN

GRATED RADISH AND PORK-RIND SALAD

GUATEMALA CITY

Chojin is one of the most popular salads in Guatemala. One sees it for sale in markets, particularly around the towns near Guatemala City. The combination of radishes and *chicharrones* is an unusual and inventive mixture of textures and seasonings.

2 cups chicharrones (fried pork rinds)
1½ cups fine-grated radish
¼ cup chopped ripe tomato
2 tablespoons chopped onion
1 tablespoon chopped mint
3 tablespoons lemon juice
½ teaspoon salt, or to taste

1. Fry the *chicharrones* in a dry skillet over low heat for 5 to 10 minutes to remove excess fat. Drain on paper towels. Chop fine.

2. Mix all the ingredients together. Serve at room temperature, as a salad, or as an appetizer with fresh tortillas or tortilla crisps.

SERVES 4 TO 6

CHIRMOL DE TOMATE

TOMATO AND ONION SALAD
FINCA PARRAXE, SAMAYAC, GUATEMALA

2 medium-size tomatoes, about ½ pound
1 large onion
4 garlic cloves, peeled, whole
3 hot green chiles, cut open and seeds removed
½ teaspoon salt, or to taste
½ cup white or cider vinegar
¼ cup water

1. Cut the tomatoes into ½-inch cubes after removing seeds and liquid.

2. Cut the onion into coarse cubes.

3. Mix all the ingredients together and let the mixture stand in the refrigerator for 1 day before serving.

4. Serve with any type of food as a small salad or condiment.

SERVES 4

Note: The green chiles and garlic are included to provide flavor and sting. The courageous will also eat them, but it may be safer to remove them before serving.

IGUASHTE

VEGETABLE SALAD IN SQUASH-SEED SAUCE

ANTIGUA, GUATEMALA

This is a pure, natural Mayan dish without oil or vinegar. The recipe is from the Spanish Colonial era in Antigua and was taught to me by a family member of that town.

1 cup shelled squash seeds
1 cup tomatillos (mil tomates)
1 garlic clove
4 medium-size potatoes (1 pound), peeled and cut into ½-inch cubes
3 cups water
1 teaspoon salt, or to taste
3 cups diagonal 1-inch pieces of green snap beans

1. Toast the squash seeds in a dry skillet over moderate to low heat for about 10 minutes, or until light brown.

2. Toast the tomatillos and garlic in a dry skillet over moderate to low heat for about 10 minutes, until the skins are slightly charred.

3. Cook the potatoes in the water with the salt until they are soft but still retain their shape. Drain well and reserve the liquid.

4. Cook the green beans in the salted water over moderate heat until soft, about 5 minutes. Drain well and reserve the liquid.

5. Prepare a smooth sauce in a processor by first putting in the squash seeds, then the tomatillos, garlic and 2 cups reserved cooking liquid. Strain the sauce through a metal sieve and discard the rough bits.

6. Toss the sauce with the potatoes and green beans. Refrigerate for 1 hour or more before serving.

SERVES 6

Variation: Other vegetables such as green peas, chayote (*huisquil*) and cauliflower can be used in place of the green beans. The potato should always be used with one or two other vegetables.

VIGORON

YUCA SNACK
COSTA RICA

Vigoron is one of those Costa Rican and Nicaraguan preparations that falls between being a salad of importance and an appetizer to serve with drinks. Since all of the ingredients can be readied in advance and refrigerated, it is the simplest of tasks to put them together on short notice.

2 cups sliced cassava, about 1 pound
2 cups water
½ teaspoon salt
2 cups chopped cabbage
½ cup chopped ripe tomato
2 tablespoons lemon or lime juice
1 tablespoon chopped fresh hot green or red chile
2 cups chicharrones (fried pork rinds), broken into ½-inch pieces

1. Boil the cassava in the water with the salt until soft, about 15 minutes. Drain well.

2. Mix the cabbage, tomato and lemon juice together. Add as much hot chile as you can tolerate.

3. Serve on individual salad plates or in a large serving bowl in this order: Put the cassava on the bottom of the plate, cover with the cabbage salad, and sprinkle generously with *chicharrones.*

SERVES 4

CHILE CON REPOLLO

HOT CHILE AND CABBAGE— A CONDIMENT

TAXISCO, GUATEMALA

2 cups fine-shredded cabbage
½ cup white vinegar
¼ cup thin-sliced onion
1 teaspoon salt
1 tablespoon thin slices of fresh hot chile, green or red
1 teaspoon sugar (optional)

1. Mix everything together and refrigerate for 24 hours before serving.

2. This is not a salad, but a condiment. It is served with any sort of entrée and eaten in small quantities. It can be described as a sort of fresh Indian chutney transported to a different continent.

SERVES 4

Variation: In Nicaragua there is a similar dish—a Cabbage Salad (Ensalada de Repollo) that substitutes ¼ cup chopped tomatoes for the fresh chile, and uses about half the amount of vinegar. This makes a drier dish—in other words, a salad rather than a pickle, but with the same combination of flavors.

ENCURTIDOS

PICKLED VEGETABLES

FINCA PARRAXE, SAMAYAC, GUATEMALA

1½ cups sliced green snap beans, cut diagonally into ½-inch slices
1½ cups cauliflower florets
1½ cups green peas, fresh or frozen
1½ cups shredded cabbage
1½ cups 2-inch-long julienne slices of carrots
1½ cups 2-inch-long julienne slices of cooked beets
½ cup small pickled onions, whole
6 hot green chiles, whole, uncooked
3 cups cider or white vinegar, diluted with ½ cup water
1 teaspoon salt

1. Cook the green beans and cauliflower separately in lightly salted boiling water for 3 minutes. Drain well. Cook the peas, shredded cabbage and carrots separately in lightly salted boiling water for 2 minutes. Drain. (Canned beets may be used.)

2. Mix all the vegetables, including the pickled onions and whole chiles, with the diluted vinegar and 1 teaspoon salt. Let the mixture stand covered and refrigerated for 1 day before using. Using all the vegetables will make the pickle more interesting; however, good results are obtained if a minimum of any four are used.

MAKES ABOUT 10 CUPS

Variations: *To Serve as a Salad:* Mix ¾ cup of the pickled vegetables with 1 teaspoon olive oil, ¼ teaspoon orégano and ¼ teaspoon sugar. Mix this combination well and serve as a salad for 1 person.

To Serve as a Sandwich: Guatemalans make a good sandwich of the pickles with the fresh French bread found in so many small village and city bakeries there.

ESCABECHE

COOKED PICKLED SALAD

EL SALVADOR

The *escabeche* is a popular and useful condiment *cum* salad, which can be served with all meat and vegetable dishes.

½ cup corn oil
2 garlic cloves
½ cup sliced sweet red pepper
5 cups sliced onions
2 bay leaves
½-inch cube chile pasa (pasilla)
½-inch cube chile guaque (guajilla)
3 whole cloves
12 peppercorns
1½ teaspoons salt
1 teaspoon sugar
½ cup cider vinegar
¼ teaspoon thyme
¼ teaspoon orégano

1. Heat the oil over moderate heat in a large pan. Char the garlic cloves for 2 minutes. Remove and discard them.

2. Add all at once the sweet pepper, onions, bay leaves, chiles, cloves, peppercorns, salt and sugar. Fry for 3 minutes, or until onions become translucent.

3. Add the vinegar, cover the pan, and steam the contents for 3 minutes. Add the thyme and orégano, stir well, and remove from the heat.

4. Turn out the salad into a container, cool it, and refrigerate for 24 hours before serving.

MAKES ABOUT 4 CUPS

CURTIDO

PICKLED HOT SALAD—
A CONDIMENT

LIVINGSTON, GUATEMALA

This is a lightly pungent condiment, eaten with any of the Livingston dishes. The chile peppers in Livingston are most likely to be the *diente de perro* or dog's tooth peppers, so-called because these 1-inch-long, slender, brilliantly red peppers can inflict a ferocious bite on anyone who has the temerity to eat them.

1 cup thin-sliced onion
½ cup thin-sliced carrot
6 fresh red small hot chile peppers, whole
½ teaspoon salt
½ cup white vinegar
¼ cup water

1. Mix everything together. Refrigerate for 2 days before serving.

MAKES ABOUT 2 CUPS

ENCURTIDOS DE CEBOLLA

PICKLED ONIONS

FINCA PARRAXE, SAMAYAC, GUATEMALA

These pickled onions are a permanent fixture in my refrigerator. Easy to prepare and useful to have around for serving with all Guatemalan foods and anything else.

1 cup small pickling onions, peeled
½ cup white or cider vinegar
½ cup water
¼ teaspoon freshly ground black pepper
¼ teaspoon salt
¼ teaspoon thyme
2 whole cloves
1 bay leaf

1. Make a ¼-inch-deep crisscross in the stem end of each onion.

2. Cook everything together in a covered saucepan over moderate to low heat for 5 minutes.

3. Cool the mixture and refrigerate in a tightly covered jar for 24 hours before serving.

MAKES 1 CUP

VERDURAS EN ESCABECHE

PICKLED VEGETABLES
GUATEMALA CITY

This *escabeche* is a spicy, hot pickle, eaten with meat and fish dishes. The carrots can also be cut into 2-inch-long julienne sticks, a matter of appearance.

5 jalapeño chiles, each about 2 inches long (see Note)
1 tablespoon corn oil
2 cups diagonal ⅛-inch-thick slices of carrots
1 pound cauliflower, cut into 1-inch florets
1 cup sliced onion
5 garlic cloves
1 teaspoon thyme
1 teaspoon orégano
4 bay leaves
1 teaspoon salt
1 teaspoon sugar
1 cup white or cider vinegar

1. Fry the chile peppers in the oil for 2 minutes to soften the skins. Remove the chiles, slice them open vertically, and remove seeds and fibers. Set aside.

2. Blanch the carrots, cauliflower, onion and garlic separately in boiling water for 2 minutes. Drain well and mix them all together. Put them into a glass jar or stone crock.

3. Mix the thyme, orégano, bay leaves, salt and sugar in the vinegar. Pour this over the vegetables and mix well. Allow the *escabeche* to marinate for 1 day or more before using. The pickle can be refrigerated or stored at room temperature in a cool place.

MAKES ABOUT 5 CUPS

Note: Jalapeño chiles are available canned in any store that carries Spanish or Mexican foods.

SALSA PICANTE

HOT SAUCE

HUEHUETENANGO, GUATEMALA

1 cup sliced ripe tomato
1 garlic clove, sliced
½ teaspoon salt, or to taste
1 to 2 teaspoons sliced fresh hot green or red chile
1 cup water
2 tablespoons fine-chopped onion
2 teaspoons corn oil

1. In a covered pan over moderate heat cook the tomatoes, garlic, salt, chile and water for 10 minutes. Process this to a smooth sauce.

2. Fry the onion in the oil over low heat until onion changes color, about 3 minutes. Add the tomato sauce and simmer slowly until the sauce is quite thick but fluid.

3. Serve chilled or at room temperature with any type of Guatemalan food. Very often added to soups to give a brighter tang.

MAKES ABOUT 1¼ CUPS

CHIRMOL FRITO

FRIED SAUCE

PANAJACHEL, GUATEMALA

1 small whole onion
2 small ripe tomatoes, whole
3 garlic cloves, peeled, whole
1 teaspoon dried red chile flakes

½ teaspoon orégano
½ teaspoon salt
1 tablespoon corn oil

1. Toast the onion, tomatoes and garlic in a dry skillet over low heat for 10 minutes, or until lightly charred. Add the chile flakes and orégano and toast them for 2 minutes more.
2. Remove onion, tomatoes and garlic from the skillet and chop them coarse. Return them to the pan with the salt and corn oil.
3. Stir-fry the mixture over moderate heat for 5 minutes until everything is cooked and the flavors blended.
4. Cool and serve with fish or any kind of meat dish. The sauce also makes very tasty tortilla sandwiches for an appetizer with drinks.

MAKES ABOUT 1 CUP

CHIRMOL DE ZAPATERO

SHOEMAKER OR POOR MAN'S SAUCE

GUATEMALA CITY

2 cups tomatillos (mil tomates)
1 small ripe tomato
2 garlic cloves, peeled
½ teaspoon salt, or to taste

1. Toast the tomatillos, tomato and garlic in a dry skillet over moderate heat until lightly charred, about 10 minutes.
2. Process all the ingredients into a smooth sauce. Traditionally served with pork dishes.

MAKES ABOUT 1½ CUPS

CHIRMOL

SIMPLE TOMATO SAUCE

GUATEMALA

2 cups chopped peeled ripe tomatoes
¼ cup water
¼ cup chopped onion
½ teaspoon salt, or to taste

1. Simmer everything together over moderate to low heat in a covered saucepan for 10 minutes.
2. Process the mixture into a smooth sauce and press through a metal sieve. Discard the skins and seeds.
2. Serve warm with chiles. Often served with Chiles Rellenos (see Index).

MAKES ABOUT 2 CUPS

SALSA

MIXED SAUCE

EL SALVADOR

2 cups chopped ripe tomatoes
1 tablespoon chopped mint
¼ cup chopped onion
½ teaspoon salt
¼ cup sour orange juice

1. Mix everything together. Chill and serve with poultry and meat dishes.

MAKES ABOUT 2¼ CUPS

DESSERTS, SWEETS AND DRINKS

Guatemalans have a great fondness for sweets. After the introduction of sugarcane into the country in the early Colonial era, there was an explosion of sweet dishes in several forms—sweet breads, desserts using eggs and sugar, milk fudges and combinations using coconuts, fruits and even vegetables (pumpkins), richly laced with both white sugar and the brown village sugar known as *panela*. Many of these concoctions can be attributed to the Spanish nostalgia for their own desserts. Then again, almost everything available in Europe and Asia was ultimately available in Guatemala, plus the local produce whose botanical origin was Central America.

The desserts, sweet breads and sweetmeats are not in the twentieth-century tradition of France and Italy or the Austro-Hungarian chocolates, creams, soufflés and the like. They are more down to earth. Their richness lies in their intense sweetness.

Many sweets required time-consuming simmering and stirring, steps that the Colonial ladies left to the kitchen servants. We are fortunate now in being able to reduce this time by the use of food processors and gas and electric stoves, without any loss of the traditional taste.

A dessert such as Plátanos en Mole (Plantain in Chocolate Sauce, see Index), is probably of pre-Hispanic inspiration. Desserts using the European type of chocolate are in very short supply even though this is a country that has grown the cacao tree for centuries.

"Desserts New and Old" should be the title of this chapter, considering the fact that in Antigua, the old capital of Guatemala, there was a confectioners' guild in 1613. Today, the tradition still continues.

Guatemala is an important coffee-growing country with *fincas* (plantations) located near the Pacific Coast and in the highlands. Ideal growing conditions produce coffee beans of a fine quality with a highly desirable flavor.

I have been in Indian villages where the people have a few coffee trees in their backyards for their own use. Their coffee is grown, toasted and ground within a few feet of the kitchen.

BORRACHO

DRUNKARD

GUATEMALA
CITY

The *borracho* is a classic dish of the more sophisticated people of Guatemala. It is not, to my knowledge, prepared by the Indian population. It is delicious and festive. It seems more than likely that the dish has its origins in the time when English immigrants came to Guatemala in the middle of the nineteenth century to consolidate their sugarcane and coffee holdings. They brought their beloved English trifle, which this single-layer *borracho* closely resembles.

3 tablespoons flour
1 teaspoon baking powder
9 egg yolks
3 whole eggs
3 tablespoons sugar

Miel (Rum Honey)

1 cup sugar
1½ cups water
1 cinnamon stick, 2 inches
2 whole cloves
2 teaspoons grated lemon rind
1 whole allspice
¼ cup rum

1. Sift the flour and baking powder together.

2. Beat the egg yolks until they change color. Add the whole eggs, one at a time, beating well after each addition. Add the sugar and continue to beat until well mixed. Then fold in the flour and baking powder mixture.

(recipe continues)

3. Pour the mixture into a buttered and floured 9-inch-square heat-proof glass dish or 9-inch tube cake pan. Bake the tube pan in a preheated 350°F. oven for 40 minutes, or the square baking dish in a 325°F. oven for 35 to 40 minutes.

4. Bring all the ingredients for the rum honey except the rum to a boil and remove the saucepan from heat. Add the rum, stir, and set aside.

5. When the cake is removed from the oven, cool it for 5 minutes. Then, first removing the cinnamon, cloves and allspice, pour half of the rum honey over the cake. Wait for 30 minutes and pour over the other half of the honey.

6. Refrigerate for 24 hours before serving in the baking dish. If a tube pan was used, the cake must be removed from the pan before soaking it with the syrup.

MAKES 1 CAKE

Variation: Prepare a *crème anglaise* and top the *borracho* with the custard after all the rum honey has soaked into the cake. Chill well before serving.

BORRACHITOS

LITTLE DRUNKARDS

GUATEMALA CITY

These are true cupcakes rather than the soufflé-like mixture of the previous Borracho.

1 whole egg
3 egg yolks
1 tablespoon plus 1 cup sugar
½ cup flour
½ teaspoon baking powder
Pinch of salt
½ cup water
2 tablespoons rum

1. Beat the whole egg and egg yolks until creamy. Add 1 tablespoon sugar and continue to beat until the mixture is thick.

2. Add the flour, baking powder and salt all at once and beat for 1 minute, until the flour is completely absorbed.

3. Grease and flour a cupcake pan. Fill the depressions half full of batter. Bake at 350°F. for 20 minutes. Remove the cakes from the pan and cool them.

4. The next day prepare the syrup (*miel*); combine 1 cup sugar, the water and rum. Bring the mixture to a boil and simmer over low heat for 10 minutes. Cool.

5. Poke several holes in the top of each cake with a toothpick, and soak the cakes with several tablespoons of the syrup.

MAKES 6 CUPCAKES

QUESO DE ALMENDRAS

ALMOND CHEESE

EL SALVADOR

The *dulces* (sweets) recipes of El Salvador have been jealously guarded by the *dulceras* (sweet makers). It is a profession that has not changed in a century, neither the *dulceras* nor the recipes. What they were, they are now—a little difficult. The candies are called "cheese" since they are shaped like round cheeses.

10 egg yolks
3 cups water
12 ounces almonds, blanched and skins removed
6 cups sugar
1 or 2 tablespoons hot water (optional)
1 or 2 tablespoons milk
Ground cinnamon

1. Beat the egg yolks well with 1 cup water.

2. Grind the almonds with the other 2 cups water in a blender until smooth.

3. Turn the yolk and almond mixtures into a saucepan, and add the sugar. Simmer and stir the mixture over moderate to low heat, stirring constantly in one direction with a wooden spoon. When the paste comes away from the side and bottom of the pan, after about 40 minutes, it is done. To test, roll a bit of the mixture between your fingers to see that it pulverizes.

4. Remove mixture from heat and beat with a wooden spoon until it has cooled, about 5 minutes. If it's too firm, add 1 tablespoon hot water or more, but the mixture should not become sticky.

5. When the mixture is completely cool, knead it as though it were dough, adding the milk, a few drops at a time, to make the dough paste manageable.

6. Prepare round "cheeses," 1½ inches in diameter and ¼ inch thick. Dip them all around in cinnamon and wrap each one in wax paper.

MAKES ABOUT 40 "CHEESES"

QUESITOS DE ZANAHORIA

LITTLE CARROT CHEESES

EL SALVADOR

¾ cup squash seeds
2 cups water
1 pound carrots, grated (4 full cups)
2½ cups milk
4 egg yolks
1 cinnamon stick, 4 inches
4 cups sugar
1 tablespoon milk for moistening
¼ teaspoon almond extract
Ground cinnamon

1. Soak the squash seeds in the water for 1 hour. Drain well.

2. In 2 portions, process the carrots, squash seeds and milk together in a blender until smooth. Add the egg yolks during the blending.

3. Turn the mixture into a large saucepan with the cinnamon stick and add the sugar. Simmer over low heat, stirring frequently, for about 1 hour, or until the paste comes away from the sides and bottom of the pan. Remove the cinnamon stick.

4. Remove the pan from the heat and beat the mixture with a wooden spoon for 2 minutes. The cool paste should pulverize when rubbed between the fingers.

5. Knead half of the mixture with a few drops of milk as though it were bread dough. At this time add a few drops of almond extract. Knead the other half in the same way.

6. Shape round cakes (cheeses) 1½ inches in diameter and ¼ inch thick. Dip both sides in ground cinnamon and rub it around the edges. Wrap each one in wax paper. The cheeses taste better the second day when the flavors have matured.

MAKES ABOUT 40 "LITTLE CHEESES"

TURRÓN

EGG WHITE CREAM
EL SALVADOR

2 cups sugar
1 cup honey
1 cup water
4 large egg whites
Grated lemon rind
Ground cinnamon
Chopped toasted almonds
Chopped toasted cashews

1. Bring to a boil over moderate to low heat the sugar, honey and water; simmer for about 20 minutes. Skim off the thick foam that may accumulate.

2. To test when the syrup is ready, put a drop in a dish of cold water. If the syrup makes a firm ball, or reaches 242° to 252°F. on a candy thermometer, the syrup is ready to be used. Or drop a syrup ball onto a plate; if you hear the "clink," then the syrup is ready (this method of testing is more folklore than science).

3. Beat the egg whites with an electric beater until very stiff. Pour the hot syrup into the whites in a slow, steady stream, beating continuously. Beat for 2 minutes more after all the syrup has been added. The *turrón* will rise into firm creamy peaks.

4. Serve as a dessert, sprinkled with as much as you wish of the lemon rind and cinnamon. My own preference is lemon rind and cinnamon alone, but you may wish to add these and chopped nuts.

5. The *turrón* may also be served in a modern way with ice cream. Put the *turrón* underneath a generous scoop. Or serve fresh fruits such as mango and strawberries over the *turrón*.

SERVES 8

MARQUESOTE

SPONGE CAKE

EL SALVADOR

Marquesote is a basic sponge cake that can be used with various other desserts such as ice cream, rum-soaked fruits, or Turrón (Egg White Cream, see Index).

8 eggs, separated
½ teaspoon lemon juice
1 cup sugar
2 cups flour, sifted with 1 teaspoon ground cinnamon
Butter for pan

1. Beat the egg whites until stiff. Add the yolks one by one and continue beating. Add the lemon juice.

2. Beat in the sugar, then fold in the flour and cinnamon. Mix well.

3. Turn out the mixture into 2 buttered cake pans, 1 inch deep and 7 × 10 inches in size. Fill the pans only halfway to allow for rising.

4. Bake in a 350°F. oven for 25 to 30 minutes. Cool.

MAKES 2 CAKES

Variation: This variation makes a smaller cake and uses a distinctive and typical flavoring—aniseed.

2 eggs, separated
¾ cup sugar
¾ cup flour sifted together with ½ teaspoon baking powder
⅛ teaspoon ground aniseed
Butter for pan

1. Beat the yolks until creamy and add the sugar little by little. Fold in the flour and baking powder and the aniseed.

2. Beat the egg whites until stiff and fold them into the mixture.

3. Turn the mixture into a buttered pan and bake in a 350°F. oven for 30 minutes.

LA SEMITA—PASTEL DE PIÑA

PINEAPPLE TORTE

EL SALVADOR

3 cups whole-wheat flour
2 cups all-purpose flour
4 teaspoons baking powder
2 cups light brown sugar
2 cups vegetable shortening
2 tablespoons cold water
1 large egg
1½ cups Pineapple Jam (recipe follows)
¼ cup dark brown sugar
White Flour Pastry (recipe follows)
2 teaspoons white sugar

1. Cut 2 rectangles of wax paper each 1 inch larger than a jelly-roll pan, 10 × 15 inches. Coat the jelly-roll pan with vegetable shortening. Press a rectangle of wax paper firmly to the bottom, with the extra inch folded over the rim of the pan. Coat the paper lightly with shortening.

2. Sift the flours and baking powder together. Add the 2 cups light brown sugar and mix well. Cut the 2 cups shortening into the flour mixture; this may be done in a processor.

3. Beat the water and egg together. Add the mixture to the pastry and mix well. Knead the pastry for 2 minutes as though it were bread dough. The mixture will be damp.

4. Divide the pastry into halves. Remove about ½ cup of the pastry from one half and add it to the other half. Put the smaller half into the center of the jelly-roll pan and press it out to the edges. Dust your fingers well with flour during this procedure. The flattened pastry should be about ¼ inch thick. Poke the pastry 10 times overall with a fork.

5. Spread the jam over the pastry to within 1 inch of the edges. Sprinkle with ¼ cup dark brown sugar.

6. Press out the balance of the pastry onto the second sheet of wax paper right to the edge. Ease it carefully onto the first layer on top of the jam, and press it down around the edges with the tines of a fork dipped into flour. Poke the top all over with a fork.

7. Decorate the top of the torte with strips of the white flour pastry, placing them diagonally in both directions over the torte 2 inches apart. Sprinkle 2 teaspoons white sugar over all.

8. Bake in a preheated 350°F. oven for 55 minutes to 1 hour. Cool well before cutting the torte into 2- to 3-inch-square pieces.

Jalea de Piña (Pineapple Jam)

2 cups fresh ripe pineapple and juice
½ cup sugar

1. Simmer together over moderate to low heat for about 15 minutes, until the jam thickens. Cool before using.

Note: A 20-ounce can of crushed pineapple can be used instead of the fresh pineapple. Use the same amount of sugar and simmer together until thick, for 15 or more minutes over moderate to low heat.

White Flour Pastry for Decorative Strips

6 tablespoons vegetable shortening
⅔ cup all-purpose flour
1 to 2 tablespoons ice water

1. Cut the shortening into the flour. Sprinkle with just enough water to form a firm dough.

2. Roll out the dough into a thin sheet and cut it into strips. Roll out the strips to round, thin pencils ¼ inch in diameter. Use to decorate the Semita.

MAKES 1 LARGE CAKE

BUÑUELOS DE YUCA EN MIEL

CASSAVA FRITTERS IN SYRUP

NICARAGUA

2 cups fine-grated peeled cassava
¼ teaspoon salt
1 cup dark brown sugar
2 cups water
1 cinnamon stick, 1 inch
Corn oil for deep-frying

1. Mix the cassava and salt together. Shape 4 round balls and set aside.

2. Cook the sugar, water and cinnamon stick together over moderate to low heat for 15 minutes. The syrup should thicken slightly.

3. Heat the oil in a wok or skillet for deep-frying. The oil should be at least 2 inches deep. Fry the cassava balls on all sides for 3 minutes. Remove them to a platter and with 2 forks open up the center of the balls like an opening flower bud. Return them to the oil and fry over moderate heat for 3 minutes more, until crisp and brown.

4. Drain on paper towels. Serve warm, spooning as much syrup as desired over the fritters.

MAKES 4 FRITTERS

PASTEL DE YUCA CON COCO

CASSAVA AND COCONUT CAKE

COSTA RICA

This pudding/cake is a peasant dessert from Costa Rica. A bit solid, filling, sweet and nourishing—a traditional dish of great popularity in the countryside. This can be served at tea or during coffee hours.

2 eggs, separated
2 cups sugar
¼ cup butter or margarine, melted
2 tablespoons baking powder
2 cups grated peeled raw cassava
2 cups fine-grated fresh coconut

1. Beat the egg whites until stiff.
2. Stir the sugar and butter together to a creamy consistency. Add the yolks and mix well. Fold in the whites. Add the baking powder, grated cassava and coconut.
3. Turn the mixture into a well-buttered baking pan, 7 × 11 inches. Bake it in a preheated 350°F. oven for 30 minutes, until browned on top. Cool the cake and cut into 2-inch cubes.

MAKES 1 CAKE

SOUFLÉ DE YUCA

CASSAVA SOUFFLÉ
COSTA RICA

This is not a high-rising soufflé like a French soufflé as the name might suggest. It is used in Costa Rica as a sweet. However, it is more of a pudding, and it can be served with meat and poultry dishes.

4 cups cubed peeled cassava
2 cups water
½ teaspoon salt, plus more to taste
2 eggs, beaten
4 tablespoons butter, melted
¼ teaspoon pepper

1. Boil the cassava in the water with ½ teaspoon salt until soft, about 15 minutes. Drain well and pull out any stringy fibers. Mash the cassava while still warm. Add the eggs, butter, pepper and more salt to taste.

2. Turn the mixture into a well-buttered 8-cup soufflé dish. Bake in a preheated 350°F. oven for 30 minutes, or until well browned. Serve warm.

SERVES 6 TO 8

HUEVO CHIMBO

EGG YOLK SOUFFLÉ IN SYRUP
GUATEMALA CITY

Here is a soufflé without egg whites. Even though it is not a high, light soufflé, the egg yolks will rise and the slices will be absorbent enough to soak up the syrup.

1 cup water
1 cup sugar
1 teaspoon lemon juice
¼ cup blanched almonds, cut into lengthwise strips
¼ cup raisins
6 dried prunes
12 egg yolks
¼ cup sherry or rum

1. Mix the water, sugar and lemon juice together. Bring to a boil in a saucepan over moderate heat and simmer for 3 minutes. Add the almonds, raisins and prunes, and simmer for 2 minutes more. Set aside.

2. Beat the egg yolks until creamy and thick, preferably with an electric beater. Pour them into a well-buttered glass baking dish 8 inches in diameter and 3 inches deep.

3. Bake in a preheated 300°F. oven for 30 minutes. The soufflé will rise. Remove it from the oven and cover the dish with a dry cloth for 15 minutes as it cools. Turn out the firm soufflé and cut it into ½-inch-thick slices.

4. Pour the syrup mixture and sherry or rum into a skillet and simmer over low heat for 2 minutes. Add the soufflé slices, one at a time, for 10 seconds, then turn them over for 10 seconds to absorb the syrup.

5. Remove the slices to a serving platter and scatter the raisins, almonds and prunes over all. Spoon the balance of the syrup over the slices. Serve at room temperature, or chill briefly in the refrigerator.

SERVES 4 TO 6

PUDÍN DE ELOTE

CORN PUDDING

COSTA RICA

There are several of these vegetable puddings that are traditionally served for dessert. If you prefer these puddings as accompaniments to the meat course, by all means serve them then.

6 ears of corn
½ cup milk
1 cup farmer cheese
½ cup sugar
2 eggs, beaten
1 tablespoon melted butter

1. Scrape the kernels off the corn cobs. This will make about 3 cups. Grind the kernels in a processor. Add the milk and strain the mixture through a metal sieve. To the milk mixture add the cheese, sugar, eggs and butter. Beat well.
2. Turn into a buttered baking dish wide enough so that the pudding mixture is about 2 inches deep. Bake in a 350°F. oven for 40 minutes, until lightly browned on top. Serve warm or at room temperature.

SERVES 6

BUÑUELOS EN MIEL

CORN DUMPLINGS IN HONEY

HONDURAS

The *buñuelos* are firm, unsweetened corn dumplings that provide a nutlike contrast to the thickened, richly sweet syrup. A simple but very popular dessert.

Dumplings

1 pound masa (tortilla flour moistened with water)
2 eggs, beaten
½ cup farmer cheese, mashed

Syrup

2 cups dark brown sugar
½ cup water
1 cinnamon stick, 2 inches

½ cup corn oil

1. Mix together the *masa,* eggs and cheese.

2. Prepare a dumpling by rolling 1 heaping teaspoon of the mixture into a ball. Flatten the ball to about ¼ inch thick and 1¼ inches in diameter. Continue until all dumplings are shaped.

3. Make the syrup: Mix the ingredients together and simmer over low heat for 15 to 20 minutes, until the syrup develops the same consistency as maple syrup, which it resembles.

4. Heat the oil in a skillet and fry the dumplings over moderate heat for 2 minutes to brown lightly.

5. Remove dumplings from the oil and add them to the slowly simmering syrup. Simmer them for 5 minutes.

6. Remove syrup from the heat and let the dumplings soak for 30 minutes before serving. Serve 2 or 3 dumplings and some syrup to each person.

MAKES ABOUT 20 DUMPLINGS

BUÑUELOS

FRIED DUMPLINGS IN HONEY

GUATEMALA CITY

According to a resident of Cobán, it used to be the custom in one household there to decorate the *buñuelos* with small lacy branches of fennel and a few red rose petals when serving them with the spiced syrup. But this was in the earlier days of the century and, alas, is no longer done; the frills are gone.

Miel Blanco (*White Honey*)

2 cups water
¾ cup sugar
1 whole clove
1 whole allspice
1 cinnamon stick, 2 inches
¼ cup red wine or port

Dumplings

½ cup water
4 tablespoons margarine
⅔ cup flour
3 large eggs
3 cups corn oil

1. Make the syrup: Mix everything together and bring to a boil. Simmer over low heat for 15 to 20 minutes to thicken the syrup somewhat. This cooked syrup is known as *miel blanco*, or white honey, because it is made with sugar and water. It could also be flavored with rum.

2. Make the dumplings: Bring the water to a boil. Add the margarine and let it melt. Add the flour all at once, and stir quickly to form a dough ball. Cool for 5 minutes.

3. Add the eggs, one at a time, and beat the dough into a smooth purée.

4. Heat the oil in a heavy saucepan or a wok over moderate heat to 375°F. Drop 1 rounded tablespoon of the dough into the oil and fry for 2 to 3 minutes. Remove the dumpling from the oil and drain on paper towels. The dumpling should be a light brown color and in the oil will expand quickly into a round ball.

When stored in plastic bags, these remain fresh for 1 day. They cannot be frozen. Two minutes in a hot oven will warm them.

5. Serve the dumplings and warm syrup separately. Pour as much syrup as wanted over the dumplings.

MAKES 18 TO 20 DUMPLINGS

Variation: This version of the syrup is from Chiquimulilla.

2 cups water
1 cup sugar
1 fresh fig leaf
1 fresh geranium leaf from a red flowering plant

1. Simmer the water and sugar together over low heat for 10 minutes.

2. Add the leaves and simmer for 2 minutes more. Serve warm with the *buñuelos.*

TAMALE ASADO

BAKED TAMALE

COSTA RICA

1 cup sugar
1 cup sour milk or yogurt
1 pound (4 cups) masa (tortilla flour moistened with water)
2 eggs, beaten
2 tablespoons butter, melted
½ cup farmer cheese, mashed
¼ teaspoon salt
¼ teaspoon ground aniseed

1. Mix the sugar and sour milk into the *masa*. Add the eggs and the melted butter. Blend in the cheese, salt and aniseed.
2. Turn the mixture into a well-buttered baking dish, 7 × 10 inches. Bake the tamale in a preheated 350°F. oven for about 30 minutes, until the top is brown. Serve warm or at room temperature.

SERVES 6 TO 8

NUÉGADOS

SUGARED MOUNTAIN PEAKS

GUATEMALA CITY

There are many recipes of this type throughout Central America. Dough, bread or egg ribbons are soaked in a syrup, sometimes spiced and sometimes plain. This is one of the simplest and most often served.

¾ cup flour
1 whole egg
2 egg yolks
1 tablespoon orange juice
¼ teaspoon baking powder
1 cup oil
1 cup sugar
½ cup water

1. Mix the flour, whole egg, egg yolks, orange juice and baking powder together and knead it into a soft dough for about 2 minutes.

2. Cut the dough into 4 equal pieces. Roll out each piece into a long, slender "cigarette." Cut these into ¼-inch balls.

3. Heat the oil in a heavy skillet over moderate heat and add the dough balls for about 10 seconds. They will puff up and brown quickly. Remove them with a slotted spoon and set aside.

4. Make the syrup: Simmer the sugar and water together over low heat for about 15 minutes, until the syrup produces a long thread (*punto de hilo*) when the wooden spoon which you are using to stir is dipped into the syrup and held high. At this point the syrup is ready.

5. Dump the fried balls into the syrup all at once and simmer and stir over low heat for 2 minutes. Scoop out 5 or 6 balls and heap them into a peak on a sheet of wax paper. Let them air-dry for 1 hour before removing them from the paper. These are the *nuégados*.

SERVES 12 TO 14

Variation: The dough balls can be baked, rather than fried, in a 350°F. oven for about 5 minutes, just enough to puff up and brown lightly. Put them on an oiled cookie sheet in the oven. When ready, proceed as for those that are fried.

NUÉGADOS ANTIGUEÑOS

SUGARED MOUNTAIN TOPS

ANTIGUA, GUATEMALA

In Antigua the "mountain tops" are covered with snow, in the form of stiffly beaten egg whites.

1 cup water
1 cup sugar
1 teaspoon ground aniseed
2 cups flour
3 egg yolks
2 teaspoons baking powder
1/8 teaspoon salt
1 cup corn oil
2 egg whites
1 teaspoon lemon juice
1 cup confectioners' sugar

1. Prepare the syrup (*miel*) by simmering together the water, sugar and aniseed over low heat for 10 to 12 minutes. Cool well.

2. Mix together in a processor or by hand the flour, cool syrup, egg yolks, baking powder and salt. Knead the dough on a lightly floured board for a few minutes.

3. Prepare a series of long "cigars" 1/4 inch in diameter with the dough. Roll out the strips in the palm of your hand. Cut these strips into 1/2-inch pieces.

4. Heat the oil in a wok or skillet over moderate heat. Fry the small dough balls for a few seconds. Remove them from the oil when light brown.

5. Beat the egg whites until they form soft peaks. Add the lemon juice and confectioners' sugar and fold in well.

6. Dip 5 or 6 fried balls into the beaten whites and pile them into small hills on a sheet of wax paper. Air-dry them for at least 2 hours. Store them in a container with a tight cover.

MAKES ABOUT 20

TORREJAS

BATTER SWEET BREAD IN SYRUP

GUATEMALA CITY

Torrejas are a popular if not classic dessert in Guatemala City. The bread used for this recipe is usually Pan de Coco (Coconut Bread) or Pan Bun (Bun Bread); see Index for recipes.

4 eggs, separated
Miel Blanco (White Honey, see Index)
10 slices of sweet bread or rolls, about 4 inches in diameter and ½
    inch thick
1 tablespoon margarine or butter
1 cup corn oil

1. Beat the egg whites until stiff. Fold in the beaten yolks and combine.

2. Prepare the *miel blanco* in a saucepan, simmering slowly over low heat.

3. Coat one side of the bread lightly with margarine. Dip it into the egg batter. Heat the oil in a skillet over moderate heat and brown both sides of the *torreja* for 3 to 4 minutes.

4. Remove each *torreja* from the oil and drain it briefly and carefully (to prevent its breaking) on paper towels. Add it to the *miel blanco* and simmer slowly for 15 minutes.

5. Serve the *torrejas* and the syrup immediately. Or remove them to a platter with a generous amount of syrup and refrigerate. These may be eaten hot or cold.

SERVES 6 TO 8

TORTA DE HUICOY

STUFFED PUMPKIN

FINCA PARRAXE, SAMAYAC, GUATEMALA

The *torta* is a beautiful, festive and authentic recipe that can be prepared several hours in advance and baked just before dining.

1 pumpkin or winter squash, 2 to 3 pounds
2 cups water
½ cup plus 2 teaspoons toasted crumbs, made from Danish pastry
    or sweet roll
1 tablespoon butter
2 tablespoons sweet or dry sherry
2 tablespoons sugar
½ teaspoon salt, or to taste
¼ cup raisins
¼ teaspoon ground cinnamon

1. Put the whole pumpkin or squash in a pan large enough to hold it with the 2 cups of water. Bring to a boil and cover the pan. Cook over moderate heat for about 20 minutes, until the pumpkin is soft enough to penetrate with a fork. Remove the pumpkin and cool it.

2. Cut a circle 4 inches in diameter around the stem and lift off the top. Scoop out the flesh and seeds without cracking the shell. Discard the seeds.

3. Mash the pumpkin flesh and put it in a saucepan with ½ cup crumbs, the butter, sherry, sugar, salt and raisins. Mix well and simmer over low heat for 10 minutes to thicken and dry out the purée.

4. Return the purée to the pumpkin shell and sprinkle it with the cinnamon and remaining 2 teaspoons crumbs. Cover it with the top. Bake in a 375°F. oven for 15 minutes.

5. Serve warm from the shell container.

SERVES 6

MANJAR DE LECHE

CINNAMON CUSTARD

GUATEMALA CITY

1 quart milk
1 cinnamon stick, 6 inches
3 egg yolks
5 tablespoons cornstarch, dissolved in 3 tablespoons water
¾ cup sugar
½ teaspoon vanilla extract
¼ cup raisins
½ teaspoon ground cinnamon

1. Bring the milk and cinnamon stick to a boil in a saucepan over low heat. Simmer slowly for 10 minutes to extract the cinnamon flavor.

2. Beat the egg yolks until golden. Add the cornstarch mixture and combine. Pour the hot milk through a metal strainer into the egg mixture, stirring constantly.

3. Pour the egg and milk mixture into a saucepan and set over heat. Add the sugar and vanilla. Simmer for 10 minutes, until quite thick.

4. Put 1 tablespoon raisins in the bottom of a 6-cup glass casserole. Pour the custard into the dish. Sprinkle with the balance of the raisins and the ground cinnamon.

5. Cool, then refrigerate for several hours. Serve cold.

SERVES 6

PLÁTANOS AL HORNO

BAKED PLANTAINS
GUATEMALA CITY

Throughout Central America the plantain is eaten daily in many forms—as a vegetable or in a dessert, baked, fried or boiled, and dressed with a sweet spicy sauce. Dessert variations are endless. The recipes given here all have slight variations in flavorings or cooking technique.

2 tablespoons sugar
1 teaspoon ground cinnamon
2 ripe plantains, with black skins
2 tablespoons butter

1. Mix the sugar and cinnamon together.

2. Peel the plantains and split them open lengthwise but do not cut completely through. Sprinkle them inside and out with the sugar mixture. Cut dabs of butter into the slits.

3. Coat a baking dish with butter and add the plantains. Bake in a 350°F. oven for 20 to 30 minutes, or until soft and brown. Serve warm with fresh cream and honey.

SERVES 4 TO 6

PLÁTANOS EN MIEL

HONEYED PLANTAINS
EL SALVADOR

Most of the plantain desserts come from Guatemala City, but this one is the El Salvadoran version and is traditionally served with a corn drink, Chilate de Maíz (see Index).

3 plantains, medium ripe with some black skin
2 cups water
2 cups dark brown sugar
1 cinnamon stick, 3 inches, broken up

1. Peel the plantains and cut into ½-inch-thick slices.
2. Simmer the water, sugar and cinnamon over moderate to low heat until the sugar has dissolved. Add the plantain slices and continue to simmer for about 30 minutes. The syrup will thicken. The plantain will absorb some of the syrup and will be cooked through.
   Should the syrup become too thick and the water evaporate, add ½ cup more water.
3. Serve warm, for dessert, afternoon coffee hour or any other time as a snack.

SERVES 6

PLÁTANOS EN GLORIA

GLORIOUS PLANTAINS IN SYRUP

GUATEMALA CITY

2 cups water
½ cup sugar
1 cinnamon stick, 3 inches, broken into halves
4 ripe plantains with black skins, cut into ½-inch-thick diagonal
   slices
¼ cup corn oil

1. Simmer the water, sugar and cinnamon stick together over moderate heat for 5 minutes.
2. Meanwhile, fry the plantain slices in oil in a skillet over moderate heat, until brown on both sides. Drain the slices briefly on paper towels.
3. Add the slices to the syrup. Simmer slowly for 10 minutes more. Serve warm.

SERVES 6 TO 8

RELLENITOS DE PLÁTANOS

LITTLE STUFFED PLANTAINS

GUATEMALA

The *rellenitos* are served as snacks with tea or coffee or as a dessert. They may be refrigerated and may be lightly heated up the following day. I have served them with success with any Guatemalan meat or poultry dish. The reserved liquid from the plantain is drunk as a flavored tea with the plantain, providing a mild drink that is reputed to be strengthening as well as refreshing.

2 cups dried black beans
9 cups water
1 garlic clove, chopped
1 small onion, chopped
6 tablespoons corn oil
4 tablespoons sugar
½ teaspoon ground cinnamon
4 plantains, with partially black skin, half ripe and firm
3 tablespoons flour

1. Soak the dried beans in 6 cups of the water overnight.

2. The next day cook the beans in the soaking water with garlic and onion until soft.

3. Process the bean mixture until smooth. Fry in 2 tablespoons of the oil in a skillet over moderate heat until beans are smooth and dry.

4. Add 1 tablespoon of the sugar and the cinnamon. Stir-fry for 2 minutes, until everything is well mixed. Set aside.

5. Cut each plantain into 4 equal pieces and peel it.

6. Cook the plantains in remaining 3 cups water and 3 tablespoons sugar over moderate heat until half soft, 5 to 6 minutes. Do not overcook. Drain the plantain and mash into a smooth purée.

7. Take 1 heaping tablespoon of the mashed plantain; with well-floured palms, flatten it out like a tortilla to 3 inches in diameter.

8. Place 1 heaping teaspoon of the bean purée on one end of the flattened plantain and roll it over to the other side, to make a round sausage shape. Seal any openings with an additional dab of plantain. Dust the fritter with flour.

9. Heat remaining 4 tablespoons oil in a skillet. Over moderate heat brown each fritter all around for about 3 minutes. Drain well on paper towels. Serve warm or at room temperature.

MAKES 18 FRITTERS

PLÁTANOS AL HORNO CON NARANJA

BAKED PLANTAINS IN ORANGE SAUCE

GUATEMALA

The plantain is a fruit that may be served with meat dishes as a vegetable or as a dessert with whipped cream or *crème fraîche*.

2 tablespoons butter or margarine
3 very ripe plantains, with black skins
¾ cup fresh orange juice
1 teaspoon grated orange rind

1. Coat a baking dish with 2 teaspoons butter. Preheat the oven to 375°F.

2. Peel the plantains and discard the skins. Make 3-inch-long diagonal slashes every ½ inch the length of the plantains, but do not cut all the way through the fruit. About ¼ inch should remain uncut to keep the plantain in one piece.

3. Put the plantains in the baking dish and dot them with the balance of the butter. Pour the orange juice over all and sprinkle with the orange rind. Bake for 20 to 25 minutes, basting occasionally.

SERVES 6

PLÁTANOS EN GLORIA

BAKED PLANTAINS IN CREAM

HONDURAS

Plantains are produced in huge quantities in Honduras and are certainly one of the most popular and useful foods to be found. This recipe is one of the many ways plantain can be prepared. It is a rich, creamy, outstanding dessert.

4 ripe plantains, with black skins
½ cup corn oil
1 cup heavy cream
1 cup dark brown sugar
1 teaspoon ground cinnamon

1. Peel the plantains and cut them lengthwise into halves. Cut each half crosswise into 3 slices.

2. Heat the oil in a skillet over moderate heat. Lightly brown the slices of plantain on each side for about 3 minutes.

3. Put half of the plantains in a baking dish in one layer. Cover the slices with half of the cream; sprinkle with half of the sugar and the cinnamon. Complete the second layer the same way.

4. Bake in a 350°F. oven for 20 minutes. Serve warm.

SERVES 8

PLÁTANOS EN MOLE

PLANTAINS IN CHOCOLATE SAUCE

GUATEMALA CITY

¼ cup corn oil
6 ripe plantains, peeled and cut into ½-inch-thick diagonal slices
½ cup sesame seeds
2 tablespoons squash seeds (pepitoria)
4 or 5 small ripe tomatoes, or 2 cups canned (drained)
¼ cup tomatillos (mil tomates)
1 chile pasa, seeds and stem removed, soaked in ½ cup water for
    30 minutes
1 ounce bitter chocolate, melted in 1 cup water
½ cup sugar
½ teaspoon ground cinnamon
2 to 3 tablespoons toasted bread crumbs

1. Heat the oil in a skillet over moderate heat and fry the plantain slices until light brown, about 5 minutes. Drain well and set aside.

2. In a dry skillet over low heat, toast the sesame seeds, squash seeds, tomatoes and tomatillos for 5 minutes or more, until lightly browned.

3. Prepare a smooth sauce in a food processor with the chile and its soaking liquid, the sesame and squash seeds, tomatoes and tomatillos. Force the sauce through a metal strainer and discard the remains.

4. Fry the sauce (*recado*) in a skillet for 5 minutes. Add the chocolate and water, sugar and cinnamon. Cook over moderate heat for 5 minutes. Add the bread crumbs to thicken the sauce.

5. Add the plantain slices and continue to simmer slowly for 15 minutes more. A thick, rich sauce will coat the plantain slices. Serve warm or at room temperature.

SERVES 8

Note: This mole is served all over Guatemala but especially during Holy Week (*Semana Santa*).

TORTA DE PLÁTANO

PLANTAIN TORTE
GUATEMALA CITY

1 large ripe plantain, cut into 4 pieces
2 cups water
¼ teaspoon ground cinnamon
1 egg
½ cup graham-cracker crumbs
2 teaspoons sugar
¼ cup raisins
2 tablespoons corn oil

1. Cook the plantain in its skin in the water for 5 minutes. Discard the skin.

2. Mash the plantain in a food processor. Add the cinnamon, egg, graham-cracker crumbs and sugar. Process to a fairly smooth paste. Stir in the raisins.

3. Heat the oil in a skillet over moderate to low heat. Add the plantain mixture and smooth over the surface. Fry this large pancake for 5 minutes. Turn it over and brown the other side. Serve warm, cut into wedges, as though it were a pie.

SERVES 6

BANANA EN AZÚCAR QUEMADO

BANANAS BAKED IN CARAMELIZED SUGAR

COBÁN, GUATEMALA

½ cup sugar
8 small ripe bananas, about 2 pounds, peeled
1½ cups hot water

1. Melt the sugar in a dry skillet over low heat, stirring occasionally, until the sugar has melted and turned bronze color.

2. Put the bananas in a heatproof glass or metal baking dish and pour the caramelized syrup over them. Pour the hot water into the skillet, swirl it around, and pour the water over the bananas.

3. Bake in a 350°F. oven for 20 to 25 minutes, until the bananas have turned a rich brown color. Baste now and then. Turn the bananas over once.

4. Serve warm or at room temperature with *crème fraîche*, thick fresh cream, sour cream, or nothing at all.

SERVES 6

CHANCLETAS

STUFFED CHAYOTE
GUATEMALA CITY

Chancletas are actually the leather sandals that the Indians wear, especially around Chichicastenango. These baked sweets are supposed to resemble the sandals. They do not resemble anything but what they are; however, the name has an amusing connotation.

3 chayotes (huisquils)
4 cups water
2 teaspoons sugar
¼ teaspoon ground cinnamon
3 egg yolks
1 tablespoon chopped blanched almonds
1 tablespoon chopped raisins
¼ cup sherry or port wine
1 tablespoon butter
1 to 2 tablespoons graham-cracker or any sweet cookie crumbs

1. Cook the whole chayotes in water until they are soft, about 30 minutes. Cut them into halves and scoop out the pulp without damaging the skins.
2. Mix the pulp with the sugar, cinnamon, egg yolks, almonds, raisins and wine. Melt the butter in a skillet and over low heat cook the pulp mixture for 10 minutes to evaporate some of the liquid.
3. Stuff the 6 chayote skins with the mixture and sprinkle them with the cookie crumbs. Put them in a greased baking dish and brown in a 350°F. oven for 20 minutes. Serve warm.

SERVES 6

COCADA

COCONUT CONSERVE

FINCA PARRAXE, SAMAYAC, GUATEMALA

To make this amount of conserve requires 2 or 3 coconuts. I suggest that you halve the recipe the first time you make it; it is a very sweet dessert.

4½ cups coconut water
4 cups sugar
5 cups freshly grated coconut
2 egg yolks
½ cup rum

1. Combine the sugar and coconut water. Bring to a boil over moderate to low heat, then add the coconut and mix well. Simmer for 30 minutes. Remove pan from heat.

2. Beat the egg yolks with the rum and add this to the coconut mixture; mix well. Pour the whole mixture into a buttered 3-quart heatproof glass baking dish. Bake in a 350°F. oven for 30 minutes.

3. Remove from the oven and cool. The conserve will have the consistency of marmalade. Divide into small servings, since this is a very sweet dessert, and offer as an accompaniment to dark espresso coffee.

SERVES 8

HIGOS SECOS

DRY SUGARED FIGS

GUATEMALA CITY

In Antigua, the center of traditional sweets, the figs are known as *maletas de higos,* or "figs packed like a suitcase," with sugar, of course.

2 pounds firm green figs, 48 figs
1 tablespoon slaked lime (see Note)
9 cups water
8 cups sugar
1 cinnamon stick, 6 inches, broken in several pieces

1. Cut a crisscross ¼ inch deep into the stem end of each fig. Peel the figs, but leave the stem intact.

2. Dissolve the lime in 6 cups of the water, and add figs. Soak overnight.

3. The next day drain the figs well and put them, the other 3 cups water, the sugar and cinnamon stick together in a large saucepan. Bring to a boil and reduce the heat immediately to a low simmer. Simmer slowly for 4 hours, or until all the liquid has evaporated. The pan should remain covered, or almost so, for the first 2 hours; then simmer uncovered during the last 2 hours.

3. Remove the figs from the pan and air-dry them individually on a wooden tray for several hours or more.

MAKES 48 FIGS

Variation: Sweet potatoes (*camotes*) can be prepared the same way with half the amount of water (1½ cups) when cooking with the sugar. Cut the sweet potatoes into 2-inch cubes.

Note: The lime is used to firm the figs so they will not disintegrate in cooking. It is usually available in drugstores or stores selling preserving equipment.

CAMOTE EN DULCE TINA

SWEET SWEET POTATOES
ANTIGUA, GUATEMALA

1 pound sweet potatoes or yams, peeled and sliced
1 very ripe plantain, peeled and sliced
1 cinnamon stick, 3 inches, broken in two
3 tablespoons honey
½ cup water
½ cup milk
2 tablespoons butter
½ teaspoon vanilla extract
1 tablespoon raisins

1. Cook together in a covered saucepan over moderate heat the sweet potatoes, plantain, cinnamon, honey and water for 15 minutes, or until vegetables are soft.

2. Pour the mixture into a food processor and purée. Return the purée to the saucepan and add the milk, butter and vanilla. Simmer over low heat for 10 minutes, stirring frequently.

3. Serve warm, at room temperature or chilled. Sprinkle the raisins over the serving dish.

SERVES 6

CONSERVA DE DURAZNO CON CEREZAS

FRUIT COMPOTE OF PEACHES AND CHERRIES

GUATEMALA CITY

Guatemala peaches are not beautiful to look at, especially those grown in the Indian highlands. But they are full of flavor and particularly firm for cooking purposes. They have not yet been ruined by horticulturists who try to improve them. The small, *marrón* village cherries ripen during July and August, the same time as the peaches, and combine into an especially delicious compote.

4 pounds peaches
4 cups water
1 cup sugar
1 cinnamon stick, 3 inches, broken into several pieces
1 pound fresh cherries

1. Peel the peaches and slash them lengthwise in 4 places.

2. Bring the water, sugar and cinnamon to a boil and simmer over low heat for 5 minutes. Add the peaches and continue to simmer for 20 minutes so that they may absorb the syrup.

3. Add the cherries and simmer for 10 minutes more.

4. Cool and refrigerate for several hours or overnight before serving.

SERVES 8

CONSERVA DE PAPAYA VERDE

GREEN PAPAYA COMPOTE

GUAZACAPÁN, GUATEMALA

This recipe is traditional with rural families, where really green papayas are available. The slaked lime firms the fruit and results in a pickle somewhat like watermelon rind pickle. Difficult to make here because of a lack of really green papayas, it is of interest as an example of a typical village pickle.

10 cups water
1 teaspoon slaked lime (optional)
1 green papaya, about 3 pounds, peeled and cut into 1-inch cubes
1½ cups sugar
1 cinnamon stick, 2 inches, broken in half

1. Boil 5 cups water and the lime if used. Pour this over the papaya cubes, stir for a moment, and immediately drain well. Rinse with cold water and drain again.

2. Bring 5 cups water to a boil over moderate to low heat and add the sugar, cinnamon and papaya. Simmer for 15 minutes to soften the papaya and "conserve" the fruit.

3. Cool and refrigerate. Serve plain or with cream.

SERVES 8 TO 10

CANILLAS O TABLETAS DE LECHE

MILK FUDGE

GUATEMALA CITY

This type of fudge is found everywhere in Guatemala City, sold on street corners all over town. It may be one of the most popular and very typical sweets available.

1 quart evaporated milk
1¼ cups sugar
1 cinnamon stick, 1 inch, broken

1. Put everything together in a heavy saucepan and bring to a boil over moderate heat. Reduce heat to low and simmer for about 1½ hours. Stir frequently with a wooden spoon so the mixture does not stick. When thick and caramel-colored, the fudge will come away from the sides of the pan, but one should be prepared to simmer the mixture for at least 1 hour or more.

2. Remove pan from heat and beat the fudge with a wooden spoon for 5 minutes. Discard the cinnamon stick.

3. Scoop 1 tablespoon of the batter onto a sheet of wax paper in the shape of a 3-inch-long finger. These are the *canillas*. Or, you may pour the milk dough into a glass pie plate and, when cool, dry and firm, cut it into squares. These are the *tabletas*.

4. Air-dry the fingers and squares for about 4 hours.

MAKES ABOUT 50 PIECES

CONSERVA DE COCO NEGRA

DARK COCONUT FUDGE

GUAZACAPÁN, GUATEMALA

I helped prepare this *conserva* in the adobe kitchen of Josefa in Guazacapán. This unobtrusive town, noted for agriculture, has a narrow river flowing freely through boulders that line its bank, and tropical trees such as coconut, tamarind, banana, coffee and cashew grow there in untamed profusion. This scene has not changed for perhaps centuries, or for at least as long as the recipe itself.

It was hot that day, about 85°F., and the *conserva* was cooked outdoors in a flat clay dish over a wood fire, smoking steadily. The sugar we used was a soft, dark brown sugar made village-style and purchased in half-moon cakes weighing about 4 pounds each. They are found and used in villages and towns all over Guatemala and are often wrapped, two by two, in woven baskets. It is much stronger in flavor than our commercial brown sugar and can be compared to Mexican *piloncillo* and the palm sugar of Indonesia.

The *conserva*, a rich brown, slightly sticky, marvelously sweet, chewy caramelized concoction, can be eaten warm and served with a strong cup of homegrown coffee. Beans from the garden are harvested from October to January, toasted on a handmade clay platter (*comal*), and ground on a chunk of gray lava stone (*piedra*). The smoky aroma of the coffee is irresistible with the *conserva*. None of this romantic scenario can be duplicated in the United States. Alas!

2 ripe coconuts
4 cups dark brown sugar (*rapadura*)
1 cup water

1. Open the coconuts and remove the meat. Cut away and discard the brown skin from the white meat. Grate the meat by hand or in a processor. Two coconuts should provide about 12 cups grated meat.

2. Dissolve the sugar in the water in a large skillet or wok over low heat. Add the coconut and cook slowly for 30 to 35 minutes, stirring with a wooden spoon constantly to prevent burning. The mixture will thicken as you go along, and when ready the confection falls away easily from the side of the skillet.

3. When ready, turn the *conserva* out on a wooden board and roll it out with a wooden rolling pin to ½-inch thickness. Moisten the pin with cold water now and then. Remember that the *conserva* is extremely hot and must be handled with care.

4. While still warm, cut the fudge with a wet knife into diamond-shaped 2-inch pieces. Cool well, and store in a jar or tin with a tight cover.

MAKES 40 PIECES

MOZAMORRA

CORN FUDGE
COSTA RICA

The *mozamorra* has a gelatin type of texture and may be served warm when it has the texture of Cream of Wheat cereal. This is an old-time sort of recipe that is served at tea time or the coffee hour. It is the fermentation that produces the distinct flavor.

6 ears of corn, kernels scraped off
¼ cup water
½ cup dark brown sugar

1. Let the corn kernels mixed with the water ferment in a warm place, or in the sun in a covered dish, for 24 hours.

2. Pour the mixture through a cheesecloth and squeeze or twist out the liquid and the inner kernels. This will remove the skins of the kernels, which are discarded.

3. For 2 cups of corn liquid, which should be slightly fermented, add the brown sugar. Bring this to a boil and cook over moderate to low heat, stirring constantly, for 15 minutes, or until the liquid has evaporated and only a thick syrup remains.

4. Turn out the fudge in a dish to make a layer 1 inch thick. Cool and cut into cubes.

MAKES 30 PIECES

DULCE DE ZANAHORIA

CARROT GLACÉ

GUATEMALA CITY

This carrot glacé was served to me in Guatemala with tiny citrus leaves, possibly from mandarin oranges, alternating with the balls on a large platter. It was a fragrant and colorful method of presenting the glacé with dark coffee.

1 pound carrots
½ cup sugar plus 2 tablespoons
2 teaspoons water

1. Grate the carrots on the coarse side of a grater or in a processor. Mix carrots with ½ cup sugar and the water.

2. Fry the mixture in a large dry skillet over low heat for 30 minutes, stirring and mixing constantly to prevent scorching. The carrots will cook and reduce to a relatively softened texture. Do not undercook since the carrot balls will ooze sugar; although the flavor will be acceptable, they will be difficult to handle. Turn the mixture out on a platter and cool it for 30 minutes.

3. Press together 1 tablespoon or a bit more of the cooked carrot to make a round ball 1½ inches in diameter. Continue until all the mixture is shaped. Put the 2 tablespoons sugar on a flat plate and roll the carrot balls in the sugar.

4. Air-dry the balls on wax paper for 2 or more hours. When completely dry, store in an airtight container.

MAKES ABOUT 20 PIECES

DULCE GLACÉ DE MANGO

MANGO GLACÉ

GUATEMALA CITY

4 pounds large ripe firm mangoes
1 cup sugar

1. Peel the mangoes and cut the flesh from the seed in slices. Discard seeds and peels. Put the slices in a large skillet with ½ cup sugar. Over moderate heat, bring the mixture to a simmer, mixing the ingredients well. Then turn the heat to low and stir constantly for 40 to 45 minutes.

The mango pulp will thicken considerably and must be stirred with a wooden spoon to prevent burning while the liquid is evaporating. At the end of the cooking time, the mixture will be thick and fairly dry. Remove from the heat and turn out in a platter.

2. Put ½ cup sugar on a platter. Scoop out 1 tablespoon of the cool mango mixture with a spoon and roll it in the sugar in the shape of a thumb. Continue until all the mixture is shaped. Remove the sweets to foil or wax paper and let them air-dry for 1 hour or more.

MAKES 22 PIECES

Note: If you want smaller "thumbs," scoop out 1 heaping teaspoon of the mango mixture and roll it in the sugar.

The sweets do not stand up too well and should be eaten, as they no doubt will be, within 3 days. They can be refrigerated, uncovered, to remain dry.

Variation: Strawberry glacé can be made in the same manner. For 2 pounds of fresh strawberries, cut into halves, use ½ cup sugar and prepare them like the mangoes.

JALEA DE BANANA

BANANA JELLY

GUATEMALA CITY

This is an extraordinary breakfast jelly with the flavors of the tropics—orange and banana. It is apparently a modern invention.

1 pound ripe bananas, peeled and sliced
2 cups sugar
4 cups orange juice

1. Process everything into a paste. Simmer over low heat in a heavy pan for 1 hour and 20 minutes, or a bit more. Stir constantly to prevent burning. Remove the foam from the surface as it develops. The color of the mixture as it approaches readiness will turn to a dark orange/amber.

2. Test firmness by dropping 1 or 2 drops into cold water. If the drops scatter, more cooking is needed. The jelly should not have a firm gelatinlike consistency, but should be smooth and flowing.

3. Pour the jelly into small jars, cool well, then cover. It is a jelly that is to be eaten at once rather than stored for future use.

MAKES 4 SMALL JARS

DULCE DE TAMARINDO

TAMARIND SUGAR BALL
QUEZALTENANGO, GUATEMALA

Tamarind is a tropical tree that grows in the coastal areas of Guatemala. The acid flavor contrasts pleasantly with the sugar. When I was in Quezaltenango market vendors, women, were selling their sweets on the curb in one of the principal plazas and doing a brisk trade at 5 cents each. Tamarind paste is available in Asian markets.

1 pound tamarind paste
5 tablespoons water
4 cups sugar, plus enough more to glaze the balls

1. Moisten the tamarind paste in the water for two hours, mixing the paste with your fingers from time to time to separate the seeds and fibers that are in it.
2. Strain the paste through a metal strainer. Discard the seeds and fibers.
3. Put 4 cups sugar in a mixing bowl and add the cleaned tamarind paste. Mix this with your fingers into a moist, but not too moist, sugar paste.
4. Shape the paste into balls 1 inch in diameter, and roll them in dry sugar. Air-dry for several hours. The center of the balls should be moist and the exterior firm and dry. Store in a jar with a tight cover.

MAKES ABOUT 40 BALLS

TRIFLE

COCONUT MILK CAKE

LIVINGSTON, GUATEMALA

½ cup butter or margarine, at room temperature
1 cup sugar
2 eggs
3 cups Rich Coconut Milk (see Index)
½ teaspoon grated nutmeg
1 teaspoon vanilla extract
¼ cup freshly grated coconut
⅛ teaspoon salt
3¾ cups flour
2 teaspoons baking soda

1. Cream the butter and sugar. Add the eggs and coconut milk. Combine smoothly. Then add the nutmeg, vanilla, coconut, salt, flour and baking soda. Mix into a smooth batter.

2. Butter a cake pan and/or cupcake tins. Pour batter into pan or tins. Bake in a 350°F. oven for 30 minutes.

SERVES 6 TO 8

Variation: One-half teaspoon ground aniseed may be substituted for the nutmeg. Or you may use ¼ teaspoon grated nutmeg and ¼ teaspoon aniseed.

MARQUESOTES

SPONGE CUPCAKES
GUATEMALA CITY

2 tablespoons cornstarch
2 tablespoons flour
½ teaspoon baking powder
4 large eggs, separated
1 cup sugar
1 teaspoon grated lemon rind
4 tablespoons melted butter or margarine
Powdered sugar

1. Sift the cornstarch, flour and baking powder together.

2. Beat the egg whites until stiff. Add the sugar slowly and continue to beat. Then fold in the beaten egg yolks and the lemon rind.

3. Add the melted butter slowly and mix well. Add the flour mixture all at once and fold it into the batter. Stop mixing when the flour has been absorbed.

4. Fill cupcake tins with the batter. Bake in a 350°F. oven for 20 to 25 minutes. When lightly brown, remove the *marquesotes* from the tins and sprinkle the tops with powdered sugar.

SERVES 6 TO 8

QUESADILLA DE ARROZ

CHEESECAKE

GUATEMALA CITY

1¼ cups all-purpose flour
½ cup plus 1 tablespoon grated Parmesan-type cheese
1 cup rice flour
3 teaspoons baking powder
4 tablespoons butter or margarine
1½ cups sugar
5 large eggs
½ cup sour cream

1. Sift the flour, grated cheese, rice flour and baking powder together.

2. Cream the butter and sugar together until smooth. Add the eggs, one by one, beating well after each addition.

3. Add the sifted dry ingredients and combine everything smoothly. Lastly, add the sour cream.

4. Pour the mixture into a buttered and floured 9-inch-square pan, 2 inches deep. Bake in a preheated 350°F oven for 30 minutes, or a bit more if needed after testing with a thin wooden skewer.

5. Remove the pan to a cake rack and cool before slicing.

MAKES 1 CAKE

QUESADILLA

CHEESE SPONGE CAKE
GUATEMALA CITY

This type of cheesecake may have originated in the town of Zacapa, for the famous cheese from that town is known all over Guatemala. This cheese making is essentially a cottage industry. The cheese is white, salted, crumbly, hard and dry; it is made in wheels and air-dried for about 1 month before it is sold.

The cheese is grated and used in the *quesadillas* as well as in many other types of regional dishes when it is necessary to use grated cheese, for example, the *tostados* of various types.

I have also used the Zacapa cheese on pastas to good account. On the other hand, a reasonable substitute for Zacapa cheese is Parmesan.

This cake was usually made for large groups and family gatherings and so I suggest that you cut this recipe into halves for a moderate-size result.

1 pound unsalted butter or margarine, at room temperature
3 cups sugar
8 large eggs
3 cups rice flour
½ cup heavy cream
1½ cups white cornmeal, sifted once
3 teaspoons baking powder
1 cup grated Parmesan-type cheese
1 cup milk
Powdered sugar

1. Cream the butter thoroughly. Add the sugar and beat until smooth. Add the eggs, one at a time, alternating these with the rice flour. Add the cream and continue to beat. Then add the cornmeal, baking powder and cheese.

2. Add the milk last and beat the mixture for a considerable length of time, about 15 minutes, until light and smooth. An electric beater is ideal for converting the ingredients into a light sponge cake. To test the batter to see if it has been beaten sufficiently, put 1 teaspoon in a glass of cold water. If the batter floats, it is then sufficiently light and airy to result in a sponge type of cake.

3. Pour the mixture into 4 buttered and floured loaf pans, 9 × 5 × 3 inches, or into 1 large round or square cake pan. *Tip:* When you have filled the pans with the batter, tap them several times on the table to eliminate any trapped air. Bake on the middle rack of a preheated 325°F. oven for 1 hour for the large pan or 50 minutes for the loaf pans.

4. Cool the cake for 10 minutes before turning out onto a cake rack. Sprinkle liberally with the powdered sugar.

MAKES 4 CAKES

POTAPON

NUTMEG COOKIES

LIVINGSTON, GUATEMALA

The mothers of Livingston send their young boys and girls out to sell these *potapons* in covered woven baskets. The better cooks in town do a brisk trade.

1 package (¼ ounce) dry yeast
1 teaspoon plus ¾ cup sugar
2 tablespoons warm water
3½ cups all-purpose flour
¼ teaspoon salt
½ teaspoon grated nutmeg
1 teaspoon vanilla extract
2 teaspoons baking soda
4 tablespoons margarine
1 cup Rich Coconut Milk (see Index)

1. Dissolve the yeast and 1 teaspoon sugar in the warm water. Set aside for 10 minutes to allow the mixture to proof.

2. Mix the flour, salt, nutmeg, vanilla, baking soda, ¾ cup sugar, the margarine and the coconut milk together. Add the yeast mixture and combine well. Knead on a floured board for 5 minutes. Dust with flour for easy handling. Let the dough rise, covered with a towel, for 45 minutes.

3. Dust your hands with flour and cut the dough into 2-ounce pieces, the size of a large egg. There should be 12 to 14 pieces. Push each into a round 3 inches in diameter and ½ inch thick. Let these rise for 15 minutes. They will rise 1 inch.

4. Grease a baking sheet and arrange the risen cookies on it. Bake the cookies in a 350°F. oven for 20 minutes. The cookies should be light brown and lightly crispy with a spongy center, not quite a cookie.

MAKES 12 TO 14 COOKIES

HOJUELAS

HONEY CRISPS

GUATEMALA CITY

The *hojuelas* can be stored in plastic bags for a day or two but are really at their best when eaten immediately. However, they can be heated briefly in a hot oven to renew the original crispness. These popular sweets are sold at country fairs and on market days in Guatemala. In the countryside they are almost always made in the shape of large plates, but the city folk make them in triangles.

1⅔ cups all-purpose flour
½ teaspoon baking powder
5 tablespoons orange juice
1 whole egg
1 egg yolk
⅛ teaspoon salt
2 cups corn oil
Honey

1. Mix the flour, baking powder, orange juice, whole egg, egg yolk and salt together into a soft dough. Knead it for 2 minutes until it is smooth and flexible.

2. Cut the dough into 3 equal pieces. Roll out each piece on a floured board to a circle about ¹⁄₁₆ inch thick, more or less the same thickness as a piecrust.

3. Cut each circle into 3-inch triangles. Or you may also cut the rolled-out dough into 6-inch-diameter circles, using a coffee saucer as a guide. For variety, cut the dough into both shapes.

4. Heat the oil in a skillet over moderate heat. Brown the triangles and circles on both sides for 1 to 2 minutes. Drain well.

5. Serve warm with honey drizzled over all.

MAKES 12 TO 18 PIECES

QUESADILLAS DE ARROZ

RICE-FLOUR CHEESE CUPCAKES

GUATEMALA CITY

½ pound margarine
½ pound cream cheese
1 pound confectioners' sugar
1 pound (4 cups) rice flour
8 eggs
Additional sugar for topping

1. Cream the margarine and cream cheese at room temperature until soft and smooth. Add the confectioners' sugar and mix well.

2. Add the rice flour alternately with the eggs. Beat well after each egg.

3. Put paper liners into cupcake tins. Fill the depressions almost to the top. Bake in a 350°F. oven for 20 to 25 minutes.

4. Remove cakes from the oven and sprinkle them with a light covering of sifted confectioners' sugar.

MAKES 30 CUPCAKES

Note: This recipe is a modern adaptation of a traditional cake. A Guatemala City cook developed it for a member of her family who was unable to digest wheat flour. By substituting rice flour, my friends could have their cake and eat it.

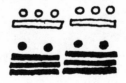

BULÉ

GINGER COOKIES
LIVINGSTON, GUATEMALA

1 cup brown sugar
1 cup water
½ pound butter or margarine
1 teaspoon baking soda
3½ cups all-purpose flour
2 tablespoons fine-grated fresh gingerroot

1. Dissolve the brown sugar in the water over low heat. Add the butter and let it melt. Cool the mixture for 5 minutes.

2. Mix the baking soda, flour and grated gingerroot together. Add the syrup mixture. Knead the batter together as though it were bread.

3. Roll the dough out to ⅜-inch thickness and cut it with a 4-inch cookie cutter. Press 3 fingers into the surface as a design.

4. Bake on an ungreased cookie sheet in a preheated 375°F. oven for 15 to 20 minutes. The cookies should appear brown and dry to the touch. Cool and remove from the cookie sheet.

MAKES ABOUT 20 COOKIES

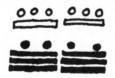

TORTITAS DE ANÍS

ANISE PANCAKES
COBÁN, GUATEMALA

The *tortita* is a specialty of Cobán. Anise is grown in the highlands of Guatemala and is used to flavor foods as well as some of the local liquor.

2 cups tortilla flour (masa harina)
1 cup water
½ teaspoon ground aniseed
2 eggs, beaten
¼ cup brown sugar
¼ teaspoon ground cinnamon
½ teaspoon salt
2 teaspoons baking powder
1 tablespoon butter

1. Mix the tortilla flour, water, ground aniseed, eggs, brown sugar, cinnamon, salt and baking powder into a smooth batter.

2. Melt the butter in a skillet over moderate heat. Drop in 2 tablespoons of the batter at a time and brown the *tortitas* on both sides for several minutes.

3. Serve warm, with honey if desired.

SERVES 4

Variation: Use the same ingredients but omit the baking powder. This will result in a crisp fritter with its own set of textures and flavors.

THE CHOCOLATE OF MIXCO

GUATEMALA

Since Colonial times and probably much earlier the women of Mixco, a town on the outskirts of Guatemala City, have ground the roasted cacao bean and mixed it with sugar and enough ground cinnamon to flavor the mixture. It was then pressed into round or square cakes about ½ inch thick, dried, and sold by the piece or the pound. In those days, the cacao bean was brought up from the tropical coastal area of the Pacific Coast and sold from private homes as a cottage industry.

The cacao bean, which looks like a dried fava bean or a good-size brown lima bean, is roasted in a dry pan for about 30 minutes, or until it becomes dry with a light charcoal look around the edges. A thin husk is peeled from the bean and the inner toasted cocoa is ground up in a mortar with a pestle; the mortar is the same *piedra* as used for making tortillas.

The ground cocoa is then mixed with the local sugar, which has a tendency to be crunchy rather than smooth, and the cinnamon. The chocolate cakes can be eaten out of the hand or used in cooking, principally as a chocolate drink made with hot water or milk.

The roasted cacao bean tastes like a bitter cooking chocolate found in any U.S. supermarket. The treatment it receives dilutes the strength and the cinnamon alters the taste completely. Its texture is gritty rather than smooth. It is used in native dishes rather than in sophisticated European or American pastries.

Nowadays, the chocolate is still made by hand in the homes of Mixco, but a modern factory has replaced a lot of the handwork although not the taste of this specially concocted mixture.

The cacao tree originated in the valley of Mexico and Guatemala and was distributed to other parts of the world after the Spanish Conquest.

QUESO BLANCO

WHITE CHEESE IN JALAPA
GUATEMALA

In a home in the outskirts of Jalapa, I was fortunate enough to be able to watch the whole process of making this cheese. First, the whole milk is poured into containers resembling canoes (troughs— they really look like wooden caskets) and mixed with the rennet tablets (*cuajo*). Formerly, the rennet was made in the home from the stomach of a cow, but now the rennet tablets are cheap and easily purchased in drug stores in Guatemala.

The milk at room temperature coagulates in 8 to 10 hours. This family had a canoe that contained 350 liters of whey and another contained 750 liters.

After coagulation, the curds are scooped out of the liquid that remains and put into a heavy cotton bag that is hung from a rafter and allowed to drip for several hours or more. A certain amount of gentle squeezing is done to press out the liquid.

The dry curds are then treated as a dough and kneaded by hand for about 1 hour to break down the lactate into grainy particles so characteristic of the Zacapa-style cheese now being made. Enough salt is kneaded into the curds to flavor the cheese. It is then pressed into round wood frames and weighed down with stone for 1 month or more, depending upon the custom of the cheese maker.

In the early stage of preparing the cheese, the milk in the canoe rests long enough for the cream to float to the top. Much or most of it is skimmed off to be used as a bath for the cheeses once they have been pressed into the wood frames. A thin layer of cream is painted over each cheese to form a crust that protects the inner texture. The cheese may be coated with cream one or more times.

It should be pointed out that the cheese is made in private homes and is essentially a family activity with both men and women contributing some muscle. They may keep a few cows but generally the milk is purchased from others since a steady supply of milk is needed all year to meet the continuous demand for the cheese.

The whey (*suero*) that remains after the curds have been removed is poured into large metal vats that contain 75 to 100 liters. This is brought to a slow simmer over an outdoor wood fire and as it simmers a second batch of curds (*requesón*) floats to the top as a bland but infinitely delicious creamy solid. The curds are skimmed off and sold to be used in rice and cornmeal dishes. They can also be eaten as is, sprinkled with salt or sugar, my own preference being sugar.

The liquid that remains from this second process is fed to the hogs. The entire milk is used for something or other.

QUESO BLANCO

COUNTRY CHEESE

FINCA PARRAXE,
SAMAYAC, GUATEMALA

The white cakes of cheese are sold all over Guatemala in the daily or weekly markets, or on some street corners in Guatemala City. It is a delicious and useful cheese that is made in every village where there is a cow or two. The texture varies from a smooth creamy consistency when cream is added to the milk, to the more crumbly texture of farmer cheese when the milk has been skimmed.

I have made this cheese in my Brooklyn Heights apartment without any special equipment or effort. Of course, one has to find milk that is not homogenized and preferably not pasteurized.

½ rennet tablet (cuajo)
5 quarts whole milk, at room temperature
Salt

1. Crush the rennet tablet and dissolve it in ¼ cup milk. Mix this with the balance of the milk. Let the rennet work at room temperature for 8 to 10 hours to coagulate the milk.

2. Pour the mixture through a fine metal sieve or colander to separate the cheese from the whey. Press the liquid out of the curds gently through a light cotton towel. Mix curds with 1 teaspoon salt or to taste. The salt may be omitted; however, a small amount enhances the flavor.

3. Pack the curd firmly into a wooden mold or a small bowl. Turn this out and wrap it in a mashan leaf, or in wax paper or aluminum foil.

This is a fresh cheese that is usually eaten within a few days.

MAKES 1 TO 1½ POUNDS CHEESE

BOJ

FERMENTED SUGARCANE DRINK

COBÁN, GUATEMALA

Boj is the national drink of the Kekchi Indians of Cobán. It is a contraband liquor that contains a punch, a small one.

I saw this prepared in a *rancho* (palm-thatched house) on the outskirts of the town of Cobán. It was a simple, small farm with the usual delegation of yapping dogs, giggling children and a profusion of vegetation of all kinds growing in no particular arrangement. There was the one-room *rancho* and another open shed in which the *boj* was made and which housed the press.

The drink is made with the ranch sugarcane of no special botanical classification. It was cane that just grew everywhere and there it was to be picked. The juice is extracted from the stalks of cane in a wooden press, a wheel arrangement by which the cane is inserted between two revolving wood logs turned by two men, one on each side of the press. One wheel turns clockwise and the other counterclockwise, propelled by nothing more than muscle.

The cane juice that is squeezed out runs down a wood trough into a clay pot. In the demonstration in the *rancho*, 4 long stalks of cane were pressed through the wheels three times. This provided about 3 quarts of juice. It was then mixed with ½ pound cornmeal (*masa*) and fermented for 3 days. The murky liquid is ready to drink as a sweet, softly fermented preparation.

Boj is not an alcoholic drink at that stage, but it can be kept for a day or two longer to develop a stronger punch. I was told by one local citizen that the *boj* was drunk in quantities and that it fermented in the stomach. The Kekchi men can and do tilt in various directions after drinking quantities of *boj*, which they consider their "alimentation" or food.

ROMPOPO

RUM CREAM
GUATEMALA CITY

1 cup canned sweetened condensed milk
5 egg yolks
¾ cup light or dark rum
6 ice cubes
10 drops of yellow food coloring (optional)

1. Beat everything together in a blender or food processor until the mixture is thick and creamy. Refrigerate.

2. Serve as an apéritif. Also does well as a sauce on ice cream or sherbet.

MAKES 1 QUART

ATOL DE MAÍZ TIERNO

A DRINK FROM YOUNG CORN

GUATEMALA CITY

This is an extraordinary and delicious beverage of pre-Hispanic origin, consumed everywhere and always available in the municipal markets. Ideal for chilly days and evenings as a refreshment.

8 young ears of corn
6 cups cold water
1 cinnamon stick, 6 inches, broken
1½ cups sugar
2 teaspoons salt
4 cups hot water

1. Cut the kernels from cobs; there should be 4 cups. Process them into a paste. Press it through a metal sieve and discard residue.

2. Put the corn paste in a large saucepan with the cold water, cinnamon, 1 cup sugar and the salt. Bring the mixture to a boil over high heat, then reduce the heat to low, stirring continuously. The mixture will thicken quickly, so add the hot water and ½ cup more sugar. Continue to simmer and stir over low heat for 20 minutes more.

3. Remove pan from heat and cover it with a damp cloth to prevent the formation of a "skin" over the *atol*. Serve hot, warm or chilled, but hot is best.

MAKES 2 QUARTS

CHILATE DE MAÍZ

ATOL—A CORN DRINK
EL SALVADOR

This mildly flavored drink, with the taste of toasted corn predominating, is probably of pre-Hispanic origin. It is usually drunk at the same time as eating Plátanos en Miel (Honeyed Plantains, see Index), the corn flavor and the sweet plantain complementing each other.

1½ pounds dry corn kernels
1 inch of gingerroot, chopped
20 cups water
10 whole allspice berries

1. Toast the corn in a dry skillet over moderate to low heat until lightly brown. Grind the corn and gingerroot together in a food processor with 2 cups water to prepare a thick paste. Add the balance of the water and mix well.

2. Pour the mixture through several thicknesses of cheesecloth to remove the coarse pieces and fragments that may remain. Add the whole allspice to the liquid.

3. Simmer the mixture over moderate to low heat for about 40 minutes, stirring frequently to prevent scorching. The drink will thicken and the flavors blend.

4. Drink hot, warm or at room temperature.

SERVES 12

TISTE

SIMPLE CORN AND COCOA DRINK

NICARAGUA

Of more historical than practical interest, the *tiste* is a popular refreshment. By virtue of its simplicity we know it is of pre-Hispanic origin like its more complex sister, the *pinolillo*. Both the corn and the cacao beans are ground with a pestle on a *piedra*—a stone mortar of ancient origin found all through Central America. The cacao is crushed on the stone in a back-and-forth motion of the round, rolling-pin pestle while adding a few drops of water to lubricate the mixture. I have seen the same process performed on the same type of stone grinder in Calcutta except that it was a mixture of toasted spice seeds and barks.

1 pound dry corn kernels
4 ounces cacao beans
Sugar
Water

1. Toast the corn in a dry skillet over moderate heat until it is a light beige color. Grind this to a fine powder.

2. Toast the cacao beans in a dry skillet over moderate heat until lightly charred. Remove the skins and discard them. Grind the cacao to a fine powder. Mix the corn and cacao together and add enough water to form a thick dough (masa).

3. Take 2 tablespoons of the dough and add it to 2 cups water with sugar to taste. Beat this to a froth. Serve chilled.

PINOLILLO

SPICED CHOCOLATE AND CORN DRINK

NICARAGUA

1 pound dry corn kernels
4 ounces cacao beans
6 whole cloves
6 whole allspice berries
¼ teaspoon ground cinnamon
Water
Sugar

1. Toast the corn in a dry skillet over moderate to low heat until the kernels are light brown.

2. Toast the cacao beans in a dry skillet over moderate to low heat until lightly charred. Remove and discard the dried skins.

3. Process to a fine powder the corn, cacao, cloves, allspice and cinnamon.

4. Take 2 tablespoons of the powder and mix it with 2 cups water and sugar to taste. Beat this to a froth, add ice, and serve cold.

Note: This is the most popular drink or refreshment in Nicaragua and probably of pre-Hispanic origin since corn, cacao and allspice originated botanically in Central America.

Supermarket cornmeal and cocoa powder can be substituted for the corn kernels and the cacao beans. The cornmeal can be lightly toasted in a dry skillet until it turns a beige color. The cocoa powder has already been processed and does not require toasting. Proceed with the same steps as above.

MAKES 1 QUART

CHICHA—CALDO DE FRUTAS

COUNTRY FRUIT LIQUOR
SALCAJÁ, GUATEMALA

This recipe is presented as a description of the wine rather than as a serious suggestion that you make it. If, however, you want to try it, substitute sour cherries for the nance and omit the mammee. This fruit is also called sapote and was one of the fruits eaten by the ancient Maya. It is available in the tropical and temperate regions of Guatemala. It is a large, egg-shaped fruit, weighing about 1 pound each, and has a dark brown skin and rich, pumpkin-colored flesh.

1 pound apples
1 pound quinces
1 pound peaches
1 pound cherries
1 pound nance
1 pound mammee
1 teaspoon ground cinnamon
1 pound sugar
1¼ quarts white rum

1. Wash the fruits and cut large fruits into slices. Leave the cherries whole. Put the fruits in a clay pot or stone crock large enough to hold them all.

2. Mix the cinnamon, sugar and rum together and pour this over the fruits. Cover the pot or crock and allow the mixture to ferment for not less than 3 months. Store the crock in a cool place during this interval.

3. Strain the liquor and bottle it for easy use. Serve it chilled as a liquor, and use it to prepare the various dishes that require *chicha*.

MAKES 1 GALLON

SUGGESTED MENUS

The following menus have been made up of compatible, though not traditional, combinations of food. They are based on my own preferences and those of my guests. May you enjoy them as I have!

1. Plato Chapín—Typical Guatemalan Lunch or Dinner Menu

The word "typical" crops up in conversations in Guatemala. It refers to the traditional weavings of the Indians and it also refers to traditional foods of the country. It is everyday dishes.

> **Black Bean Soup**
> **Guacamole (Avocado Salad)**
> **Frijoles Negros Volteados (Fried Black Bean Paste)**
> **Queso Blanco (Country Cheese)**
> **Carne Asado (broiled steak served with Chirmol)**
> **Plátano Frito (Fried Plantain Slices)**

SERVES 6

2. Vegetarian Menu, Cold

Pico de Gallo (Fruit Salad)
Guacamole (Avocado Salad)
Iguashte (Vegetable Salad in Squash-Seed Sauce)
Tostados (Plain Crisp-Fried Tortillas)

SERVES 6

3. Vegetarian Menu, Hot

Sopa de Pepino (Cucumber Soup)
Berenjena Guisada (Eggplant Stew)
Sopa de Arroz Chapín (Guatemalan Rice)
Encurtidos de Cebolla (Pickled Onions)
Fresh tortillas or tostados

SERVES 6

4. Winter Menu

Sopa de Albóndigas (Meatball and Vegetable Soup)
Estofado (Braised Beef)
Sopa de Arroz Chapín (Guatemalan Rice)
Ensalada de Remolacha (Beet Salad)
Banana en Azúcar Quemado (Bananas Baked in
Caramelized Sugar)
Fresh tortillas or *tostados*

SERVES 6

5. Mayan Menu

Chunto (Spiced Turkey Stew)
Tamalitas Paches (Little Cornmeal Tamales)
Tortillas
Fresh tropical fruit
Coffee

SERVES 6 TO 8

6. Buffet Menu, Hot

Arroz Con Pollo Chapina (Chicken and Rice,
Guatemalan Style)
Encurtidos (Pickled Vegetables)
Salsa Picante (Hot Sauce)
Dobladas (Doubled-Over Tortillas)
Tortitas de Papa (Potato Fritters)
Borracho (Drunkard)

SERVES 10 OR MORE

7. Buffet Menu, Cold

Lomo de Marrano Relleno Prensado (Pressed
Stuffed Boneless Pork)
Enchiladas (Crisp Tortilla)
Ensalada de Naranja (Sliced Orange Salad)
Pan de Maíz (Tortilla Flour Cornbread, with
Cream)
Borracho (Drunkard)

SERVES 10 OR MORE

8. Caribbean Menu

Camarones al Ajo (Garlic Shrimps)
Arroz y Frijoles Colorados (Rice and Beans)
Plátanos con Salsa (Green Plantains with Sauce)
Curtido (Pickled Hot Salad)
Trifle (Coconut Milk Cake)

SERVES 6

9. Modern Menu

Pollo Festivo (Festive Chicken)
Chojin (Grated Radish and Pork-Rind Salad)
Garbanzo en Tomate (Chick-Peas in Tomato)
Chirmol Frito (Fried Sauce)
Plátanos al Horno con Naranja (Baked Plantains in Orange Sauce)

SERVES 6 TO 8

10. Cocktail Party

* Butifarra (Anise-Flavored Sausage Patties)
  Picado de Zanahoria (Tortilla Crisps with Carrot)
* Salpicón (Chopped Beef Appetizer)
  Dobladas (Doubled-Over Tortillas)
* Rellenitos de Plátanos (Little Stuffed Plantains)
* Encurtidos de Cebolla (Pickled Onions)
* Plátanos Verdes Frito (Green Plantain Chips)

SERVES 20 OR MORE

* Can be prepared the previous day.

BIBLIOGRAPHY

Coe, Michael D. *The Maya.* New York: Praeger Publishers, 1966.

Goetz, Delia, and Morley, Sylvanus G., trans. *Popul Vuh, the Sacred Book of the Ancient Quiché Maya.* Norman, Okla.: University of Oklahoma Press, 1950.

Masefield, G. B.; Wallis, M.; Harrison, S. G.; and Nicholson, B. E. *The Oxford Book of Food Plants.* Oxford, England: Oxford University Press, 1969.

Oakes, Maud. *The Two Crosses of Todos Santos.* Bollingen Series XXVII. Princeton, N.J.: Princeton University Press, 1951.

Recinos, Adrian, and Goetz, Delia, trans. *The Annals of the Cakchiquels.* Norman, Okla.: University of Oklahoma Press, 1953.

Rosengarten, Frederic, Jr. *The Book of Spices.* New York: Pyramid Books, 1973.

Stephens, John L. *Incidents of Travel in Central America, Chiapas and Yucatán.* Illustrations by Frederic Catherwood. New York: Harper & Brothers, 1841.

Thompson, J. Eric S. *Maya Hieroglyphic Writing.* Norman, Okla.: University of Oklahoma Press, 1971.

Villacorta, J. Antonio, and Villacorta, Carlos A. *Codices Mayas.* 2d ed. Impresse en la Tipografia Nacional, Guatemala, 1977.

Von Hagen, Victor W. *World of the Maya.* New York: New American Library, 1960.

INDEX